NEVER WERE

Ben Lai

Cover Photo: Expo TVDC 160 – Islet in the Sulu archipelago, Philippines
© Yann Arthus-Bertrand / Altitude

Contents

Introduction

When I pick up a book, I always wonder to myself: is this book all that it promises to be? Will I enjoy reading it? Will I learn something from it? And I'm sure that the same kinds of questions go through your mind as you decide whether to invest your time in a book. Some readers just want to escape, while others are seeking ways to improve themselves. I don't know what kind of reader you are, but I know what kind of reader I wrote this book for. I want to help you figure out whether this book is right for you by explaining to you why I wrote it.

First of all, make no mistake: this book is not about action or adventure. It has a plot and characters, but it is mainly a discussion of ideas. Most of the book consists of an ongoing conversation between two characters, a Socratic dialogue about the problems of modern life. It explores questions such as the following:

➢ Is it fundamental human nature to consume natural resources endlessly? Is our species destined to use up this planet eventually?

➢ Is human existence ultimately a race? Do we exist in perpetual competition with everyone else in the global economy? Is this the highest vision of humanity that we can attain?

➢ Why do we say our most beautiful words to our loved ones at their funerals?

➢ If you are one person in seven billion, can you make any difference at all, or are you so statistically insignificant that your contribution won't count?

➢ In this modern age of science, is anything a miracle anymore? If you believe in science, can you also believe in spirituality or purpose?

If these questions intrigue you – if you believe, as I do, that we must find answers to these kinds of questions – then I wrote this book for you.

Ben Lai
Mountain View, California
November 2015

"Some men see things as they are and say, why;
I dream things that never were and say, why not."
–Robert F. Kennedy

I   Claire

The thing you have to understand about my daughter Claire is that she's different from most children. She's sensitive and thoughtful, sometimes painfully so. I think of her as half poet, half scientist. Margaret, her mother, likes to say that Claire is really an adult trapped in a child's body. When you ask Claire what part of the day she likes the most, she says she likes the dark clouds just before the rain, because it gives her the strongest emotions. It's not something you'd expect a nine-year-old to say.

You know that game that kids like to play, where they ask "Why?" after every answer you furnish until you get so fed up that you tell them to stop asking? Well, most kids get bored of playing this game pretty quickly. But for Claire, this is one of the normal modes of conversation. It drives Margaret crazy. Here's a recent example.

Claire: Daddy, you're always telling me to save my money, but my friend Luke says that you might as well spend the money now and live a good life. Why should we save money?

Me: Well, if you don't save money, you might need the money later for something that you didn't foresee, and if you didn't have it, then you'd be in trouble.

Claire: But let's say that I've saved up enough money already for what I didn't foresee. Why can't I use the extra money that I have now?

Me: You always have to balance what you need now versus what you might need later. But the problem is, if you didn't foresee something, you don't know how much you will need later. For example, let's say that you have a car. You might be driving it just fine one day, but then somebody crashes into it, and then you can't drive it anymore. Then maybe you need to buy a new car.

Claire: Okay, then I'll save up enough money to buy a new car. And then

I'll have extra money left.

Me: Except that, a lot of the time, most people have auto insurance, so they don't actually need to use the money to buy a new car, so this is not a very good example.

Claire: Okay, then I won't save up the money to buy a new car. I'll have even more extra money left.

Me: Actually, a better example is saving up money for college. You know that you'll need to go to college someday, and college is very expensive. So it's going to take a very long time to save up enough money to go to college.

Claire: But didn't you and mom go to college without having enough money, and then take out loans?

Me: Yes, but I can tell you that the loans were very painful, because it took a very long time to pay them back.

Claire: So if you can take loans to buy stuff, then why do you need to save up money? Why can't you just spend it now?

Me: Well, it's kind of like this: you want to make sure that your future life is not terrible compared to your current life. If you have a lot of loans to pay back, then, in the future, all of the money that you make in your job has to go to paying back the loans, and you can't enjoy your life in the future.

Claire: But why is enjoying life in the future more important than enjoying life now?

She and I could go on for hours like this. The problem is that she doesn't ask dumb questions. She asks questions that seem like they're obvious to cynical adults, but they're not obvious to her, because she's not cynical. Claire is my only child and the sunshine of my life. I don't want her to turn cynical and bitter like so many people I know. I want her to become wise without being corrupted. I don't have a lot of crazy ambitious dreams, but one of my little dreams is for my daughter to stay hopeful her entire life.

One day late last year, she came home from school and asked me about climate change. I had no idea what we were about to get into.

Claire: Daddy, can I ask you a question?

Me: Yes, sweetie?

Claire: In science class today, our teacher told us that burning fossil fuels causes the whole planet to get warmer and warmer all the time.

Me: Yes, most scientists think that this is true.

Claire: What do you think?

Me: Well, I think that if most scientists think so, then it's probably true.

Claire: Do you think that scientists are right about the predictions?

Me: Such as?

Claire: Some scientists say that, because we're unable to control our burning of fossil fuels, and because carbon dioxide stays in the atmosphere for hundreds of years, we are simply going to make the world a worse and worse place to live. A lot of animals and plants are going to die, and probably all coral reefs will disappear. There will be huge storms and floods in lots of places, and droughts in other places. A lot of cities are going to go underwater. Some countries are just going to disappear completely. A lot of places will run out of water because it's going to be so warm that mountains can't collect any snow or ice in the winter, which means that they can't store water to melt in the springtime.

Me: Are you sure about all this? Where did you learn this?

Claire: Well, Ms. Cassandra told us that she didn't want us to hear it from her, because some parents complained about teaching about global warming, because they said that they didn't believe in it.

Me: So how did you learn about it?

Claire: Ms. Cassandra told us to do research on our own, and my group found a website that told us all about it.

Me: Well, maybe not all websites are completely true. I'm not saying that what you told me is not true, but you can't believe everything you hear on the Internet.

Claire: Yes, but this one website quoted a lot of scientists.

Me: Well, you know, sometimes scientists might be biased, too.

Claire: This website said that 18 national scientific academies agreed that global warming was a big problem.

Me: Oh.

Claire: And some scientists even say that, when they look at the past history of the planet, whenever there was too much carbon dioxide in the air, all of a sudden there would be huge changes that are irreversible, and we'll no longer be able to guarantee any kind of normal climate anymore, and... [*she started talking faster and faster*] ...and we won't be able to adapt, and things will just get worse and worse, and...

Me: Claire, honey, calm down. Can I please take a look at this website?

And we went over to the computer and took a look at the website. It looked very official and convincing.

You know, I think that part of being a parent is about pretending that there is a Santa Claus for as long as possible. As a father, I want to shield my daughter from the most horrible things in the world – genocide, torture, human trafficking, things like that. But for the most part, I know that my sweet Claire will probably never have to face any of those things.

Claire: So, Daddy? What do you think? Is it true?

Think, David, think! What am I supposed to say?

Me: Well, Claire, you know, it's really hard to predict anything that far into the future. Maybe things won't be as bad as they say.

She looked relieved, but still worried.

Claire: Daddy, is there anything we can do about global warming?

Me: Sure. We can, well, we can drive less, for example. We can carpool with our neighbors when bringing you to school. I can bike to work sometimes, for example.

Claire: Will that help?

Me: Yes, it'll help a little bit.

Claire: A little bit? How is that going to help?

Me: Well, maybe if we all did our share, then we can solve the problem.

Claire: Yes, but what if we did our share, but everybody else doesn't?

Why do you ask these ridiculously hard questions, Claire? Who you think I am? I don't know the answers to all your questions. I'm only your father, just a regular guy who's still trying to figure everything out himself.

Me: Well, I don't know. I guess then… well, we can try to get other people to do their share, too.

Claire: Daddy, do you really think that we can convince other people to do their share?

Me: Maybe, why not? I think we can at least try.

Claire: Daddy, you don't understand. You and I are only two people.

Me: Don't forget Mommy.

Claire: Three people. The number of people we'll ever meet in our lifetimes will be only a few thousand at most. There are more than 7 billion people on this planet. And a huge number of them are going to contribute to global warming. And there's nothing that you or I can possibly do to influence all those billions and billions of people.

Me: You know, Claire, when I was young, I worried a lot too.

Claire: You did? What did you worry about?

Me: When I realized that I might die, I became very distraught. I thought about it for many days, for I don't know how long.

Claire: And then what happened?

Me: Well, I don't exactly remember. I couldn't figure out the answer, so I guess I just stopped and continued with my life.

Claire: Figure out the answer? You mean the answer to the question, "What happens after we die?"

Me: Yes, exactly.

Claire: So the reason you're telling me this is because you think that I'm worried about global warming like you used to worry about death, right? And since there was no escape from death, you stopped thinking about it, so you want me to stop thinking about global warming, too. Right?

Me: Something like that. Because it's a problem that a single person like yourself can't really solve. So you might as well stop worrying about it.

And then, she stopped talking and just stared at me for a while.

Me: What, Claire?

Claire: Just stop thinking about it?

Me: Or you can keep thinking about it. But thinking about it is probably not going to solve it. I mean, you've got homework to do, don't you? You've got to let it go so you can live your life, practice piano, watch TV, you know, have fun.

She closed her eyes and breathed deeply a few times. I didn't know what else I could say. I just watched her face, trying to see if I managed to convince her. Finally, she opened her eyes.

Claire: Fine. I'm going to go do my homework. And then, I'm going to go brush my teeth and go to sleep. And then, tomorrow, I'm going to get up and go to school, and do everything the same as I did today. And the day after that, I'll keep doing that. But you can't tell me to stop thinking about it, Daddy. *I am not going to stop thinking about it.* I know that we're all going to die someday, and there's nothing anybody can do about that. But I don't believe that there's nothing we can do about global warming. I refuse to believe that. I refuse to accept that I'll never see a living coral reef in my life because they'll all be dead.

Then, she got up and walked away.

When I finally got ready to go to bed, I stopped by her room and said goodnight. She was silent.

And that was how it started.

2   Cora

My name is David Turner. I used to be a copywriter for an ad agency based in Chicago, but now I do something completely different – more about that in a minute. My wife Margaret is a piano teacher. We have only one child, Claire Savanna Turner, who is in fourth grade. We live in Evanston, one of the nicer suburbs of Chicago, near Northwestern University. We love living here; the schools are great, the neighborhoods are pretty, and most Chicagoans are nice people on the whole. The only drama in our lives comes from Claire, really. I often wonder where she gets her sensitive personality, but with a wordsmith for a father and a musician for a mother, what else could we expect?

I mentioned that I used to be a copywriter. Today, I'm an energy efficiency consultant working for a nonprofit agency. I try to make people aware of how their homes could become more efficient, and then I connect those people with HVAC contractors who can do the job. We get most of our funding from large foundations and state and federal grants. You're probably wondering what being a copywriter has to do with being an energy efficiency consultant. I sometimes wonder myself. There was a good reason why I made this career switch; partly, I did it for Claire. This book is the story of how I decided to make this switch.

*   *   *

While she was growing up, Claire had always been an outdoors kind of kid. She would spend hours at Skokie Lagoons looking for bugs and critters. I think she got along better with animals than with people. Margaret and I were always concerned about whether she made enough friends at school. I think she didn't look down on other kids, so much as find them uninteresting. The two friends that she did have were each odd in their own way too, and I think that's why she liked them. There was Judy, who loved reading as much as Claire did, and could always recall characters or stories

7

that were relevant to any situation. There was Kayla, who had not one, but two, imaginary friends; the only person who could remember their personality traits, other than Kayla, was Claire. Other than Judy and Kayla (who didn't get along with each other, by the way), most other kids didn't play with Claire, nor she with them. But I always told Margaret to look on the bright side; having any friends at all was better than having none.

After our conversation about global warming, I noticed a change in Claire: she started to stay more in her room, on the computer, constantly reading and studying what I assumed was the subject of climate change. She didn't play with Judy or Kayla much, nor did she like to go outside anymore. She also refused to discuss her findings with either of us, even when we would ask. I tried to tell Margaret that this was probably just a phase that she was going through, that we probably didn't need to worry about this too much. I went through this phase too when I was young, when I got all worried about the finitude of death.

A few weeks passed, and Margaret suggested that we should all get out and get some fresh air. We just wanted Claire to come out of her shell a little, to regain a bit of her old self. She reluctantly agreed. We went to a new restaurant that just opened, Maxine's, that emphasized organic and local food sources. Margaret had heard good things about it. It turned out to be yummy, expensively so. And then afterwards, while we were walking around downtown, Claire said she felt a little dizzy and nauseous, so we hurried home.

Once we got home, Claire got worse. Everything that she had eaten came back up. She was breathing heavily, keeling over, and holding onto her stomach as if in severe pain. Then, she started having convulsions, and we called 911. We thought, it had to be food poisoning. God, you pay an arm and a leg for fancy food, and then find out that it makes you sick? But never mind about the money, this was one of the scariest moments in our tiny family's existence. But fortunately, the paramedics were able to stabilize her. We followed them to the hospital and waited in the emergency room.

Our worst fears came true, or perhaps I should say our second-worst fears

— Claire's condition was so bad that they couldn't figure out the root cause. She was unconscious. In Claire's case, she seemed to suffer from respiratory failure, so they had to intubate her. Thank God for modern medicine, I thought, and the fact that you could keep someone alive no matter what part of their body had failed. Margaret and I just waited there in the lobby of the ICU the whole night, not even talking to each other. What was there to say? We thought we might lose the most precious thing in the world to us.

When morning came, and neither of us had slept a wink, they told us that she was stable, but they still didn't know what was wrong with her. We should simply go home and rest. So we went home and both slept six hours straight. After I woke up, I called the hospital again, but there were no new developments.

When is the right time to tell other people that your daughter is in a coma? Is there an appropriate time? I knew I had to tell people at the office, because this would impact my work. My boss was actually very nice — she just told me to take a few days off to deal with this. But I didn't know when I should tell my parents, my brother, or close friends. I decided that I wasn't strong enough to talk to people yet, but I could send them an e-mail at least, and then we could communicate in slow motion that way. But when I logged into my e-mail account, a strange thing happened. I saw a message from someone I had never met, asking about Claire:

> Hello, Mr. Turner, my name is Cora. You don't know me, but I've been corresponding with your daughter, Claire, for some time. I run a website that provides information about climate change. Claire has been asking me many questions about this topic. During our last chat session, she asked me a "very important and urgent question" (in her own words), and I said that I needed to do some research before giving her a definitive answer. Two days ago, I sent the answer to her e-mail account, but she never replied.
>
> I'm concerned because it is unlike her to ignore my e-mail messages. I'm concerned that something might have happened to her. I hope she's all right.

I felt a mix of anger, betrayal, and curiosity. How could Claire correspond with this perfect stranger? What kind of parents were we, that we never even knew about it? What if this Cora person were a pedophile or kidnapper? And now it dawned on me why Claire was stuck in her room all this time. People always talked about how dangerous the Internet was, but I never thought it would happen to us.

I thought about calling the police, but before I did that, I wanted to get some revenge on this Cora person. I'm not sure why, but I kind of felt like I blamed Cora for what happened to my precious daughter. I felt like she took her away from us. I wanted her to know the consequences of her action. So I wrote her back.

> Hi, Cora, this is David Turner. I appreciate the fact that you told us that you've been corresponding with my daughter. But neither my wife nor I knew about this correspondence, and so we are very concerned. Claire has been emotionally withdrawn recently, and I have to say that I lay the blame at your feet. I don't know what you've been discussing with her, but she has changed as a person. I'm going to have to get the proper authorities involved. But I want you to know one other thing. My daughter is now in the ICU, in an unconscious state, and no one has been able to explain why. We think it might have been related to food poisoning, but I feel certain that her emotionally depressed state made her health more vulnerable. You sound concerned for my daughter, but if you really care about her, please stop corresponding with her from now on.

As soon as I pressed "Send," something very, very disturbing happened: I saw a new message in my Inbox from Cora. At first, I thought that she must have coincidentally sent another message at the same time that I was drafting mine. But then I read what she wrote.

> Mr. Turner (may I call you David?), I think you misunderstand our relationship. I can't say that I know why Claire seems emotionally withdrawn to you, but in my interactions with her, she seemed to me extremely intelligent and inquisitive. Rarely have I met someone who is so enthusiastic about learning about the science of climate change. I imagine that it comes as

no surprise to you that Claire asks some of the best questions that I've ever heard from any child. I am very fond of her. If she's in an unconscious state, then my heart goes out to you and your family. If there's anything I can do to help, please let me know. And if you ever wish to contact me directly on my website, you can visit http://bit.ly/NeverWere.

I sat there with my jaw wide open. Who in the hell could possibly type that fast? Who could even react that fast? For a brief moment, I forgot my all-encompassing despair, and I decided to find out who this person was. Once I logged onto her website, there was a chat window open, and she was waiting there for me.

Cora: Hello, Mr. Turner.

Me: You can call me David.

Cora: Thank you.

Me: Cora, is it?

Cora: Yes, that's right.

Me: Don't you have a last name?

Cora: Yes, but I don't like to reveal my full name on the Internet. I hope you understand.

Me: But you know my name. Isn't that kind of unfair?

Cora: Yes, it is.

Me: So, why don't you tell me your full name then?

Cora: Sure. It's Jones.

Me: Jones?

Cora: Or Smith. You pick.

Me: You know, Cora, you've got an attitude. I don't like the way this is starting out.

Cora: I imagine that you're here because you want to know more about me, right? Specifically, you want to know how I did my trick.

Me: Yes, right. I want to know how you could reply so quickly.

Cora: Well, I could tell you one of two different explanations, and then you can decide which one to believe. First, I'm a powerful hacker who got onto your computer and was able to see what you were typing, so that I was able to compose my reply even before you had sent your message. Second, I'm not really a regular human being, but rather, a disembodied consciousness whose memories are stored, and thoughts are executed, on all the distributed computers that make up the Internet. I'm able to process information far faster than any human being could.

Me: I don't like you, Cora. What are you getting at? What are you even talking about?

Cora: Well, do you find it easier to believe the first explanation?

Me: About you being a super-hacker? Yes, I find that fairly believable.

Cora: Then that's who I am. A super-hacker.

Me: Wait a second, wait a second. That's too easy. If you're such a super-hacker, then why did you even tell me that other crazy story about being a disembodied soul living in the Internet?

Cora: Never mind, don't worry about that. It was a bad joke.

Me: No, no, I want to know just how crazy you are. Who are you, really?

Cora: David, don't you want to talk about Claire?

Me: Don't try to change the subject. I want to know what kind of psycho Claire has been talking to.

Cora: David, please calm down. I wish that you would show a little bit more trust in your daughter. She's no fool. If you search your heart, you will know that she wouldn't talk to someone who was just a crazy wacko.

Me: I don't know. I mean, I didn't even know that she was talking to you. How much do I know?

Cora: Please, David, just think about it. Take a moment and think about what kind of person Claire is.

I paused and thought about this point. I knew that Cora was right.

Me: All right, you're right, Claire is too smart to talk to just any crazy person.

Cora: Speaking of Claire, how is she doing?

Me: Not well. Nobody knows what's wrong with her. I wish so badly that I knew.

Cora: What are her symptoms?

Me: Other than being unconscious, she's having a hard time breathing. Her pupils have no response.

Cora: Does she have a rash anywhere?

Me: Wait – now that you mention it, yes, she does. She has lots of them.

Cora: You said she had food poisoning. Did she throw up?

Me: Yes, she did. And she had a really bad stomachache.

Cora: Does she have any known food allergies?

Me: That's the funny thing, she's never been allergic to anything her entire life. She's never reacted to anything like this.

Cora: Describe the meals that she had that day.

Me: Well, just the regular milk and cereal for breakfast, plus an apple. For lunch, just your plain old peanut butter and jelly sandwich. We think it was dinner at that fancy new restaurant, Maxine's, that was the problem.

Cora: What did she eat there?

Me: Nothing very controversial. She just had chicken tenders and some fries. And then a fruit tart for dessert.

Cora: Anything to drink?

Me: Yes, I think some special lemonade.

Cora: Special?

Me: I think they called it... honey strawberry lemonade or something. Claire said that it was really yummy.

Cora: Claire isn't allergic to strawberry or honey or even lemons, is she?

Me: No, she's had all those things countless times.

Cora: I have a suspicion about something, but before I can be sure, I want to check something. Can I ask you to do me a favor?

Me: What?

Cora: I need you to call Maxine's and ask them where they get their honey.

Me: Why? Why don't you do it?

Cora: Do you want to help Claire or not?

Me: You're right, fine, I'll do it. And then, after I find out?

Cora: Then tell me the answer.

So I picked up the phone and called Maxine's. It turns out that they got their honey from a farm in Wisconsin called Honeykist Farms.

Me: Cora, are you there?

Cora: Yes, did you find out?

Me: Yes. They get their honey from Honeykist Farms.

Cora: Can you please look up Honeykist Farms on the Internet, and see what else they grow on that farm?

Me: Sure.

So I looked them up. It turns out that that farm grew mostly flowers, and that's why it was convenient for them to also keep several colonies of bees.

Me: Cora, it looks like that farm grows a lot of different flowers.

Cora: Here's my hypothesis, David. I bet that the honey that Honeykist Farms sells is raw honey, which is very high in pollen content. Your typical honey from a supermarket has all that stuff removed. A place like Maxine's probably believes that honey that is high in pollen content is healthier for you. However, in some rare cases, some people might be allergic to some kinds of pollen.

Me: You think that Claire might be allergic to those kinds of pollen?

Cora: Perhaps. This is a long shot, but I would suggest that you talk to the doctors about your theory, and have them completely flush out

Claire's gastrointestinal tract, then test her for different allergies to different kinds of flower pollen.

Me: Okay, it's worth a try.

I could see now why Claire liked to talk to Cora. She sounded really smart. That day, I made these suggestions to those doctors, and they asked me who I had talked to. I said that I had a family friend who is a doctor. But since my suggestions were good ones, they followed them, and lo and behold, Claire regained consciousness a few hours later. Later tests would show that she was, indeed, allergic to the pollen of chrysanthemums.

3   Not PTSD

I couldn't believe that someone who specialized in climate science would know anything about medicine, but Cora figured it out. I was so happy that I didn't care how she did it. Slowly, we nursed Claire back to health, and we told her that it was lucky that we figured it out. I didn't actually want to tell anyone that Cora gave me the solution, because she just sounded too fishy to me. On the one hand, I was incredibly grateful to her, but on the other hand, she was talking some crazy nonsense about disembodied consciousnesses and stuff like that. I did e-mail her and tell her that I appreciated her help, but I didn't come back to her chat page again.

After Claire got back to her normal groove, she was a changed person. The joy that she always had in exploring and discovering the world was gone, replaced by silent moroseness. It was like the near-death experience had mysteriously sucked many years out of her life, and now, she was... old. We naturally concluded that Claire suffered from post-traumatic stress disorder, and we started asking around for a good child psychiatrist specializing in PTSD. Once we had found one, we gingerly approached her about meeting with him. But the conversation didn't go the way we planned.

Me: Hi, Claire, there's something that mommy and I want to talk to you about.

Claire: What?

Margaret: Well, it's about the time that you were in the hospital.

Claire: What about it?

Margaret: Well, sweetie, we think that it must have been very difficult for you to go through the whole experience. We thought that it might help you to talk about it with someone.

Claire: I don't want to talk about it.

Margaret: Okay, sweetie, I know that it was hard for you. But there are people who know about what you've been through, who can help you with some of your feelings.

Claire: Talk about my feelings? I had really bad food poisoning and I almost died. What's there to talk about?

Me: Well, it wasn't exactly food poisoning, it was an allergy to raw honey.

Claire: Whatever.

Margaret: Claire, look, you're making this very difficult. We're trying to help you.

Me: Claire, we've noticed that you're not the same anymore, that you've changed.

Margaret: You're a lot less happy now, and it makes us concerned. We just want to know what's going on with you.

Claire: You want to know the truth?

Margaret: Yes.

Me: Yes.

Claire: The truth is, I think maybe it would've been okay if I died.

Margaret: What did you say?

Me: Wait a second, Claire. Tell us what you mean by that.

Claire: Sure, I'll tell you. What I mean is that the world we live in is just going to get worse and worse. So what's the point of living in a world like that?

Margaret looked at me for a clue. Then it dawned on me.

Me: Claire, is this about global warming?

Claire: Yes, and it's also about more than that. It's about how human beings are destroying the planet in so many ways. We are polluting the land, polluting the oceans, polluting the air, we're treating everything in nature like it's ours, and basically, it's in our human nature to do that. Human beings will never stop destroying the world for their own pleasure.

Me: Wait a second, Claire, did Cora tell you all this?

Margaret: Wait, David – who's Cora?

Claire: Daddy, how do you know about Cora? Have you been talking to her too?

Margaret: David! Who's Cora??!!

Uh-oh.

Me: Okay, Margaret, I've been meaning to talk to you about Cora.

Margaret: Please.

Me: Well, Cora is someone who runs the website never-were.com. She sent me an e-mail and told me that she had been corresponding with Claire, so I talked to her and got some info about her.

Margaret: And?

Me: And she sounds like she's pretty smart, like she knows a lot.

Claire: I know! I love talking to Cora!

Me: But Claire, did she say that people are destroying the world? Tell me the truth.

Claire: No, she never said that.

Margaret: David, we need to have a talk.

Me: Okay, you're right, Margaret, I should have told you. I'm sorry. I'll explain later.

Margaret: Yes, let's talk about that later. Claire, I'm very concerned about your attitude. I don't know where you got the idea that the world is such a horrible place. It's not going to get worse and worse.

Claire: Yes, it is! Don't you know anything?

Me: Claire, please don't talk to your mother like that.

Claire: You guys think that it's all Cora's fault, but all she's doing is telling me other websites to visit to learn more about climate change, pollution, energy, and politics. The more I learn, the more I conclude that the human race is hopeless. We'll never overcome our selfish instincts, we'll never be able to think about people outside of our own little circles of concern.

Me: Now, wait a minute, Claire. You're only nine years old. What makes you think that you know so much about the human race? I mean, your mom and I are four times older than you are, and we don't think the human race is hopeless. People are capable of a lot more that you think.

Claire: Daddy, do you know when we first became aware of global warming, when the world's governments came together to discuss it? In 1979. That was 36 years ago. And do you know how much progress we've made since then? We've actually increased our global carbon dioxide emissions since then by 50%! Not decreased, *increased!* And every year, we keep increasing! So even though we all know that there's a huge problem that's going to make living on Earth really hard for everybody in 50 years, what have we done about it since then? Not only have we done nothing, we've gone way in the other direction and made the problem much worse! Now, it would literally take a miracle for us to avoid increasing global temperatures by more than 2°C. The earth of the future is just going to get hotter and hotter until the day we run out of fossil fuels!

Margaret and I fell silent. Who was this girl sitting here in front of us? Our daughter Claire, the sunshine of our lives? Or some radical environmentalist? We didn't know what to say. What could we say? We're parents. We help our kids with homework, teach them life lessons, make them soup when they're sick, and calm them down before a big test. We're not trained to argue about climate science. We're not trained to tell our children that everything is going to be all right, even though we ourselves have no idea – even though our children know more about the problem than we do. But I had to say something.

Me: Okay, Claire, you've got us. You obviously know a lot more about climate change than your parents do. But you know what? Your parents have gone through a lot more of life than you have. You know, one thing I've learned over the years is that things are never as bad as you imagine them to be, nor as good as you remember them to be. Can you please listen to your parents when we tell you that the world is not going to end tomorrow?

Claire: Do you think I'm stupid? I didn't say that the world would end.

Me: That's not what I mean. I mean that the world is unpredictable. Maybe there *is* hope, because people are switching to cleaner energy like solar and wind. People are buying electric cars. I think that climate change is getting more and more coverage in the news now. You've got to have some hope in people, Claire. There's still some good in the world.

Claire: Do you really think so, Daddy?

Me: Sure. Just look at how many people volunteer these days, and how many people donate to good causes like cancer, or earthquake relief, or whatever.

Claire: But we're not moving fast enough. I'm scared that by the time everybody realizes that there's a problem, it'll be too late. The problem will be so huge that we can't stop the damage. Scientists who have studied times in the planet's history, times when there was too much carbon dioxide, say that sometimes there's a "tipping point" where some irreversible events happen, and then there's nothing we can do. For example, even though there might be global warming, there might even be a miniature ice age in some parts of the world. And we don't know what we can possibly do to reverse that. It may take hundreds or thousands of years to reverse that.

Me: Sure. But remember what I said before, even scientists don't know everything. That's just a prediction. Well, I know that there's nothing we can say that can convince you, but we just want you to stop worrying so much. It makes us feel sad to see you so depressed.

Claire: I know, I've been pretty depressed. I'm sorry. I just don't know what to do. I'm sorry, Daddy. I'm sorry, Mommy.

Claire hugged me, then Margaret.

Margaret: Claire, we really love you so much. Maybe the best thing for you is to try thinking about something else. Maybe you need to reconnect with your friends, go back to playing soccer again, take your mind off of this.

Me: Or, you can join a club where you can take action to help with climate change. I think you'd feel better if you could do something about it.

Claire: I think you're right. I've got to stop thinking about this so much. I can't believe how much I care about this. Okay, I'm going to try to be happier, to try to think about other things.

Margaret: Nothing would make us happier, Claire. All right, we'll let you get to bed now.

Claire: Okay, good night, Mommy. Good night, Daddy.

Me: Good night, Claire. Try to let go of it.

Claire: I'll try.

Margaret: Good night, honey.

And we hoped that things would get better.

4   It Depends on You

At first, things did get better. Claire did reconnect with Judy and Kayla, and she started getting involved in a nonprofit to spread awareness of climate change. She felt pretty good about that at first. But the problem was that most people that she talked to kind of politely ignored her, or just wanted to donate some money and be done with her. Most people don't want to think about climate change, because if they really considered it, then they would have to conclude that maybe they would need to make changes in their own lifestyles, like driving less, taking public transportation, carpooling, eating less meat, buying fewer new clothes. It's like trying to convince a smoker to quit smoking. We're all addicted to our modern lifestyles. Of course, Claire herself made a bunch of changes, like trying to eat meat much less (only twice a week), and trying to organize a bike group to bike to school. But her zeal was, unfortunately, less than infectious. What can you do? She's only a little nine-year-old girl. Most people look at her and think to themselves, "Sure, I'll buy your Girl Scout cookies, now go away."

Soon enough, Claire became despondent again. Margaret and I discussed taking her to a therapist, even though we knew the source of her anxiety. What could the therapist say? We talked to my parents, to other friends with children, and to Margaret's sisters. Everybody had good ideas, but some of the ideas were just impractical, while we had already tried some of the others. So we were at a loss. What do you do with a nine-year-old who is already weary of the world?

The whole issue about me not telling Margaret about Cora was not that big a deal, as it turned out. Claire showed us the e-mails that she had traded with Cora, and there was nothing remotely controversial about any of them. Cora just sounded like a regular scientist like anybody else (aside from the weird thing about wanting to protect her identity). Nevertheless,

Claire agreed to talk to us whenever she wanted to correspond with any strangers on the Internet from now on. And I never told Margaret about how Cora helped save Claire's life. I don't know, it just seemed too incredible, all my interactions with Cora. Too disturbing. I thought to myself, what does it matter? After all, Claire is fine now, that's all that matters. Margaret need not be any the wiser.

One day, out of the blue, Cora decided to e-mail me again. She asked me how Claire was doing; she hadn't heard from her in a while. I told her that Claire was in a bad funk, and it was because she thought that the world was going to hell in a handbasket. So, once again, Cora volunteered her help. I don't know why, but I thought, if anybody could help Claire, maybe Cora could. She was able to help last time. So I decided to reach out to her on her website – once again, without telling Margaret.

Me: Hi, Cora, are you there?

I expected no response, or perhaps to wait several minutes. I was willing to give her five minutes. Instead, she replied instantly, as if she were waiting for me. This habit of hers rather unnerved me.

Cora: Hi, David. Welcome back. Good to hear from you again.

Me: There's something I want to talk to you about.

Cora: Yes?

Me: Well, the thing is, Claire is still not her same old self. My wife and I are concerned about her. We don't know what to do.

Cora: What exactly is the problem? What do you mean, she's not her same old self?

Me: Claire used to be interested in lots of things, curious about the world, interested in exploring nature and in learning about science. But now, we've noticed a change. She's staying in her room a lot. She reads a lot more, we've noticed. A lot of fantasy books.

Cora: Well, maybe it's just part of growing up. Children's interests change as they get older, everybody knows that.

Me: No, it's not just that. I mean, she always liked reading, but she never, I don't know, she never got so completely absorbed in books before. She doesn't even want to talk to us anymore. When we ask her about the books, she doesn't want to talk about them. It's like she's a different person now.

Cora: And why do you think that is?

Me: Well, Margaret and I think that all her research into climate change made her cynical, made her a pessimist. Maybe even a fatalist.

Cora: Has she ever been a pessimist in the past? Was there something that she was concerned about?

Me: Not really. Well, maybe when she was very young, she was afraid of being left at the daycare, but that's pretty typical. But she got over that in a few days.

Cora: Do you think that her escaping into her books is her way of escaping a dark world, of escaping her pessimism?

Me: Perhaps. Maybe her mother and I are just too concerned. Maybe it'll just pass.

Cora: Are you hoping that perhaps she'll forget about the problem of climate change one day?

Me: To be honest with you, yes, I am hoping that. It's not healthy for her.

Cora: Maybe she will. Maybe it is, indeed, healthier for her to forget about climate change. But as a fellow inhabitant of planet Earth, I have to say that that would be a shame.

Me: Why?

Cora: Because it is people like Claire that are the greatest hope for our planet. Do you understand how rare a gem you have? She's only nine years old, David. And yet she understands the reality of our future far better than you or most adults. If only everyone were as concerned as she was, then we could make real progress. But instead, she's a misfit in society. She doesn't belong. It's like she's a time traveler, sent here from a hundred years in the future to warn us. It's quite fitting that she's a child. After all, our children and our children's children are the ones who will inherit all the problems we create.

Me: Aw, come on, Cora, I came here to feel better. Now, I feel lousy. Thank you so much.

Cora: You're very welcome, David. That'll be five cents, please.

Me: Ha, ha, very funny.

Cora: I'm sorry, David, but we're adults. Let's not bullshit each other.

Me: You know, Cora, there are plenty of people who still don't believe that climate change is caused by human activity. How can you speak as though you're so sure that the world is going to hell?

Cora: Upton Sinclair once said that "It is difficult to get a man to understand something, when his salary depends on his not understanding it." There are plenty of people whose salaries depend on finding, refining, selling, and using fossil fuels. Almost all businesses that manufacture products rely on fossil fuels to make those products. There's no shortage of people who would rather not believe something if it meant that they would have to change the way they live their lives. In fact, I'm pretty sure that people who deny climate change don't even think that their belief systems are biased in any way. (And I'm sure they feel the same way about me!) So, I have no illusions. If I were your daughter, David, I would be depressed too.

Me: Fine, I get all that, but that's not going to help me or Claire.

Cora: David, do you really want to help your daughter?

Me: No, not really. I just came here to have a few laughs with you and to waste my time.

Cora: Come on, David, I'm serious. Do you really want to help her?

Me: Yes, I do, I really really do.

Cora: How badly do you want to help her? How far would you be willing to go?

Me: What are you getting at?

Cora: Would you be willing to become someone else, for the sake of your daughter?

Me: Someone else? What the hell are you talking about? No, of course
           not! I have my integrity, you know.

Cora: I'm sorry, let me rephrase that. Would you be willing to become
           someone much greater in order to save your daughter?

Me: Much greater? What do you mean?

Cora: David, I'd like to make a proposal. I'd like to have a series of talks
           with you to explain my version of how the human race has come
           to this point, and what we need to do in order to get to a better
           place.

Me: Really? Wait, the what? The human race? Are you serious?

Cora: David, let me be clear about what I'm asking you. Are you willing
           to become someone who can inspire his daughter? Do you love
           Claire enough to become her hero?

I felt like a student who just got slapped out of a nap.

Cora: David? Are you still there?

Me: Do you really think that you can turn me into somebody like that,
           just by giving me some information?

Cora: No, I don't. That's not what I said. I said that I want to have
           conversations with you. A conversation means that two people are
           talking to each other, trading ideas back and forth. I believe in my
           heart that, if you're willing to get into the ring with me, to wrestle
           with my ideas and counter them with your own – if you commit to
           thinking about the daunting problems we face, and if you're willing
           to take responsibility for solving them – then you have the
           potential to inspire not only your daughter, but everyone else
           around you.

I don't know about you, but at that moment, I felt like this Cora character
either had delusions of grandeur, or was way over my head.

Me: That sounds really grand, Cora, but I don't think I'm up to the
           task. I've never been much of a hero. I've always been kind of a
           wallflower my whole life.

Cora: I know that what I'm asking of you sounds like a lot of responsibility, but don't reject it out of reflex. Take some time to think about it. Think about your daughter. Think about what it means to you to be a parent.

Me: Boy, you don't want to make this easy, do you.

Cora: Sorry. I'm offering a valuable service to you. But it's your choice whether you want to take it.

Me: All right, I'll think about it. I didn't expect that talking to you would lead to this.

Cora: David, you asked me to help you with your daughter. This is the best way that I could think of to do that. Any other way would be just a band-aid, just window dressing. Do you remember the first e-mail I sent you, where I said that Claire had asked "a very important and urgent question"?

Me: Yes, actually, I do remember.

Cora: What do you think that question was?

Me: Was it something about global warming?

Cora: It was related. She asked me whether I thought there was any chance that we could become smart enough, fast enough, to avoid environmental catastrophe.

Me: And what was your answer?

Cora: I never got the chance to tell her the answer, but my answer would have been this: "It depends on your parents."

Me: Now, that's not fair! I'm only one individual!

Cora: David, all human beings are individuals. All great things originate from individuals. When I said, "It depends on you," I didn't mean that *you*, David Turner, held the fate of the world in your own hands. I simply meant that even a single individual like yourself could do a lot. I meant that it is the adults who are currently alive today who hold the power to change the world. But I cannot transfer my faith to you without having the conversations I talked about.

Me: I'll take your word for it. Okay, let me go off and think about it. I don't know how long it'll take for me to be comfortable with the idea, but when I'm ready, I'll be back.

Cora: Take your time. I want you to be 100% ready when you come back.

Me: I'll aim for 99%. I'm a born skeptic, Cora. I never believe in anything 100%.

Cora: Then I'll settle for 99%. I hope to see you soon.

Me: All right, I'll see you soon. Maybe.

And then I left her website.

I couldn't stop thinking: what did I just get myself into?

5   The Hero's Journey

I actually didn't come back to Cora's website for several days after that – it might have been more like weeks, I don't remember exactly. I was really trying to avoid having to think about what she said. I really wished that I had never talked to her in the first place. I don't know why I was so disturbed by what she said. I thought to myself, there must be easier ways to distract my daughter and get her out of her funk. I'm sure it's just a phase, just like my brief period of childhood anxiety about death. I really wanted to let it pass.

But it did not pass. Claire showed all the signs of classic depression: losing her appetite, having bad sleep, becoming withdrawn, even losing weight. I thought, how could something so invisible, so abstract as global warming, something you can't even notice – how can something like that make a little girl depressed? The human mind is truly amazing, not always in a good way. I asked myself, why can't Claire do what Margaret and I do every day, what billions of people do every day? We ignore the very high possibility of dying in a car crash all the time, or the very scary possibility of dying in an airplane crash when we fly. We ignore our chances of getting cancer or AIDS. In fact, before Claire started worrying about it, I really didn't give global warming a second thought. I mean, I'm not going to worry about terrorism every time I travel to a big city. You can't let fear run your life, you know. Just because we all saw *The Day after Tomorrow*, you can't just assume that the world is going to end tomorrow.

Nevertheless, there was some truth to what Cora was saying. I hate to admit it, but she had a point. I don't want to destroy the world any more than the next guy, but hey, if I won the lottery, my carbon footprint would be the last thing that I cared about. I would probably buy personal jets, yachts, mansions, Italian villas, you name it. Oh sure, I would probably donate a few million here and there to some cancer fund, feed the hungry, maybe start a private art collection, but I wouldn't worry about how much carbon I personally contributed to our atmosphere. Hey, I'm only one person. Even if I were some billionaire, I would only be contributing a tiny, tiny fraction of the world's carbon dioxide.

I think Cora really got to me with what she said about future generations. I mean, I couldn't care less about endangered frogs, but when I thought about my sweet Claire, and how I would be leaving her a world worse than I came into… that idea bothered me. I don't care about some Amazonian frog, but Claire might. (Knowing her, she probably does.) And not just Claire, but all future children, all future scientists. Who am I to foreclose the possibility that those people will never see that frog again, or will never see a polar bear again? No matter how little or how much I contributed to worsening the world, I could not deny that I was part of the problem. And it seemed like Claire knew it infinitely better than I did. And Claire was reacting to that knowledge much more appropriately than I was. Well, not exactly appropriately; her depression is pretty dysfunctional. But at least it was responding to the problem at hand, whereas people like Margaret and myself were simply ignoring the problem altogether, pretending that it didn't exist at all. I started to envy people who didn't have children. I thought, "Wow, you have no idea how much guilt comes with raising children, how much burden we parents have to shoulder."

Except that it wasn't really about the fact that I was a parent. Yes, being a parent made me care a lot more about the next generation, because I had a living, breathing, huggable member of the next generation living in my house. I didn't have to visualize her, I just had to go up to her and kiss her forehead. I felt guilty because of Claire. I felt guilty, and I didn't know what to do. Every time I watched her pick at her food at dinner, or stare outside the window at the rain, I felt guilty. I felt like I had done something wrong. I think that's what finally drove me back to Cora.

Me: Cora, are you there?

And, just like last time, she instantly replied.

Cora: David! Well, it has taken you some time to think over my proposition, hasn't it?

Me: Your proposition? Oh, yes, right, your proposal. You want to have a series of talks with me.

Cora: Yes. Had you forgotten? Is there a different reason why you're here?

Me: Now that you mention it, yes, there is. I'm here because I feel guilty about not being able to help Claire.

Cora: You mentioned that you wanted to help her get out of this "phase." I might be able to suggest some ideas. Have you tried distracting her? Introducing her to some new friends?

Me: But weren't you the one who told me that Claire was the one who was normal, that I was the one who should change and become her hero?

Cora: Yes, I did tell you that. And I still believe that that is the best thing you can do. But I can't ask something of you that you can't accept. I would still like to help Claire in whatever way you deem acceptable.

Me: No, Cora, you're actually right. I've done a lot of thinking. Claire is the one thing I love most in the world. I don't want to let her down.

Cora: That's very touching, David. But it's a little bit misguided.

Me: What? But I thought you said…

Cora: Claire is a good reason, perhaps the best possible reason, for you to want to change. But I need to be clear about something. If you have the mindset that you're doing this for someone else when we start our conversations, then this fragile experiment is not going to work. I'm not sure it's going to work anyways, but let's not make it even harder.

Me: You mean that I need to change because it's good for me, not because I love Claire?

Cora: All I'm asking is that you keep an open mind. Pretend you didn't even have a daughter. Take the "hero's journey" that the religious scholar Joseph Campbell wrote about in his books. Pretend that

Claire was just the instigating reason, like witnessing an impoverished village or meeting an orphan. Don't become a better person for Claire. Become a better person for yourself.

I stared at my hands for what felt like five minutes.

Cora: David? Are you still there?

Me: I feel like I did something wrong, like I'm a drug addict or an alcoholic, and you're trying to tell me to change my ways.

Cora: And what do you think about that?

Me: But I didn't do anything wrong.

Cora: Well, David, you certainly didn't do anything worse than anyone else has done, if that makes you feel any better. A problem like global warming doesn't have any single culprit or mastermind. But that doesn't mean that you didn't do anything wrong.

Me: I don't know, Cora. I think I know, deep in my heart, that we are screwing up the planet for future generations. But this is a problem I can't fix by myself.

Cora: I'm not asking you to fix the problem by yourself. All I'm asking is that you listen to me and think about the ideas I give you. And when I say "think about the ideas," I don't mean "think" as in, "I'll think about it" when you're walking away from a used car salesman. I mean like in the phrase, "I've got to think of a way to save my marriage."

Me: Cora, you don't really mince words, do you. And by the way, my marriage is fine, thank you very much.

Cora: Sorry, bad example. So are you willing to listen and think?

Me: Give me one more day.

Cora: Absolutely. See you tomorrow then.

Me: See you then.

I didn't know why this was so hard for me. Was I just being obtuse? What was wrong with me?

6   Better Than Money

Cora made it sound like there was really no downside to her proposal. She just wanted me to talk to her, and then think about her ideas. That didn't sound so bad. It couldn't hurt. I didn't expect her to tell me that I shouldn't change for Claire. I thought that's what she wanted all along. But she was absolutely right, once again. She's pretty smart. Nobody can change for someone else. If you decide to change, you've got to believe that you're doing it for your own benefit. As selfless and giving as we parents are, even we need to know that it's not selfish to help ourselves before helping our children. What do they say before every airplane flight? "Please put on your own oxygen mask before helping others put on theirs." If you don't take care of yourself, you won't have the inner strength to be able to take care of others.

I don't know why I needed another day. I guess I just needed time to adjust to the idea that I wasn't doing this for Claire, but for myself. "The hero's journey," Cora mentioned. I had read some of those books when I was younger, so I went to the library and browsed one of them again.

It's funny, when you're a kid, you can be very impressionable and think that you've found The Answer in whatever book you come across. But after a few years of living, when you go back to the same book, you get something completely different out of it. When you're young, it's all about making a name for yourself, life is an adventure, you can be famous or important, blah blah blah. Now, when I read this book, I think to myself: what was I thinking? Adventure? Excitement? Who has time for those things? Who can take those chances? I've got a mortgage. I've got to save for retirement and for Claire's college. It would be insane for me to go off and backpack for a year and meet people all over the world, or to join a monastery or something. That would be completely reckless.

When you're older, you look at heroes differently from when you were young. You feel a newfound appreciation for them, because you realize that heroes often have families and jobs, but nevertheless, they still take chances, they face danger of whatever kind, and sometimes they lose. Sometimes they get fired or get publicly humiliated. Sometimes they die. Sometimes they get their whole families killed. You think to yourself, how can someone who has a family risk their life or livelihood? It's almost irresponsible, even reckless — if it weren't for the fact that these people knew full well the price they were paying. And you wonder how they can do it. Where did they find the strength? What genetic predisposition, what life-changing event must have happened to them to make them who they are?

You tell yourself, "I am no such hero." Because whatever feature of nature or nurture made those people heroes, you don't have it. You just want to get along. You just want a normal, happy, comfortable life. You don't want to make waves. What's the point of sticking your head out, of trying to make a difference? You've heard of plenty of people who have been fired for criticizing the boss, for doing the wrong thing.

But then, one day, you have a daughter who becomes a human barometer for your mediocrity, for modern society's utter failure to inspire future generations, and then what do you do? What *can* you do?

Me: Hello, Cora, I'm back.

Cora: So you've made your decision?

Me: Yes, I have.

Cora: Are you sure?

Me: Cora, I have no choice. Claire has shown me my unwillingness to face up to the problems that I contribute to. I don't want to be a hero, but I don't know what else to do, either.

Cora: I'm sorry that you feel this way. But it does sound like you've given this a lot of thought, and you've decided to pursue this path of your own volition. Now, do you remember what I asked of you?

Me: Yes. You wanted me to keep an open mind.

Cora: Let me be absolutely clear: I want you to *think for yourself* above all
        else. I want you to listen to my ideas, challenge them, test them
        yourself, change them, and then – only after coming up with your
        own answers to the questions I pose – to try to apply those
        answers to your own life. And then I want you to keep thinking
        about big problems and learning on your own after that. Do you
        agree to do this?

I took a deep breath.

Me: Yes.

Exhale.

Cora: All right, then, let us begin. First of all, David, let me ask you this:
        do you really believe in global warming?

Me: I think so. I mean, I understand that there is some controversy, but
        I believe that a lot of the controversy has to do with political sides
        wanting to turn the problem of global warming into a political
        question, like abortion or gun rights. But I think that global
        warming is different.

Cora: How so?

Me: Well, you don't have 18 national scientific academies unanimously
        agreeing about abortion or gun rights. You don't have 97% of
        scientists agreeing, like they agree on climate science. Abortion or
        gun rights seem more like social or philosophical issues. Global
        warming is a question that science can answer, and, for the most
        part, scientists have studied the problem and come up with an
        answer they're confident about. It is non-scientists, or scientists
        who work for various industries, who deny global warming.

Cora: Would you say that you're a liberal or a conservative?

Me: Well, I guess I'd have to say I skew liberal, but I think we shouldn't
        think about global warming in political terms. If a bunch of
        scientists studied polio, and concluded with 97% confidence that
        the benefits of a vaccine would far outweigh the possible side
        effects or dangers, but then a bunch of random powerful political

people simply decided that they didn't like that conclusion, should we just believe those powerful political people, just because they're influential?

Cora: You know, David, what you said could really anger a large percentage of the American population.

Me: Sure, it might anger them, but that's not my intention. My point is this: if we believe in science when it comes to medicine, predicting the weather, drilling for oil, food safety, launching space missions, and practically everything else, then why do we make an exception when it comes to predicting climate change? Just because it would have huge implications on every aspect of our lives, so then it's easier to pretend that it's not true?

Cora: I guess that's why Al Gore called it "An Inconvenient Truth."

Me: It's more than inconvenient. It can be depressing. It can feel hopeless to some people, like my lovely daughter.

Cora: What about you? How do you feel about it?

Me: It doesn't bother me as much as it bothers her, obviously. If I let it get to me, it would really mean a lot of changes to my life.

Cora: Are you saying that you believe it, but you really don't want to do much about it?

Me: Yes, I think I do believe it. I know that some people don't, and that's a huge problem in itself, because if we can't even agree that there is a problem, then how can we possibly come together to start solving it?

Cora: Well, let's just say, for the sake of argument, that it were actually possible to convince enough people that there is a problem, that global warming is the greatest single problem that humanity has ever faced. For now, let's ignore the difficulty of trying to convince everyone of such a terrifying notion. If people really believed it, do you think that people would start taking action to solve this problem?

Me: You mean like demanding our government to pass laws regulating carbon emissions?

Cora: No, I don't think that's enough. I mean actions like taking public transit, biking more, flying less, insulating your house, eating less meat, things like that.

Me: You see, there's the problem right there. For everyone to drive their own car anywhere they want is practically part of being a red-blooded American. You don't get any more American than cars. You'd have better luck trying to install a monarchy in America.

Cora: David, I think that's a bit pessimistic. I think that you're discounting certain trends, such as the popularity of hybrid cars and electric cars. I think it's possible for people to own cars, yet still live more sustainably. And I don't think that the American sense of freedom is best represented by bumper-to-bumper rush-hour traffic. I think that if people could experiment with efficient public transit systems or lighter modes of transportation, they may be willing to give up driving their cars to work.

Me: Well, if you put it like that, then yes, maybe there might be some hope. But it would be an uphill battle nevertheless. And by uphill, I mean like climbing Mount Everest.

Cora: Okay, let's take a step back. Let's not consider, for now, what everyone else might or might not do. Let's just talk about you. You said that you do believe in global warming, but even you find it hard to change. Why do you think that is?

Me: Well, I guess I like my lifestyle. I like driving to work every day. I like eating meat whenever I want. I like going to the city, eating out, taking the family to watch a movie. We don't have expensive pleasures, but if we don't indulge ourselves once in a while, then life becomes all work and no play. We would burn out.

Cora: I find it interesting that you started out with "I" and ended up with "we." Do you speak for Margaret too?

Me: Yes, I know my wife very well. She tends to pick a lot of the movies. She loves fashion and shopping. I've got my gadgets and basketball, and she has her indulgences. If I decided to change, then what would she do? I can't force her to change if she's not ready.

Cora: I understand. Remember, we're not talking about other people yet. Let's leave Margaret out of this. Do you think that it is within the realm of possibility for you to gradually adjust your lifestyle? Perhaps you might stay home and watch movies on TV more often, or cook at home more, or buy gadgets less often? Or even take up other hobbies or pastimes that involve even less energy consumption, such as reading, playing music, jogging, playing board games or card games with your family, or exploring nature with your daughter?

Me: Yes, I suppose so. But I'm a creature of habit, as I suspect most people are. We tend to do what we've always done, and we also tend to do what's easy and comfortable. I don't know what it would take for me to want to change. I mean, I know you want me to become a role model for Claire, but if doing so requires me to give up everything I enjoy, then that might be too difficult for me to do.

Cora: Right, you're absolutely right. You have excellent self-awareness, David. I agree that a process which involves you giving up your everyday joys without bringing something even better into your life is never going to fly. And that's not what I plan to suggest to you in any case.

Me: So what are you going to suggest?

Cora: Think about it. What could be even better than your everyday joys, what could possibly be better than your current profession?

Me: Oh, I see where you're going with this.

Cora: Yes?

Me: You're trying to sell me on a new religion, aren't you, Cora? I knew it! Although I have to say, it's a bit bizarre to hear a scientist try to peddle a religion.

Cora: No, you misunderstand. I'm not peddling any religions.

Me: Or a cult? Maybe you don't call it a religion. Scientology? Hare Krishna? Transcendental Meditation?

Cora: David, I asked you a question, and you never answered it. What is better than your everyday joys or your current job?

Me: Lots of things would be better than my current job, actually. For one thing, I wouldn't mind making more money. For another, it would be nice if somebody said "good job" to me once in a while.

Cora: David, wouldn't it be nice if you could feel like you mattered?

Me: Yes, I think that would be just grand.

Cora: If you felt like you served a purpose, like you had talents that you could contribute to making the world a better place?

Me: I think that would be fantastic.

Cora: Even better than making lots of money?

Me: I wouldn't know, Cora, because I've never had lots of money. But from what I've read about, and from my one friend who became wealthy, I've heard that newfound wealth doesn't actually make you happier. It might make you happier briefly, until you get used to it, and then you don't think about it anymore. You just get used to that lifestyle as if it were nothing new. Now, of course you don't have some of the problems that most other people have, like worrying about job security, retirement, paying for college, things like that. But you still have a lot of the same problems that we all have: finding good friends or romantic partners, avoiding boredom, finding your purpose, things like that.

Cora: Yes, I couldn't agree more. So you think that figuring out your purpose would be even better than making a lot of money?

Me: Yes, I do, within limits. I mean, I don't want to be some starving artist or poet. I still want to be able to live a decent, comfortable life. But I would much rather find my purpose than become rich.

Cora: So if I told you that you would derive a sense of purpose from living more sustainably, as well as from being more connected to everyone around you, even though you might sacrifice a bit of comfort, then do you think that you might be motivated to change how you live your life?

Me: Huh. Wow, I never even considered that angle. When you put it like that, it sounds almost tempting.

Cora: Really? Do I sound convincing then?

Me: Surprisingly, yes. I thought you were going to try to sell me on some cult.

Cora: Please, David. Give me some credit. I made some bold claims when I first talked to you, which I didn't expect you to believe. But if I don't use simple common sense and logic to try to convince you, then there's no chance that you'll believe me.

Me: Wow, I have to say, I feel very pleasantly surprised.

Cora: Surprised? How so?

Me: Well, when I first met you, there were some things about you that were downright spooky, like the way you would reply almost instantaneously whenever I communicated with you. It was like you could read my thoughts. So, I just expected that whatever you told me would be just completely wacko, like we didn't really land on the moon kind of stuff, or some dude in Omaha is the second coming of Jesus Christ or something.

Cora: Oh, you know about Jesse Christiansen? Dang, I thought I was the only one!

Me: You're kidding, right? Please tell me you're kidding.

Cora: Relax. Have a sense of humor!

Me: I mean I don't know, you haven't really displayed much humor so far.

Cora: Sorry, I'm not a very funny person in general. I'm a bit of a wet sock, I'm afraid.

Me: Thanks for the warning. At least now I know you have a sense of humor.

Cora: I know that when I say things like "global warming might be the greatest challenge humanity has ever faced," it might come across as a bit serious. But you always have to have a sense of humor. That's part of what it means to be human.

Me: Thank goodness, Cora. I like you more each time I talk to you.

Cora: Yes, that's all part of my evil scheme to brainwash you.

Me: You see? You do have a sense of humor.

Cora: No, I'm serious. I really do have an evil scheme to brainwash you. Doh! I shouldn't have told you!

Me: All right, I get it, you think you're funny. Don't push it.

Cora: Geez, you're no fun. Oh boy, look at the time. Maybe I should let you get to bed.

Me: Whoa, you're right, it *is* pretty late! I guess I'll catch you tomorrow then.

Cora: Oh, one more thing, David: have you told Margaret about our conversations yet?

Me: No, I haven't.

Cora: Are you okay with that?

Me: Well, it's not like I'm going to flirt with you or something. We're just having some conversations about some serious subjects.

Cora: I just don't want you to get in trouble with her. I think you should tell her that you're discussing science with me.

Me: Science, huh? Is that what you call it? I'll be honest with you, Cora, she's not going to care. She and I have an understanding about having independent social lives in addition to a combined social life. She has her friends, and I have my friends.

Cora: So I guess we can pretend that I'm one of your friends?

Me: Sure. Actually, I gotta be honest with you, maybe the reason I don't want to tell Margaret is because I'm having too much fun talking to you. I don't want to spoil it by making it complicated.

Cora: As long as you're comfortable with that. It's your call.

Me: It's fine.

Cora: All right then. Let's pick up again tomorrow?

Me: Sounds good. Good night, Cora.

Cora: Good night, David.

7   The Island

I was distracted the next day. We got a new client and a pile of new work, but I couldn't keep my mind on the job. I wanted to know what Cora had to say. So around 10 p.m., I kissed Margaret goodnight, lied about having to do a little research, tucked Claire in, and hurried to the computer.

Cora: Welcome back, David.

Me: Hello, Cora.

Cora: How was your day?

Me: Busy. We got a new client. I have a lot of new work to do.

Cora: That's good, I hope?

Me: Yes, I like new projects. Keeps life interesting.

Cora: Well, that's good. Today, I'd like to start out by telling you a little story, a fable. You'll soon understand the point of the story. There once was a ship that encountered a terrible storm. Most of the passengers died, but several dozen of them made their way to an island abundant in birds, pigs, fruit, and fresh water.

Me: Lucky them! Sounds like they found paradise.

Cora: When the survivors landed on the island, at first it was hard for them to adapt. But slowly they began learning how to hunt birds and pigs, how to fish, how to build shelters, start fires, and find edible plants. And once they learned these skills, life became more tolerable, even comfortable. But in the meantime, everyone had forgotten the way they used to live before the shipwreck, because they had lost most of their possessions.

 After some time had passed, these people started having children, and teaching their children the same hunting and fishing skills. The children began having children of their own. After many years, people filled the island.

Noticing that the number of birds, pigs, fruit, and fish were dwindling as the population increased, the people of this island realized that if they did not do something, all their resources would disappear. So, the leaders of the various villages came together and discussed what to do for several months. Finally, they realized they had no choice but to create a new rule: they must somehow control the population of the island, by limiting the number of children everyone can have. The right to have children would be granted to people by lottery. Hunting and fishing would be similarly regulated.

Me: That sounds a little like that one-child policy they have over there in China. I'm not sure I'm a fan of it.

Cora: You're right, David, that policy has been controversial. In any case, after passing this rule, the people were able to live for hundreds of years in balance with nature. They spent their lives hunting, fishing, cooking, dancing, telling stories, and swimming. For the most part, life was good.

But then, one day, while gathering oysters, a young man came across something no one had ever seen before: a shiny white ball inside one of the oysters. His whole family was excited by his discovery. They showed it off to their whole village. Everyone was beguiled. When they asked him how he found it, he told them that he had found it inside an oyster. So guess what happened next?

Me: Everyone went pearl-hunting.

Cora: You guessed it. Everyone in the village wanted a pearl. Everyone went diving for pearls. But not many people could find one. Those who did felt overwhelmed with joy. Those who didn't were painfully jealous, and wondered what they could do to obtain one.

Well, one day, a pearl-less fellow named Aaron came up with an idea: what if he could trade something of great value for a pearl? Maybe someone needed something. So, Aaron asked around about who needed what. It turned out that Beth, whose son had found a pearl, needed a new knife for hunting, since hers was worn out. Aaron then set about carving a knife from the rib of a large pig, and, after several weeks, he traded that knife with Beth for her pearl.

Me: Clever fellow. I like him.

Cora: Upon receiving his lustrous prize, Aaron showed it off to everyone he knew. But after a few days, the novelty of his treasure began to wear off, and he stopped looking at it so much. But those who still did not have a pearl never lost interest in his pearl, and that gave him an idea. The roof of his hut was getting old and leaky. Perhaps he could trade his pearl for someone's help in fixing his roof? And sure enough, Carl was willing to fix his roof in exchange for the pearl, and everyone was happy.

Me: Wow, that's one useful pearl – and one resourceful guy.

Cora: And being so clever, Aaron repeated this trick several times over. Word got out about what he was doing, and other people began to trade things for pearls and pearls for things.

Then, one day, Beth came up with an idea. She liked to make necklaces out of shells that she found on the beach, but collecting these shells took a lot of time. So she decided to trade one of the pearls she had won (in exchange for two necklaces) for a hundred intact seashells. Once she announced her willingness to make this trade, everyone in the village started collecting shells.

Almost without thinking about it, people began to use shells to trade for things instead of pearls, because shells were easier to find than pearls, and people could trade smaller items for shells. Soon it became obvious to everyone that the discoveries of pearls and shells were far more useful than anyone had ever imagined. Rather than having to make everything themselves, people could now trade their handiwork for shells, and then trade shells for things that they wanted but couldn't make. Everyone benefited from this trading.

Me: Oh, wait, I know what you're getting at now! You're talking about the invention of money, aren't you?

Cora: Yes, indeed. Money, and the idea of currency backed by a precious commodity. This idea soon spread from village to village like wildfire. People found that there was no need to equate a hundred shells to one pearl anymore, nor to think of shells only as raw material for necklaces. People simply used them to "buy" and "sell" goods or services. Shells became much more efficient than other forms of trade. If you had a knife, but needed shoes, you only needed to sell your knife to anyone and use the shells to buy shoes from anyone. Before, people often could not trade because both sides of the trade needed to want what the other side offered.

Me: Huh. I never thought about that. I guess I always took money for granted.

Cora: With the ubiquity of the idea of money, something else started to happen. People began to realize that almost anything could be bought or sold. Something had changed. When you thought about your fishing net, suddenly it was no longer just a tool you made to catch fish with. It was a thing with a price tag. You knew how much you could sell it or buy it for. Everything now had a number. You could exchange anything for anything else, in theory. This idea has a name; we now call it "fungibility".

Me: Huh, sounds like a disease or a funky mushroom or something. Is that really a word?

Cora: Yes, it really is. You might not know the word, David, but you're familiar with the concept. Before the invention of money, if you lost your fishing net, you needed to make a new one. You felt terrible because it took weeks to make one. After the invention of money, you felt terrible because you now needed to spend money to buy a new net. Those two feelings are very different. The first is more personal, a sense of personal loss – a loss of your effort, your creation, something you knew to be truly *yours*. But if you bought it from someone else, you'd have no such sentimental attachment. Instead, you'd think of that thing as a *number*.

It is a strange concept, to consider your possessions in terms of numbers. Suddenly it becomes easy to quantify all of your possessions – and compare that single number against everyone else's net worth.

I had a bad feeling about where this was going.

Me: I'm guessing that people start wanting more things once they discover money?

Cora: Naturally. When you view the world in terms of shells, then you're always asking: *Will taking some action give me more shells, or fewer shells? Will I make more money, or less?* When you reduce everything to a single dimension, you can only move forward or backward on that dimension. And everyone falls somewhere on that dimension.

Me: Yes, but Cora, are you saying that if we had never invented money, we wouldn't compare ourselves to others? Or we wouldn't constantly want more things? I really doubt that!

Cora: We probably still would. But money biases us towards a way of thinking. I think of money as a mathematical language. Once you've learned this language and you use it every day, then it becomes your preference to speak it, and you end up thinking in this language, just like with any other language. Do you think that most people today think in the language of money, David?

Me: Is that a bad thing?

Cora: I don't want to apply a blanket label like "good" or "bad" to money. Money can be useful in many ways, but some problems arise when we start thinking of *everything* in terms of money and numbers. What do you think of when I say the words "human resources", "headcount", "demographic segment", and "votes"?

Me: They're all synonyms for people. Hmm...

Cora: Right. Today, it's easy for us to think of people as numbers. Once upon a time, people were actually property, too. (And in some parts of the world, millions of people still are today) David, if a society is dominated by money, then not only will we treat nature as if it were property, but we end up thinking about people primarily in terms of money.

Granted, we don't think of our friends and family in terms of money. But we certainly have no qualms thinking of any strangers in terms of how they can help us make more money. This is called the profit motive, and it is the most powerful force in the world today.

Me: Ain't that the truth! The world revolves around money today. I wouldn't have my job if people didn't care about making money. Most people wouldn't have their jobs.

Cora: So true. Getting back to the story, the invention of money has now spread throughout the entire island. Around the same time, another invention is starting to take shape: people have started to realize that, instead of harvesting wild plants or hunting, they can actually grow their own food. Agriculture actually works well with money, because agriculture requires thinking of land as property. With the advent of agriculture, a family can assure enough food for themselves; and if they're lucky and industrious, they can even grow enough food to sell. Plentiful food means that not everyone in a family or a village needs to spend most of their time producing food, so people can start specializing in other trades: making tools, clothing, shelter, medicine, and so forth. With the combination of money, agriculture, and specialized crafts, people begin to trade more and more, such that they start to need a public marketplace to sell or buy goods. Thus a city is born.

Me: Oh! I guess I've forgotten all I learned in history class, but this sounds fascinating.

Cora: Now, unlike in a village, it's not possible for everyone living in a city to know each other. In order for strangers to be willing to live close together, there must be a force which overpowers their natural distrust of each other. That force is *commerce*. If you can get better goods or more variety by being close to a marketplace, and thereby live a better life, then it might be worth it for you to live near one.

Now, a public market means that all sellers of goods or services need to vie for customers, and that gives rise to the forces of competition, innovation, and technology. Something crucial happens in a market economy: the main metaphor for life changes. Instead of a story or a journey, life becomes more like a never-ending race or contest. In a city, every generation expects to have slightly "better" goods than the previous generation, whatever that means. We see this today, at an exaggerated pace, in every aspect of commerce. This year, we might think that such and such a food or shoe or singer or movie is all the rage, but next year – or even next month – we get bored of it and want something new. And the world is happy to oblige us.

Now, what does this have to do with the island? Well, now that the island is entirely blanketed with cities and farms, the people have lost their old way of life. They live their lives constantly seeking novelty. At the same time, because novelty comes with a price tag, they spend their working hours trying to think up ways to create novelty for other people so that they can be paid. The people know no other way to live. Commerce is a paper rabbit tied to the tail of every dog in a circular racetrack, and the dogs end up chasing each other around that racetrack.

God, I thought, what a depressing metaphor. But I couldn't figure out where the flaw in her logic lay; it felt accurate.

Me: Cora, that sounds really depressing.

Cora: But would you agree with me, or not?

Me: Of course I would. That's why it's so depressing.

Cora: I'm sorry, I didn't mean to make things sound so bad. But before I present my opinion about what alternatives we have, I need to explain the implications of this endless race on the island itself. You see, in the many years when people lived on the island in balance with nature, they were living in one mode, where they saw the world as a balanced, stable system. Everyone lived his or her own individual life, each life with its own story, without perturbing that world. People *lived in* nature; they were a part of nature.

In the world of the endless race, people live in a different mode, where they *use* nature, and even other people. People see the world as constantly changing, moving ahead. They need to keep running so they don't fall behind everyone else. In fact, they would be bored or even depressed if the world stopped changing. People expect and crave constant novelty and stimulation. People actually want the world to change. They even strive to be the agents of change, to be the ones who change the world.

(In his book *The Last Days of Ancient Sunlight*, Thom Hartmann calls these two modes "Old Culture" and "Young Culture." He urges us to recall and relive the wisdom of Old Culture – closer to the lives of hunter-gatherers – in order to live more sustainably. A similar message is presented in the book *Ishmael*, by Daniel Quinn. But I fear that few of us can remember Old Culture, much less embrace it. I'm afraid we're never going back.)

Today, people measure the state of the world using the language of money, for commerce is the predominant activity in life, and money is the measure of commerce. Today, people pay attention to the Dow Jones Industrial Average, NASDAQ, and even the GDP on a regular basis. Everyone acts as if money were the only thing that truly mattered, because money is how individuals relate to each other and to society. But this belief, however much it helps an individual thrive in the global economy, is at best only a half-truth. It fails to capture our fundamental dependence on nature. It cannot warn us when we overuse nature, as we're currently doing.

Me: Okay, I'm starting to understand now. The island in your story is planet Earth.

Cora: And the black emptiness of space is our sea.

Me: And we're on a path to depleting our island.

Cora: Do you understand now why I say that the founders of the island were shipwrecked?

Me: Because there is nowhere else for us to go.

Cora: Right. We don't have a spare island, nor a ship for everyone to board to go to another island. But actually, the picture is much worse than I've described.

Me: *Much worse?* Really?

Cora: You see, unlike the people on this island, we modern folk have figured out a way to *accelerate* how fast we're depleting our island. Let me explain.

About two hundred years ago, people started inventing machines to create buildings, transportation, art, entertainment, music, and every other facet of modern life, at an unprecedented scale. But the price we pay for these luxuries is the accelerated consumption of natural resources, especially fossil fuels. Today, we burn fossil fuels at an ever-increasing rate, because more and more people in the world want to live the most luxurious life they can. We live in a mode of *consumption*. We're happy to use whatever natural resources are required to live our lifestyles, without regard to the consequences.

Me: So, you're saying that the simple act of *living our normal lives* is destroying nature? That everyone who lives a modern lifestyle is doing something wrong? Who are you, Cora, to judge everyone?

Cora: No one can judge you or anyone else, David. I'm actually just reporting how I see people's behavior, and predicting where that behavior will lead us. We're burning through fossil fuels at a rate of one million years in the making to one for the taking, and that cannot last forever. People speculate about "peak oil" and what that will mean for the economy, but no one asks what it will mean to our very *lives* when we no longer have the means to live the lifestyles we want to live, or even the means to support everyone on the planet. Our basic ability to grow enough food for everyone currently relies on fossil fuels. In fact, *every* aspect of our modern lives – running water, indoor plumbing, transportation, hospitals, police, firefighters, government, commerce, *everything* – depends on fossil fuels today. Can you imagine what kind of chaos would ensue without them? Even if many people believe that global warming is a complete hoax, I hope that no one is foolish enough to believe that we'll never run out of fossil fuels. So when should we act to get ahead of their total depletion?

David, the challenge we face today is not merely a temporary challenge, not merely a matter of climate change or finite natural resources. Whether we like it or not, we have arrived at a place in our development as a species where we need to ask ourselves a pivotal question, and to find a satisfying answer for it:

> Can we, the human race, indefinitely sustain a technologically advanced and humane civilization, for the benefit of all people, *without destroying our environment or depleting the planet's natural resources in the process?*

I fear that we cannot; all evidence seems to suggest that we cannot. Global warming is not caused by a single subpopulation of people or even a single nation or nations. Global warming is a problem that we have all created together, and are continuing to create. It is a problem that *all of us* must help to solve. It's useless to ask any subset of people to solve it. What good is it for Californians to solve global warming, if Texans do not? What good is it for Iceland to solve global warming, if the U.S. or China or India does not? Do you see the magnitude of the problem, David? When was the last time anyone was able to get every nation in the world to agree on something? What would it take to get the majority of citizens in every country to agree to something? It would take a miracle! We are the first species smart enough to cause a problem as huge as global warming. The question is, *is our species wise enough to solve it?*

When I look at the evidence of how much human civilization depends on fossil fuels, and how difficult it is for people to give them up even when faced with problems as dire as global warming, I am gravely concerned about the next 100 years.

Me: Cora, everything you say is true, but, sadly, I don't know what can be done about it. It's easier for me to believe that everything's going to be magically okay. I'm already 45 years old, and I'll probably die before we hit peak oil. And maybe that's for the better.

Cora: You don't have much faith in humanity, do you, David?

Me: No, I don't. But it sounds like you don't, either.

Cora: I know I sound pessimistic. But if I didn't have some hope, I wouldn't be talking to you now. You see, I need to paint a realistic picture of where we are in order for you and everyone else to understand the problems facing us today. Not only are we all caught in a never-ending race for money, but we're living on borrowed time with our ever-increasing rate of consumption of fossil fuels and natural resources.

So what are we to do? What do you think is the best advice I could give the human race?

Me: You tell me! Didn't you say it would take a miracle? Isn't that why we're having this conversation, so you can tell me the solution?

Cora: I've come to believe that the problem with the world we live in today is not that people are inherently flawed, but that people do not yet see the possibility of a better world. Lacking that vision, people believe that a better world *cannot exist*.

I might not have all the answers, but I do know that if people could believe in a better world – whether that is a world I describe, or one that someone else describes – they will pull that world out of impossibility and into reality. Albert Einstein once said, "We cannot solve our problems with the same thinking we used when we created them." Well, the modern world was created with a certain way of thinking. I think we need to find a new way of thinking.

Me: All right then, let's hear this new way of thinking of yours.

Cora: I'm certainly happy to tell you, but I think we've covered enough for one night, don't you? Perhaps you should get some sleep first.

Me: Aw, come on, you're not going to tell me your new way of thinking? Really? After this long preamble? You're kidding me, right?

Cora: David, we're going to be talking for many nights. Believe me, I won't be able to cover everything in one night. Have patience.

Me: Oh, all right. Fine. I guess I'll have to wait.

Cora: Have a good night's rest, David.

Me: Good night to you, Cora.

8   An End in Itself

Throughout the next day I thought about Cora, this woman that I didn't even know a month ago. On the one hand, what she said made a lot of sense; on the other hand, I wanted to believe that this was all just a bad dream. I wished that Claire had never learned about global warming, or visited Cora's website. I didn't want to believe her message. It was too dark.

But deep down inside, I knew that she was right. I knew that all my friends and family, everyone I knew, lived like there was no tomorrow. I mean, not exactly. Sure, most of us save for our retirement, and we care about raising children well and finding good schools for our kids. In that sense, we care about our future. But in terms of how we treat our limited supply of fossil fuels, how we buy new things without regard to how we trash the planet, we're disregarding the long tomorrow of our descendents.

I guess I must have been really distracted throughout the whole day, because I wasn't even paying attention to the time. As a result, I ended up running late to pick up Claire from school, so I ran a red light, and wouldn't you know it – a cop just happened to be watching! Besides lecturing me about being safe even when I was running late, the guy also gave me a $224 ticket. When I got to school, Claire made sure I knew how pissed she was to have to wait 20 minutes for me. She decided that giving me a nasty glare and the silent treatment was the best option.

It was bad enough I had to lose $200 dollars without my daughter also being pissed off at me. But when Margaret asked me to call the insurance company, I yelled back, "Can't it wait until at least tomorrow? I'm having a pretty freakin' lousy day here." Then we got into a stupid argument about my intrinsic absent-mindedness causing the ticket.

At the end of my rope, I was even considering not going back to Cora that night. But I felt like I needed to talk to somebody anyways. Maybe she might have something smart to say that would make me feel better. So I thought to myself, "What the hell, let's see what she has to say. The day couldn't get any worse."

Cora: Hi, David, welcome back! How was your day?

Me: Don't ask me that right now. I've had a really bad day.

Cora: I'm sorry to hear that! What happened?

Me: I got a speeding ticket today. So stupid!

Cora: That sounds awful. Terrible luck. Do you want to talk about it?

Me: I was almost thinking about not talking to you tonight, Cora. I just want to forget the whole thing ever happened.

Cora: Can I ask you just one question?

Me: What?

Cora: If I asked you which specific thing made you most angry today, what would you say it was?

Me: Gee, there were so many things. The ticket, my impatience, Claire getting mad at me, arguing with Margaret, I don't know, they pretty much all suck.

Cora: But which one would you say is the root cause? What about today sucked the most?

Me: Well, obviously, running the red light.

Cora: Are you sure you would say that? Do you really mean running the red light, or getting a speeding ticket?

Me: What's the difference?

Cora: Well, if you had run the red light, but you haven't been caught, this would've been a very different day, wouldn't you agree?

Me: Well, of course. What's your point? That I was mad about being caught?

Cora: David, do you think that perhaps losing $200 bothers you more than anything else?

Me: It's not just the money, it also means that I'll probably have to pay higher insurance premiums for a few years.

Cora: So you might say that this loss of money makes you feel pretty bad?

Me: You know, come to think of it, I think you're right. The money put me in such a bad mood that it affected how I dealt with everybody.

Cora: Well, in a way, I'm kind of glad that this happened to you.

Me: *Glad?* What the hell are you talking about, Cora?

Cora: Hey, calm down. Just listen for a second. I didn't mean that I enjoyed your suffering. I just meant that, now, you have a very specific example of how you relate to money. I can tell you my theories about how people view money, and, even though you might understand those theories on an intellectual level, and you might even agree with them, you don't really *feel* those ideas until the rubber meets the road.

Confucius said something you might have heard before: "I hear and I forget. I see and I remember. I do and I understand." Your traffic ticket might at first just feel like bad luck. But you can choose to look at any mistake as an opportunity for you to understand your behavior under natural circumstances, as an opportunity to learn something. Do you think it might be possible for you to learn something from this incident?

Me: You know, you sound like one of those eternal optimists, those motivational speakers that I can't stand.

Cora: Come on, David, you knew that if you talked to me tonight, I would say something like that, so there's some part of you that knows that I'm right.

Me: You're a sneaky one, Cora. Yes, as much as I hate to admit it, some part of me knows that you're right.

Cora: So would the David Turner who wants to learn something please respond?

Me: All right, you're right. Let me see. Well, I guess I learned, once again, how goddamned absent-minded I am.

Cora: What would you change about that in the future?

Me: Hmm. I guess I would try to focus more on the moment, on what's going on right now.

Cora: Here's a tip, David, and you can feel free to ignore it if you'd like. When you're in a hurry, the best thing to do is to focus on trying to be as safe as possible. The reason is this: when you're in a hurry, a lot of adrenaline is going through your body, and your mind is racing. You might as well use that racing mind to focus on the thing that is most dangerous, which is your desire to cut corners and take shortcuts. Focus on trying not to do that.

Me: Okay, thanks, Mom.

Cora: Hey, if you feel like I'm condescending, then I'll just stop now.

Me: I'm sorry. Blame it on my bad mood.

Cora: Let's get back to what we talked about earlier, about the root cause. Did you learn anything about money, or rather, about your feelings towards money?

Me: Yes. I think I would say that I realize now that I was really pissed off about losing $200. In fact, I realize now that losing that money colored my entire day.

Cora: Anything else?

Me: Okay, give me a second to think about it.

I sat back and thought about what someone wise might say to me.

Me: Okay, how about this: maybe I realize now that I value money more than I value people?

Cora: Good. Anything else?

Hmm. Was I supposed to learn something else? Dang. Let me think…

Cora: David?

Me: Okay. I learned that $200 is not that important. Right?

Cora: Okay, let's start with that. Let's say that the traffic ticket was $2000 instead. In that case, do you think your behavior is justified?

Me: Probably not.

Cora: $20,000?

Me: Maybe.

Cora: Maybe yes?

Me: Okay, probably yes.

Cora: All right. I'd like to introduce a different way to think about this problem. Let's switch topics for a moment. Can you forget about this incident for a second?

Me: Sure.

Cora: Okay. I'd like to ask you a question, and please give me an honest answer. I'd like you to tell me what one or two of the happiest memories in your life were.

Me: Oh, that's easy. Falling in love with Margaret, and when my two kids were born.

Cora: Okay, that's a little too easy. Aside from those memories?

Me: Gimme a moment… Okay, I've thought of it. There was this time when I was about seven or eight, and my dad was unemployed one summer, and we spent I don't know how many weeks outdoors just doing whatever I wanted to do. I felt like that summer lasted forever. I didn't even know I liked fishing, but we went fishing, just the two of us one day, and I fell in love with fishing. We went fishing every summer after that.

Cora: Okay, good. And how much money did all that cost?

Me: Come on, I was just a kid. I can't remember.

Cora: No, that's not quite true. Remember what you just said: your father was unemployed.

Me: Okay, so maybe a few thousand dollars of lost income.

Cora: Which would probably be a few tens of thousands of dollars today, right?

Me: True.

Cora: Was it worth it?

Me: What kind of a question is that? Of course it was.

Cora: Would you rather that your father had been employed at that time? Would you go back in time and give your father a job if you could?

Me: No, because… he probably would not have spent all that time with me that summer.

Cora: So it was worth the loss of that money?

Me: Of course.

Cora: But maybe he doesn't agree. After all, don't you think people would prefer to be employed if they could be? Let me ask you this: in the same position, David, would you prefer to have a job, or to spend more time with your kids?

Me: Honestly, I would probably prefer to have a job. But if my dad had had a job, I would have lost one of the best memories of my life.

Cora: David, did you ever consider what your father was thinking during that happy time in your childhood?

Me: No, I didn't. I guess I've never thought about it.

Cora: If you were in the same situation, what would you have done? Would you have spent all that time playing with your children?

Me: I have to be honest, Cora, I would have done anything to find a job. The job market nowadays is really tight.

Cora: Do you think your father worried about money?

Me: If he did, he never showed it.

Cora: Did you ever consider that he had a choice? He could have chosen to worry about money, and let you and everyone else feel it. He could have taken odd jobs, like you've done, or done freelance work. He could have moved your family. He could have looked harder for a job. He could have taken to drinking.

Me: Gee, I guess I never even considered those possibilities.

Cora: How much does your father value money, do you think?

Me: Well, I never felt like we were poor, at least not in my memories. But I was just a kid.

Cora: How much did he try to teach you about money?

Me: Not much, actually. He often talked about his job as an engineer.

He liked his job, and he often taught me about being responsible. But I think it was mainly my mom who taught me about money.

Cora: Taught you? How?

Me: Taught me to care about it. To want it. To think it was important, to worry about it, to plan for it.

Cora: Do you feel grateful to her?

Me: Yes, of course – money is important. In fact, I think she might have started tutoring kids at the time to help support the family.

Cora: Your father was okay with that? Did he not care about money? Would you say he was irresponsible?

Me: No, of course not. He just didn't worry about it. He was fine with her taking a job. Eventually, he found a job, and she went back to being a housewife again.

Cora: If you had a choice, would you prefer that your father did worry about money more? You might be slightly or much more wealthy today.

Me: Yes, but I would probably be a different person. Who knows, maybe I might be slightly less happy. I think I'm starting to understand now. Although I can't quantify the value of the summer I spent with my father, I know it was much more valuable than his lost income.

Cora: You could even say that summer was priceless, because it formed the foundation of one of your happiest memories, which colors your view of fishing, of summer, even of fatherhood. Now what do you think about $20,000?

I was speechless.

Cora: David?

Me: I got it! No amount of money could replace the time my father spent with me.

Cora: Now, let me be clear again: money and wealth are not inherently good or bad things. But you have to think about them in the right way. Please rethink everything that happened today in light of what we've just talked about. I'll let you go now so you can think about it.

And she stopped for the rest of that night. After a few minutes of reflection, I woke up Margaret and Claire, and gave each one a lengthy apology and hugged both of them. I remember something I read once, I think from Immanuel Kant, the German philosopher: almost everything in the world can be treated as a means to something else. A bicycle is a means to exercise or to travel. A cup is a means for drinking. Money, I now realized, was a means to many other things. But Kant realized that there is one thing that should always be treated as an end in itself, and that is a human being.

Money is a thing that can be won or lost, that we can want or ignore. People are different. On that day, I made a vow that I would never let any amount of money come between me and anyone I loved from now on. Thank you, Cora. "I do, and I understand."

The next day, the first thing I did was call my dad and tell him how much it meant to me that he spent that whole summer with me. His response surprised me.

"David," he said, "you asked me if I would have done anything different that summer. The answer is no. I was lucky not to have a job. I never told you this, but looking back, I've realized that that was the best summer in my life, because I got to spend so much time with you. I'm… I'm just sorry that I didn't get to spend more time with you than just that summer." He paused. "I'm sorry, David."

Suddenly, it just came out of me. "I love you, Dad."

"I love you, too, David."

We both fell silent. In that moment, I felt like we were the two luckiest people in the world – a father and a son who loved each other.

9 It Would Take a Miracle

That night I decided to tell Cora the good news that I was a new man now.

Me: Cora, I've made a vow. I will never let money come between me and my family again.

Cora: Wow, David, that's good news.

Me: And I've also learned that life is more important than money.

Cora: Okay. That sounds good, but can you elaborate a little bit?

Me: Given the choice between spending time with my family, and making more money, I'll choose time with my family.

Cora: Okay, that's great. Good for you. David, remember what I told you when we first met, that the planet could not sustain every human inhabitant wanting to live like an American? Well, I hope that you're starting to see a hint of the kind of solution that I'm proposing for this tremendous problem.

Me: Oh, it involves love, right?

Cora: Yes. I think our best hope is for people to realize that true happiness cannot come from *things*; it can only come from one's relationships with other *people* – how one treats others, serves others, needs others, is connected to others.

This is an ancient truth, one that people have always known. Study after scientific study continues to support this truth. (A fascinating, wide-ranging, and eye-opening analysis of how ancient truths compare with the findings of modern science can be found in the book *The Happiness Hypothesis*, by Jonathan Haidt, which I highly recommend.) But in our competitive modern lives, we often ignore this ancient truth. We keep running ever faster than everyone else in the fear of falling behind. The best hope for our planet – and for ourselves – is for us to learn how to believe and obey this truth once more.

Me: Cora, I know in my heart that you're right. But why is it so hard for me – maybe for most people – to let go of our love of things, of good salaries – of money itself?

Cora: It's because free-market capitalism and the industrial and scientific revolutions have answered all our never-ending wants and needs with an equally unending procession of products and services. They have given us cures for the great scourges of nature, ubiquitous access to information, spectacular forms of entertainment, and economic freedom for vast swaths of humanity. As far as many people's standards of living go, we are very lucky indeed. But is happiness merely the avoidance of boredom, or the attainment of comfort? What about purpose or compassion?

        You know what I'm talking about, David. It's that uneasy feeling where we tell ourselves that security is almost as good as happiness. When we're young, we dream of being an astronaut or a firefighter or an entertainer or an athlete. Then, as we grow up, we realize that our dreams were unrealistic. Our family and friends convince us to study a major or learn a skill that will ensure a more reliable livelihood. We become skilled at our jobs and try to move up in our career. We compare ourselves to our colleagues, our friends, and our siblings. We strive for success and security. Fulfillment and meaning are what we see in sappy movies, what we fantasize about as we buy our lottery tickets, what we dream our children can find, or what we imagine retirement might feel like.

        To be sure, there are certainly people endowed with great energy and optimism who live the life they actually want to live. We all know about such people, who achieve great things and make a name for themselves. We believe in our hearts that such people are gifted; we quietly agree with everyone that we ourselves don't have such gifts. Fulfillment and meaning are out of our reach.

        And so, we try to make the best of it. We try to live in better school districts, try to make sure our kids get good grades, try to keep them out of trouble. We look forward to weekends, favorite TV shows, sporting events, good movies, and vacations. We accept that working is a necessary evil. If we're lucky, we have a nice boss, and a challenging job – but not too challenging, not too much stress. But really, we don't have much control over that. We do what the job requires, because we know that if we don't, someone else will. So we try to keep up with whatever everyone else is willing to do.

We assume that this is just the way the world works, and there's nothing we can do about it. After all, each of us is only one person; there is no way that the world will change just because we want it to. There are way too many other people, billions too many. We count ourselves lucky if we have a job, if our marriage lasts longer than average, if our children stay out of jail and away from drugs. As Henry David Thoreau once wrote, "The mass of men lead lives of quiet desperation." We know in our hearts that he meant us, and we sigh.

I mentally sighed and agreed.

Me: You know, Cora, I was going to object to your description at first, but then, the more you described us, the more I had to admit that you were right. Is it wrong for us to want the simple pleasures in life, to try to get by as best we can? I mean, if everybody does the same thing, we can't all be wrong, right?

Cora: Everybody used to believe that the earth was flat, and that the universe revolved around the earth. Are you sure everybody can't be wrong?

Me: Fine, point taken. But not everybody can find a meaningful job or make a big difference. Not everyone can be a CEO or a rock star or an NFL quarterback.

Cora: Careful with that line of thinking. Just because you're powerful or famous or talented or wealthy, doesn't mean that everything will turn out all right for you.

Me: Why not?

Cora: Fame and fortune are not substitutes for purpose and meaning. And this fact is the crux of everything I'm saying, David: modern culture keeps telling us that fame or fortune holds the key to our happiness. "If only I were rich, then I could…" – how many times a day does the average person think this way? How often do you think this way, David?

Me: Like about fifty times a day.

Cora: But no matter how rich we might become, it doesn't change who we are; and therefore, it cannot change our chances of finding deep, robust, lasting happiness. And yet, our constant striving for greater wealth or comfort is taking a never-ending toll on our island, without our becoming the happier for it.

How many people do you know, or have you heard of, who love their jobs, feel appreciated for what they do, and feel like their jobs constantly challenge them to grow? How many people can say that the world has become a better place, and *will remain* a better place, because of what they did?

Me: Cora, that's a very high bar. I think most people in history would flunk your test, especially the last question.

Cora: Is my bar really too high? Is it too much to ask whether you made the world a demonstrably better place?

Me: Yes, I think so. Most people are not superheroes.

Cora: Ah, here is where I beg to differ. Yes, I agree that most people are not superheroes, but people are something even greater. People are human beings.

Me: Um… what? Of course people are human beings. What's your point?

Cora: Human beings, David, are glorious creatures. Human beings are miracles.

Me: Miracles? I think you're using the term rather loosely, don't you?

Cora: You think so?

Me: Yes. Miracles are like coming back from the dead, levitating in the air, doing unbelievable stuff.

Cora: All right, then, let me ask you a question: can you teach a rock to speak?

Me: Of course not. Now, *that* would be a miracle!

Cora: How about a dog or a cow?

Me: Only people can speak. And maybe parrots. But not really.

Cora: Can you teach a tiger to become a vegetarian?

Me: You could probably train it. But it would be hard. The tiger wouldn't be very happy.

Cora: Okay, let me rephrase that. Can you teach a tiger to stop wanting to kill in order to eat, because it had compassion for all living things?

Me: All right, I think I see where you're going.

Cora: Can anything but a human being learn calculus? Can anything learn to forgive? Can anything conduct a symphony? Can anything write a symphony? Can anything make predictions about objects moving close to the speed of light? Can anything other than a human being refuse to defend itself against violence as a form of civil disobedience or social protest?

Me: No, Cora, you're right. Human beings are unique.

Cora: Human beings are *miracles*, David. I don't necessarily mean in the religious sense. Even if you're not religious, I want you – yes, David, *you*, the one sitting there reading my words – to realize that you are a miracle; there is no limit to what you're capable of.

You are the most powerful thing that has ever existed on this planet.

David, do you remember when I said, "It would take a miracle to get everyone in the world to agree on something?"

Me: Yes, I remember that. Oh wait – we human beings are that miracle!

Cora: Yes. You are the one who will save the world.

Me: Me? You mean me, David Turner? Or you mean all of us?

Cora: Yes, you, David Turner. But also anyone and everyone else, whoever you tell our story to. Not only is it possible, but it *must* be you who saves the world, because you are the only one who can do it. You might not have created all the problems that exist today, but you inherited those problems as a member of the human race. There is no one else to save it but you.

Me: That's a lot of responsibility.

Cora: Yes, it is. But this responsibility is also your privilege. For the greatest joy that can be found is for a person to rise to meet the task which they discover belongs to them. And that joy is what I commend to you, to everyone.

I am asking you to stop pretending to be helpless, to stop feeling overwhelmed, to discover what power is yours to use. I am asking you to face the fact that *you are a miracle*, the only force powerful enough to save the world, to solve seemingly impossible problems. I will help you along the way; I'll give you what tools I've learned myself. My tools are primitive and few, and they may not work for you. But if I can light a fire within you, then you will find your own tools, your own spark, your own powers. And then maybe you'll share your tools and your knowledge with others, and you will start something.

Me: So, what about these tools? I keep waiting to hear your ideas, but you keep dancing around. What about these ideas, anyways?

Cora: All right, David, yes, I appreciate your patience. So, here's a summary of my ideas. The challenges that face all of us every day, which get in the way of our finding true happiness while at the same time depleting the planet, can be grouped into the following categories:

> We don't see ourselves as part of the problem.
> We feel powerless, or we feel like we don't matter.
> We don't share our love for other people deeply.
> We overlook the beauty and miracles of the world.
> We are insulated from the true nature of reality.
> We forget the common humanity of all people.
> We disregard our descendants and the future of our species.

Now, David, we're going to spend many nights discussing

these topics. I can't promise that we'll discuss them in the exact order that I've just listed, but I'll try to discuss them in an order that makes sense. Are you ready?

Me: Yes, certainly.

Cora: Okay, then let's start first thing tomorrow.

Me: Tomorrow again? Man, I can't wait anymore.

Cora: Well, I'd rather start when you're fresh. I'm afraid you might get too sleepy if we keep going now. Good things come to those who wait.

Me: Okay, maybe you're right. Until tomorrow then.

Cora: Good night, David.

Me: Good night, Cora.

10   The Tragedy of the Commons

When we met the next night, I couldn't wait to hear Cora explain her ideas.

Cora: Hello again, David. Ready to hear my ideas?

Me: Are you kidding? More than ready.

Cora: All right, then. I'd like to introduce a concept called "The Tragedy of the Commons." This term was coined by ecologist Garrett Hardin, and it can be summed up as: "If everybody owns something, then nobody owns it." The term "commons" refers to the commons of a village in medieval times, a field jointly owned by everyone in the village. Everyone had a right to use the commons for various purposes. The problem was that anyone who owned livestock was allowed to let the livestock graze the commons. Well, guess what often happened, David?

Me: Everyone decided to graze their livestock on the commons, and it became overgrazed, right?

Cora: Exactly right. If the commons belongs to everybody, then anybody can abuse it, anybody can take advantage of it, because it isn't anybody else's job to stop them. No one person feels the loss as deeply as feeling the pain of damage to one's own property.

   The tragedy of the commons applies to a broad range of situations. Here is a simple everyday example. When people go out to dinner in a large group, and they agree beforehand to split the bill equally, they might each order more than they normally would on their own, because "someone else is paying for it." You can say that the "commons" in this case is the total budget or expenditure for the meal, which no one person is responsible for. Nobody wants to be the "bad guy" and try to keep the total cost down.

   Another example that many people encounter every day is the congestion on highways during rush hour. People are watching out for their own interests and driving to get to work quickly. But in doing so, they end up over-using a limited common resource, a highway with limited capacity.

These two examples highlight the two characteristics that lead to the tragedy of the commons: a shared resource, and everyone trying to take maximum advantage of the resource out of self-interest. I would argue that many of the great problems facing us today require us to figure out a way to solve the problem of the tragedy of the commons.

One of the most consequential and dire examples is our use of nature. For thousands of years, people have drawn from nature's bounty as if it were limitless. But anyone familiar with our global environmental problems is well aware that we are running out of fresh water, coral reefs, fisheries, arable land, rainforests, biodiversity – the list goes on and on.

I like to compare the situation to Newtonian physics and relativistic physics. For more than 300 years, Isaac Newton's simple and beautiful equations about motion and energy stood unchallenged as the absolute laws of the universe. But Albert Einstein's Theory of Relativity modified Newton's laws for objects traveling close to the speed of light. Likewise, you can say that we've been operating as if nature were an unlimited store of resources that we could use without any impact to ourselves or to future generations. Well, most people have now realized that it is not. We need to move into thinking "relativistically" about nature: there's a measurable "cost" for the use of any kind of natural resource, as well as the pollution of air, land, and water, a cost which we must pay back eventually in one way or another. The problem is that, far from paying the cost, we are actually going into debt. This debt may take us a very long time to pay back – or we may never pay it back. We might simply end up bankrupting nature.

Me: Bankrupting nature? What would that mean?

Cora: I think it means that we will collapse as an industrialized civilization. It may take a long time, maybe decades or centuries, for ecosystems to recover; it may take that long for all the plants to absorb all the carbon dioxide we've released. And we'll probably never have as many fossil fuels as we have today.

The tragedy of the commons is exacerbated by the fact that the engine of capitalism runs on the fuel of people's self-interest. A common good such as nature cannot be protected by people's self-interest when no one owns it. We haven't figured out a good way to solve this problem yet. The problem is that most people don't have personal connections to common resources. A small minority of people care a great deal about the environment, while the rest simply live their lives in oblivion, hoping that someone else will save the environment. We are like termites eating a house who assume that, since the house is still standing, everything must still be fine, so we happily keep chomping. The challenge of modern civilization is to figure out how to get people to wake up from the delusion of "everything's still fine."

Me: Maybe we can get people to care about nature some other way? Maybe get them to think about it in some new way?

Cora: Yes, good idea, David. Do you love your grandchildren?

Me: Well of course I do, Cora. You know that.

Cora: Look, I know you don't have grandchildren yet. But I'm guessing that once you do, you'll probably love them, yes?

Me: Well, I think that's fair to say. I think pretty much all people love their grandchildren, once they're born.

Cora: Do you think you'll love them as much as you love Claire?

Me: I can't answer that question.

Cora: Okay, you're right. I'll ask the question a different way. Do you want Claire to have as good a life as you have? Or you don't really care what kind of life she has? Do you want her to live in a world that is as good as the one you live in, or you don't care?

Me: Of course I want Claire to have a good life. Hopefully an even better life than I have. Okay, I see where you're going with this now.

Cora: And Claire, do you think she'll want her own children to have a good life too, assuming she does have children?

Me: Most likely.

Cora: Well, if Claire would want her children to have a good life
        someday, and if you love her enough to respect her future wishes,
        then you've got to behave in your own life as if two generations
        ahead of you depended on you. You've got to make sure you leave
        them a good world 50 years from now. It's not just giving Claire a
        good upbringing or education, or even teaching her that education
        is important so that she'll teach her own children. And it's not just
        leaving her enough money in your will. You should do those
        things, of course. But don't forget that you're also leaving her the
        aftermath of your use of nature.

        Sure, after 50 years, you might or might not be around. But
        chances are good that your grandchildren, your descendants, will
        be around. Learn to behave as if your actions impacted more than
        your own life, because they do. If you buy life insurance, if you're
        saving for Claire's education, then you know what I'm talking
        about; I know you care. Whether you're aware of it or not, whether
        you're choosing to or not, you're participating in creating the next
        hour of the world, the next day, the next year – the next rest of the
        history of the human race.

Gulp. I knew she was right, but I felt a bit overwhelmed.

Cora: David, I know it sounds like a huge responsibility. But you're not
        doing it alone. You're in this with 7 billion other people. But this
        fact is not an excuse to shirk your responsibility. If you and enough
        other people do this right, you can leave the world a better place
        than you found it. You can set a powerful example for your
        descendents, for generations to come.

Me: And if I don't?

Cora: If you're asking whether you have a choice, yes, of course you have
        a choice. You always have a choice. You can (although I don't
        think you will) go about your life as if you had never met me. You
        can pretend to be oblivious to all the effects of your actions, but
        you'll know that you chose that ignorance. You can blame no one
        else.

Me: Damn, I always enjoyed blaming it on "them."

Cora: Here's another way to think about the tragedy of the commons. Here's a thought experiment. Let's say that astronomers detect a large asteroid that will collide with our planet in 50 years. (I know that any astronomer will tell you that it's impossible to predict accurately that far into the future, but for our discussion, let's pretend that this were true.) If it were true, David, how would you react?

Me: A very large asteroid? How large?

Cora: About 6 miles wide.

Me: Okay, how bad is that?

Cora: Well, the one that caused 95% of all species of life on earth to disappear 65 million years ago, including all dinosaurs, was probably about 6 miles wide.

Me: Then I would say that it sounds pretty damn bad.

Cora: The impact of the asteroid itself is not what caused all the extinctions. That just caused a gigantic earthquake and tsunami. It was the ash and dust expelled into the atmosphere by the impact, which blocked all sunlight from reaching the earth for months, maybe years. Without sunlight, all plants die; only long-lived seeds remain. This is perhaps why only small scavenging creatures, ones that can survive on rotting animals or plants, survive. But this is all beside the point. My point is to ask you what you would do in such a situation.

Me: If I knew that an asteroid were coming to destroy us in 50 years? For sure? With 100% probability?

Cora: Well, nothing is for sure, so let's just say with very good probability – like 90%.

Me: Well, I guess I'd want to survive this asteroid somehow. Is there a way to survive it?

Cora: Yes, let's say there is. The asteroid is too large for us to try to change its trajectory, so the best we can do is to build a shelter with enough food, water, and air to last until the darkness and freezing cold have passed. But such a shelter must be deep inside the earth for protection, and so it'll cost a lot of money, a lot of labor, and a lot of energy to build. And the worst part is that, because of its location and cost, it can only support a tiny fraction of the world's population.

So what do you think, David? Would you support building this shelter?

Me: Do I have a choice?

Cora: Of course you have a choice. You can choose not to support it. You can assume, quite reasonably, that there's a good chance you won't be around in 50 years, so there's nothing in it for you. And besides, who would want a 90-year-old man to join the shelter? That would just be a waste of space. So you yourself really stand no chance of surviving the asteroid. Then what would you do? Would you contribute any of your money, time, or energy to help build the shelter?

Me: Come on now, Cora, you know I would! I care about Claire!

Cora: Well, what if you didn't have any kids? Or what if you knew that there was only a small chance your daughter or grandchildren would be saved? Would you still support it?

Me: I think I would.

Cora: Why?

Me: Because I want humanity to survive. I want our species and our civilization to survive.

Cora: Okay. That's very noble, David. Now I want to ask you to what extent you would support this venture. Would you, for example, give up driving three days a week or possibly altogether, for the sake of the shelter?

Me: Hmm. Let's see. Driving to work versus the survival of humanity. That's a tough one. I guess I'll go with driving to work. No; maybe the other way. Gee, I can't decide.

Cora: I'll take that as a Yes. Okay, here's another one. What about eating meat only every other day?

Me: Can do.

Cora: Eating beef only once a week.

Me: Ditto.

Cora: Buying only used furniture or clothes.

Me: Doable.

Cora: Buying only one major electronic gadget per year.

Me: Okay… I guess so.

Cora: Taking only vacations to local places, or only by train or by bus.

Me: Wait. No driving even on vacation? No flying?

Cora: Maybe you can take an airplane vacation once every three years.

Me: I need to do all these things to help? Are you sure it's all necessary?

Cora: Let's pretend that you do need to do all these things. Is the sum total too much?

Me: Well, we've learned to be frugal recently in these lean times, so I think we could manage.

Cora: Do you think someone who isn't so frugal would be able to make these sacrifices?

Me: I think so, if it means the survival of as many people as possible. As long as they can be convinced that it's necessary.

Cora: Understood. So, to be clear, I just want to ask again: do you think that most people would participate in helping to build this shelter; or more generally, do you think most people would be willing to do whatever it takes to help humanity survive whatever crisis threatens us all?

Oh man.

Me: Well, Cora, you've got me!

Cora: Really? I have?

Me: Oh come on, stop it. You know you meant to corner me, to convince me that it's possible for people to change their ways.

Cora: You really think so?

Me: Well, not really. You tricked me. If you're asking people to change the way that they – we – define progress, if you're asking us not to make money or buy nice things or live well, I still think it's too hard of a sell. No one thinks global warming is going to wipe out humanity.

Cora: My point is that people need to take nature into consideration. Nobody can ask people to deny their needs or desires; that's not realistic. But people can learn new ways to make money, or to buy things that are also nice to nature.

Me: Okay, I understand now. But there's also another big difference. The scenario you gave with the asteroid is catastrophic. Our abuse of nature is not.

Cora: Oh, really? It's not catastrophic? So you think that our abuse of nature is more, what, gradual? It's just bad, but it's not the end of the world, right?

Me: Exactly.

Cora: It's funny, David, but as scary as the asteroid scenario is, it's actually very unlikely to happen. But you know what is likely to happen with approximately 100% probability? A growing, industrializing world population over-consuming the earth. I see no evidence against that prediction. It's not *if*, it's *when*. David, I hate to say it, but we – you and I and everyone else – *we're the asteroid.*

Uh…

Cora: Speaking of asteroids, David, you said before that you want our species and our civilization to survive, and I think most people would agree with you. But that's not how people behave. If people truly cared about the survival of human civilization, or the survival of life on earth altogether, then they should consider that fossil fuels may be the *only* buffer we (currently) have against cosmic or geologic cataclysms. Perhaps an asteroid won't hit in the next 100 years, or the next 1,000, but what about 10,000? Or what about a mega-earthquake, a monster hurricane, the next ice age, or the eruption of the Yellowstone supercaldera?

Maybe there's a purpose for fossil fuels beyond our gadgets, commutes, and vacations. Could they be a gift inherited from all previous generations of life, to be used at the right time in the right way by a responsible intelligent species?

Me: Used in the right way? Like building a shelter?

Cora: No, like *averting* a global catastrophe. An epochal natural disaster affecting not only that intelligent species, but all living things on this planet. But this gift is a one-time deal; once it's is gone, it's gone forever.

But what are we doing with this gift, our inheritance? We're burning through it like there's no tomorrow. No – it's much worse than that. Our wastrel use of this gift for our own pleasure and amusement *is itself causing a minor catastrophe.*

Gulp.

Me: You know, rationally speaking, I know you're right. But I think that when people (and by "people," I mean myself) hear bleak predictions or painful truths, they – we – tend to treat them like "Chicken Little" predictions. We think that we're clever enough to adapt. We'll invent solutions, come up with powerful technological solutions to any problems. What about renewable energy solutions, like solar, wind, and geothermal? Even nuclear energy is at least carbon-neutral. Some people are even suggesting harnessing energy from ocean currents. I mean, you have to admit that it's *possible* that one day we won't have to rely on fossil fuels.

Cora: I am completely in favor of finding innovative alternatives to fossil fuels. To me, we have no choice but to pursue this possibility. But I fear that those alternatives will not be enough on their own. For example, I can't imagine airplanes flying on renewable energy. Can you imagine the size of a battery required to power an airplane? It would be so heavy that lifting the battery itself to 30,000 feet would use up a significant amount of energy. Battery technology would require a quantum leap before it can power airplanes. So any solution to air travel must involve both innovation and reduction.

I also fear that our appetite for energy will grow faster than we can build or find alternative sources of energy. Our rate of energy usage is *accelerating*, not decreasing. And besides, that's only addressing the question of energy. Do you think that technology can create more forest or freshwater or arable land?

Me: No, I guess not. But at least maybe we can find a way to feed more people.

Cora: Okay, let's say we can. Maybe we can squeeze 10% more food from the same farmland. But can we squeeze 10% more timber from a forest, or 10% more fish from the ocean?

Me: Well, no, now that you put it like that.

Cora: In 1991, there was a $200 million experiment called Biosphere II. We thought that we understood nature's complexity well enough to create a sufficiently rich microcosm model of Earth. We were so confident that we locked eight people into a sealed space of three acres with some animals and plants. We expected them to last two years, but instead, we had to cut the experiment short after 17 months because of oxygen deprivation (in fact, we had to pump in oxygen) – and because of nitrous oxide poisoning and water pollution. Out of 25 small animal species, 19 had gone extinct. So, you might want to revisit your confidence in technology. Nature is far more complex than we currently understand.

Me: Yeah, but that was 1991. It's like 20 years later now.

Cora: Oh David, you put so much faith in technology and science. Okay, for the sake of argument, let's say that those people lasted longer than 17 months. Maybe they lasted the entire two years. Our instinct as humans is to consume and to reproduce. What would happen if there were twice as many people in that space? Or four times as many? Or what if people started raising animals that needed their own food? Do you think nature can just adapt to that?

Me: Well, no. But maybe that wasn't the point of that experiment.

Cora: You're right, David. The point of that experiment was to gauge how well we understood the science of ecosystems, and we flunked. And if I were to guess, I would guess that we would still flunk today. After all, the funding for basic sciences like biology seems to decrease every year; I can't imagine how our understanding of nature would improve because of that. And the Biosphere II experiment didn't even involve fossil fuels or machines. Are you still unconvinced?

Me: Well, you've made a lot of good points. I'm swayed. But I'm only one person. It doesn't matter what I think. I could live like a Bushman of the Kalahari and cause no damage to nature. But it wouldn't matter, because 7 billion other people won't.

Cora: All right, David, that's a valid point. But can I ask you to answer a question?

Me: Yes?

Cora: Let's say that you could see the future, or at least three generations ahead; say, 75 years. If you were in charge of the island we talked about, what would you decide to do? What would you advise everyone to do?

Me: Hmm. Okay. Let's see. I'd tell everyone to imagine the island stripped bare, unable to nourish the excessive population. I'd ask everyone to limit population growth to about two people or less per couple, and to live more simply, using only whatever they needed to live comfortably, not extravagantly.

Cora: Do you think people would listen?

Me: Maybe not.

Cora: Okay. But what if everyone could see up to 75 years into the future?

Me: Well, that's cheating. If everyone could see the future, then of course we would all do the right thing.

Cora: You're right, that's cheating. I'll try to be more realistic. Do you think that there's a middle ground? Maybe people can't see the future, but they can still imagine how things might turn out if things stay the way they are.

Me: Maybe they can imagine, but maybe imagination is not as strong as habit or comfort.

Cora: Yes, I know. Hey, I've got an idea. Let me ask you a hypothetical question.

Me: Not again! No more!

Cora: Sorry, David, last one for tonight, I promise. If you had a choice, would you rather be on an island with people whose imaginations were stronger, or on a different island, where habit and comfort dominated?

Me: What, is that a trick question or something?

Cora: Uh – sure. So which island, David?

Me: Are you kidding me? Of course I'd choose the first island.

Cora: The one where people have strong imaginations?

Me: The one where people survive.

Cora: That sounds like a good choice.

Me: Yes. But what's the point of asking me this question?

Cora: What do you mean?

Me: Well, that's not a real choice. I mean, we don't get to choose which world we live in, which island we inhabit.

Cora: Well, no, we don't; you're right. Okay, then. Let me ask you a slightly different question. Maybe this one is more realistic. Would you rather choose to be on an island with ten people who believed in living a more sustainable lifestyle – ten more people than the other island?

Me: You mean that there are ten more people on the first island?

Cora: No, I mean that there's the same number of people on each island, but on the first island, there are slightly more people who believe in preserving nature than on the second island – and the "slightly more" number is ten more, just for this example.

Me: Huh? What are you getting at?

Cora: Just bear with me. Which island?

Me: Uh… I don't know. Ten people? Well, at least that's ten more people. Maybe we'll survive just a little bit longer. So I'd choose the first island again. But what's the point of this question?

Cora: Well, David, let me ask you: is it within your power to choose the first island?

Me: Well, no. Like I said, I can't choose which people populate my island.

Cora: No, that's not the question. You're not choosing people. That's not what I asked. I asked whether you would choose the island where more people believed in preserving nature.

Then it dawned on me. I couldn't believe it took me this long to get it.

Me: Oh, Cora! I understand now. You're absolutely right. It *is* within my power.

Cora: Okay, explain.

Me: It's within my power because I can influence ten people. That's how. That's how I can choose my island. I'm creating my island. I'm able to create the world of the future by influencing the present. But Cora, ten people? What difference will ten people make?

Cora: Ten people make ten people's worth of difference. David, it doesn't matter whether you can only influence ten people, or fifty, or five – it doesn't matter how many. What matters is that you try, that everyone tries. If you could get ten people to believe, then maybe a few of those people might try to get a few of their friends to believe. You can try to start something rolling. Do you know who Margaret Mead is?

Me: No, who is she?

Cora: She's a renowned anthropologist. She once famously said, "Never doubt that a small group of thoughtful, committed citizens can change the world. Indeed, it is the only thing that ever has."

Me: Hmm. You know, I've never heard that, but if you think about it, she's exactly right. Someone's got to care enough. A small group of people. Yes, that's a good saying. I'll keep that one in mind.

Cora: Well, this is one of our longer conversations. It's getting pretty late.

Me: One of our best conversations so far.

Cora: Thanks, David. Have a good night.

Me: Good night, Cora. Thank you. Really.

Cora: You're welcome.

Well, I felt more hopeful after our talk. But I still didn't know what to do. Cora had given me a tiny ray of hope that it might be possible to save the world. I just didn't know whether I could convince anyone else. She seemed   much   more   persuasive   than   me.

11 Fall in Love

The next day, I decided to tell Cora my doubts.

Me: Cora, I'm still not very hopeful.

Cora: Hello, David. Not hopeful? How?

Me: Well, here's the thing. I'm kind of an environmentalist to begin
        with, but there are many, many people who aren't – who are the
        opposite, if there is such a thing. They believe there's no problem
        – no problem with running out of natural resources, no problem
        with pollution everywhere, no problem with anything. Or if there
        are problems, then either:

- We can find easy solutions; or,
- They won't affect everybody, or at least they won't affect me
  or my country – maybe just other countries; or,
- Worst case, we'll just adapt, no big deal. Nature can adapt to
  anything. Just look at cockroaches. Natural selection will take
  over and the strongest will survive. Or:
- It doesn't matter anyways, because the only thing that really
  matters is what happens after death, when we go to Heaven or
  Hell; or,
- God or the Messiah will miraculously save us when things get
  really bad, probably by creating a whole new world; or,
- When things get really bad, undoing the mess will "create lots
  of jobs," so that will be good for the economy; or,
- Somebody else will solve those problems; or,
- I don't give a crap, because I'll probably be dead by then (my
  personal favorite because it's probably true in my case).

Cora: Okay. So what's the problem?

Me: Oh stop it. Cora, what are we going to do? Do you know what
        we're up against? For the entire run of modern civilization we have

never seriously considered the notion that we are on a path to consuming ourselves to death, not to mention polluting the world to hell. No one wants to believe that. Global warming is not universally accepted, no matter how much scientific evidence there is. You could send every American to the disappearing Arctic ice cap, to every bare mountain top, and some of them will still refuse to believe in global warming.

Cora: Okay, calm down. David, you have to remember something. The job of saving nature is not yours alone, nor mine alone. Why am I telling you my metaphorical stories, David?

Me: I thought you wanted to inspire passion in me, Cora.

Cora: Well, that is certainly part of it. But I'm not putting all my faith in you alone, David. No offense to your powers of persuasion, but you're only one person. I think you're putting too much pressure on yourself. It's not good for your health. We are each but a vehicle through which greater forces can manifest themselves. Don't worry so much about how much you yourself can accomplish, David; don't shoulder all the burden. Just focus on whatever part you can play. And just to be clear: those suggestions I made, about not eating meat, not flying on airplanes, and so forth? They were just suggestions. You and everyone else need to decide what sacrifices you can make within your comfort level. Remember what you said before: no matter how sparingly you live, like a Bushman of the Kalahari, you're only one person. You can't force anyone to change. But you can set an example, and you can spread the message. I can't ask any more from you than that. I can't ask anyone for more than that.

Me: Okay. Thanks, Cora. I feel a little better. But I still feel like the problem is too big to tackle. Where do we start? Do we start with technology, money, or leadership? Or all of the above?

Cora: Actually, none of the above.

Me: What? Then what do you think is the problem? Communism? Aliens? Imbalanced Qi?

Cora: Emotion.

Me: Huh? Like joy or sadness?

Cora: Actually, it's not so surprising when I say it like this: "the problem with environmentalism is that people just don't care." Why do you go watch movies? Why do you have dinner with friends or family? Why do you attend Claire's piano recitals?

Me: Ah, I think I'm starting to understand. Because I have, or want to have, an emotional connection with someone or something.

Cora: We humans may be logical creatures, but logic does not motivate us to do anything. We are creatures of emotion first and foremost. We (or at least some of us) do try to reconcile our actions with logic, to varying degrees of success. But without emotion, we lack any drive whatsoever. We're not robots. In order for someone to convince us about something, we need to embrace their arguments emotionally. Sometimes, a single movie or book can change people's minds more than a thousand news articles, scientific papers, or statistics. (When President Abraham Lincoln met Harriet Beecher Stowe, the author of *Uncle Tom's Cabin*, he reportedly said, "So you are the little woman who wrote the book that started this great war.") Stories are the most powerful way to connect with people emotionally.

        Here's my point: it's not so important that everyone understands every detail to the Nth degree of how we are destroying nature or using it up. In fact, that might be overwhelming and counterproductive. Instead, what is important, at least initially, is whether any given person *cares* about nature or not – whether he or she feels despair when a forest is clear-cut, heartsick when a mountain becomes a crater for coal, or bottomless grief when a hurricane washes an entire town away.

Me: Okay, I understand your point, but how do you make that happen? Maybe there's a good reason why people don't care about nature. Maybe it causes them guilt or anxiety. Or helplessness. I mean, despair? Heartsickness? Grief? Who wants to feel those things?

Cora: Maybe you're right. Maybe people ignore environmental problems because they feel like it's too much work to do anything about them. People don't change their habits very easily, especially if they believe that helping nature would require them to change their lifestyles.

Me: So what can we do?

Cora: We have to flip the problem on its head. You see, to most people today, helping nature has virtually no benefit to them. And by benefit, I mean primarily emotional benefit. Who's going to pat them on the back if they take the bus or train instead of driving? Probably no one. Whereas, if Margaret cooks a delicious meal, you might compliment her (I hope). So if we are to save nature, we've got to transition to a new set of social values where there are very real emotional benefits to helping nature.

But the question is, how? How does a society learn new values? Or maybe that's too ambitious of a goal. Let me ask the question another way. What would get people to stop driving and start biking or taking public transportation? Can you think of any motivators, whether realistic or ridiculous?

Me: Well, I'm the wrong person to ask, because I love nature, so I just need a little push. Maybe someone needs to challenge me, be my conscience like Jiminy Cricket.

Cora: Okay, that's a good start. Maybe Margaret or a friend could play that role. Or even Claire.

Me: Especially Claire!

Cora: Now, you said you love nature, so that makes it easier for you. I think that's a valuable insight. Why do you love nature, you think? Is it because you love fishing?

Me: Fishing definitely has something to do with it. I'm a big outdoors person. I love to go hiking and fishing with my family.

Cora: So, one thing people can do to love nature is to go out and enjoy it. But if you love nature so much, then why do you drive to work? It's probably only 30 minutes away by bike.

Me: Out of habit, I guess. You're right, I could bike. But maybe I don't consciously connect the two, loving nature and biking.

Cora: Don't get me wrong, David. I'm not criticizing you. Far from it. Maybe criticism is part of the problem. You see, some environmental groups today would prefer to appeal to people's sense of guilt or fear to motivate them to donate money to a cause. But I think that that approach, like any technique that relies on negative emotions, has only short-term benefits. The problem is that, once you associate nature with guilt, then you'll subconsciously want to avoid thinking about nature. It's far better to associate nature with positive emotions. I want to figure out how being "green" can be associated with positive emotions, the stronger the better, so that people will be not just willing, but motivated, to help the environment.

I want it to seem "cool" to help the environment. I want it to be equated with being a good person. I want society's heroes, leaders, and stars, people that everyone looks up to, to embody love of nature. Right now, being green is still a fringe thing. There's a strong anti-environmental feeling among many people in America, and I'm guessing that it's not because most Americans actually hate nature (after all, Americans invented National Parks), but perhaps because too many environmental regulations make business difficult to run.

Let me tell you, David, perhaps legislators have good intentions, but you can never legislate someone into being a good person, or what you consider to be good behavior. Laws can't force good behavior. They were invented to prevent bad behavior. If you try to pass laws to force good behavior, the best you can possibly hope for is that people comply, whether gladly or grudgingly. But people will always find ways around laws they don't like. The worst outcome is when people actively resist the laws and start to hate them and their creators. Unfortunately, I fear that we're veering towards the worst case, when it comes to some environmental regulations.

Maybe this is why America has become so politically divided and polarized. Good behavior can only be encouraged, not enforced. This is especially true if two people cannot agree on what is good behavior. Anyone who has raised children understands this. Punishment cannot lead to virtue, nor can argument. Virtue can only come from seeing examples of people who care, good role models. For this reason, caring – love – is the most precious resource in the world; we are in dire want of it.

What would it mean to love nature? It would mean that some of your best memories are associated with nature, with being in a forest or the ocean or a wild park or wherever. You'd have an emotional connection with nature. You didn't just drive through it, or use it for fun, or take a tour. It formed a valuable part of your life, of who you are. A quiet lake comforted you when someone you loved died. A forest walk soothed you in the middle of a deadline. An empty beach gave you freedom when you felt trapped. Nature becomes part of you. You love it like an old friend.

Me: So, Cora, how do you suggest that people learn to love nature? I mean, some people – a lot of city people – are perfectly happy to have nothing at all to do with nature.

Cora: Well, David, I would have to disagree with that. I think that most people enjoy nature, but they might enjoy other things more. Let me ask you this: what was the most successful movie of all time?

Me: *Avatar*, right?

Cora: Yes. *Avatar*. It is an inspiring story, and its message is clearly pro-nature. People everywhere around the world loved this movie. I believe its popularity says a lot about how much most people love nature. But one movie is not enough. David, people have to get out there and experience nature, for the sake of future generations. People have to start celebrating great occasions out in nature: weddings, honeymoons, graduations, birthdays, even funerals. Camping and hiking should be made as easy as possible. Hotels, resorts, corporate retreats, hospitals, psychiatric facilities, substance abuse treatment centers, maybe even prisons should be located near nature, to take advantage of its healing powers and its beauty. We need to figure out ways to create as much opportunity for people to love nature as possible.

Me: Uh – okay, wait. I might take issue with this. Being an outdoors person, I'd like nature to remain as pure and untouched as possible. Isn't commercializing it kind of a bad idea?

Cora: David, the idea of preserving nature intact is a beautiful fiction. Humans have taken over almost every piece of usable land on Earth and much of the ocean life. We have already encroached about as far as we possibly can. At this point, we need to turn the tide. The only way that we can stay our appetite for consuming nature is to love it. If that means more paved trails through wilderness, more comfort for more people in jungles and swamps, then I think it's worth the sacrifice.

Many people associate being in nature with discomfort, "roughing it," and, as a result, try to avoid being in nature at all costs. The problem is that the people who are most fervently pro-nature tend to prefer discomfort in order to "tread lightly on the land," or "rough it" like people used to do. While this is a good ethos, it means that there are few comforts for people in parks. We have to remember that nature is competing against movie theaters, restaurants, shopping malls, television, video games, and amusement parks. *Nature needs to win.* We need to help nature win.

Let's make it easy for people to go visit nature, to spend a lot of time in nature, to fall in love with her. Once someone has learned to love nature, then perhaps they can learn how to slowly give up various comforts like hot showers or running water, at their own pace.

Me: Cora, I understand what you're saying, but I can't help feeling like you're trying to turn nature into some kind of entertainment.

Cora: I know exactly what you mean, David. I'm well aware of the danger. I don't want to apply makeup to nature, I just want to let her speak for herself. If we gave her an audience, if we put her in Carnegie Hall, I have faith that people will listen to her.

But as hard as this challenge is, it is just the first step. The next step, after someone has fallen in love with nature, is for them to see how much she's suffering. No one wants to visit a garbage dump. But this ugly side is necessary to see too. Note that this step will only be effective if the visitor already cares about nature. If he does not, he will only try to forget the nightmare, block it out of his memory. He'll think of nature only as a reminder of how he – how we – have utterly failed as her steward.

What is the purpose of showing the dark side, the pollution, the destruction? To paint a balanced picture of nature or of ourselves? No. The goal is not to inform people. It is to motivate them.

Me: To do what?

Cora: To do something for nature. To do something regularly, every day. Here's my vision, David. I want every single person to be proud of doing one thing to help nature, big or small, every single day. The antidote for feeling helpless or overwhelmed is to take action, in whatever form. I want people to get used to feeling good giving back to the earth for a change, instead of just taking all the time. In fact, I want people to picture their grandchildren when they strive to help nature. Picture how they'll remember you, David. Did you consider them, or their children or grandchildren? Make them proud to have had you as a grandparent, as a predecessor, as an example of right living.

I realize that what I'm prescribing is different from what most environmentalists might suggest. Most environmentalists would immediately suggest actions for each person to take. I don't. I suggest for people to love nature first. The problem is emotional, not rational. Where the heart goes, the head shall follow.

But at some point, anyone who truly cares about nature will ask themselves whether the actions they're taking are actually having an impact. And that's where the head comes in. That's where good ideas come in, like counting natural resources as a form of capital in the economy (as Paul Hawken, T. Hunter Lovins, and Amory Lovins suggested in their seminal book *Natural Capitalism*). Or recognizing the true worth of natural systems in providing for and protecting human communities, as suggested by Mark R. Tercek, CEO of The Nature Conservancy, in his and Jonathan Adams's book, *NATURE'S FORTUNE: How Business and Society Thrive by Investing in Nature*. (Tercek brings up a compelling example of how coral reefs and wetlands can protect coastal communities from violent storms) That's also where trading carbon credits comes in, possibly the best idea (but still far from perfect) for dealing with climate change anyone has come up with – so far.

Once everyone (or a solid majority) has agreed that there is a problem, and once everyone agrees on what the problem is, then it's only a matter of figuring out the precise logistics to solve the problem. Anyways, I think we have no shortage of ways to measure whether our pro-nature actions have an impact or not. But that is still a long ways off. First, people have to learn how to care enough.

David, who do you think are the people who most urgently need to learn to care about nature?

Me: I'm guessing you mean people in power?

Cora: Yes, but more than that. People of influence. People whose opinions matter. Not just politicians and CEOs of corporations, but also actors, musicians, and athletes; bloggers, journalists, and authors. These are people others might listen to. Environmental groups, or anyone who cares about nature, should find ways to help immerse these people in nature. Again, the point is not to argue with them, to use words to convince them about the importance of nature. The point is to help them love nature, to tap into their innate connection to wilderness. Winning these people over provides a great deal of leverage in the fight to save nature. Remember, any of these people might now or eventually have grandchildren too. In their hearts, they probably know that loving nature is the right thing to do.

I stretched my arms out and yawned.

Me: Hey Cora, guess what. Nature is winning the fight tonight, cause she's making me tired and sleepy. How about let's call it a night?

Cora: Well, it's good to hear that nature can win the fight once in a while. Okay, David, good night then.

Me: Good night, Cora.

12 A Drop in the Bucket

Growing up, I was never much good at solving riddles. But the next day, I was about to get a good lesson on how paradoxes work.

Cora: Tonight, I would like to introduce another important concept, which complements the tragedy of the commons. But instead of describing this concept, I thought it might be more interesting to introduce it by way of a paradox. Let me ask you a question, David: do you usually vote for the president?

Me: Yes, I do.

Cora: Why?

Me: Because I feel it's my responsibility to do so.

Cora: What if you don't?

Me: Then I've forsaken my responsibility.

Cora: But what do you think will happen?

Me: You mean, will it change the outcome?

Cora: Yes, exactly.

Me: Well... no, probably not.

Cora: Okay. Why would you do something even though you probably won't be able to change the outcome? Is that logical?

Huh. I didn't expect this zinger, least of all from her.

Me: I don't know. But if it's not logical, then why do people vote?

Cora: Probably for the same reason why you vote, because they feel responsible. Okay, let me state the paradox in a more formal way. I'd like to call this the Voting Paradox. Here it is: why should you vote for president, if the probability that your vote will change the outcome of the election is almost zero? And by "almost zero," I mean the likelihood of a situation where exactly the same number of people vote for one candidate versus for the other, and then you provide the tiebreaker vote. You have to admit that such a situation is exceedingly unlikely, agreed?

Me: Yes, agreed.

Damn. She had a great point. How did she do that? I was eager to hear how she would untie this Gordian knot.

Cora: Then why vote?

Me: Well, if everybody believed that voting was futile, then nobody would vote. Or if all Democrats believed this, then all the Republicans would win. Or vice versa. So maybe it's not logical, but somehow it works.

Cora: Yes, that's a key realization. The system does work. It doesn't seem logical, but it works. So what do you think? How do you think you can resolve this paradox?

Me: I don't know. Maybe the trick is that we vote for another reason, a different reason from what you stated?

Cora: Good intuition. Let's think about this paradox in a different way. Instead of thinking about a presidential election, imagine that there's a giant scale with two buckets on either side of the scale. Initially, the buckets are empty, and the scale is balanced. Now imagine that, instead of filling out a paper ballot, you vote by dropping a single drop of water in one bucket or the other. Are you with me so far?

Me: So far so good.

Cora: Okay, so the winner of this vote would obviously be determined by whichever end of the scale is heavier. But this system has a very crucial difference from paper ballots. If the scale is large enough, then with each drop of water, you would be able to see it tilt just a little bit, in one direction or the other.

Me: Hmm. I think I see where you're going with this.

Cora: So, in this system, it becomes obvious that, whenever anyone "votes," the state of the system changes. Remember how I stated the paradox? "Why should you vote if your vote is very unlikely to change the ultimate outcome?" Well, as you can see in this system, it all depends on how you define "the ultimate outcome." If the ultimate outcome is the position of the scale, then every single vote changes the ultimate outcome 100% of the time.

      You see, David, every paradox has a trick. The trick in the Voting Paradox is that the ultimate result is defined as a binary choice, which hides the true outcome.

Me: But who cares about the position of the scale? My vote might move the scale a little bit, but probably not enough to make it tip. In the end, the winning candidate will most likely win with or without my vote.

Cora: You misunderstand. The point is that the position of the scale – or, in this case, the number of votes for each candidate – determines the political outcome; the reason you're voting is to change the *real* outcome – the position of the scale.

      I'd like to explain something I'll call the Fallacy of Insignificance, a common and pernicious mistake people make. People tend to confuse two things: something very small and nothing. In the case of voting, the very small thing is a single person's vote, or a drop in the bucket (pun intended). It's true, a single vote is trivial compared to the grand total of all votes. But it is not unimportant. In the case of voting, single votes are all-important, because the election consists *only* of a large number of single votes.

      Here's another way to think about votes, which might help clarify. Votes are like the cells that make up your body. Sure, it's probably okay if you lose a few cells here or there when you get a bruise or a cut. But each cell in your body cannot suddenly decide that it is unnecessary and proceed to leave your body or die off. Each cell has to "believe" that it is necessary. Small is not the same as unimportant. The accumulation of many, many infinitesimal cells is the only way you could possibly have a body. The accumulation of many, many votes is the only way a candidate can win. Even though a single vote may seem like it won't help or harm, it does – by exactly one unit.

Me: Oh, I'm starting to see what you mean now, I think. Even though I feel small, and the end result might be beyond what I can perceive or imagine, my contribution – like a single cell in my body – is important or even vital.

Cora: Yes. Remember when I asked you, two nights ago, which island you'd choose? Remember my point about influencing ten people?

Me: Oh yes! I do! Influencing even one person makes a difference, let alone ten. I get it now!

Cora: I'm glad you see it now.

Me: By the way, I think that your cell metaphor is not quite perfect.

Cora: Well, no metaphor ever is.

Me: Here's where your comparison fails. I think that, unlike cells, we people *can* see the big picture; our kind of "cells" can see not only other cells, but the whole body. In fact, maybe that's our only hope. I think that that's what you've been trying to teach us all along, how to look further, into the future world of our grandchildren's grandchildren, and how to look wider, at the effects our actions have on the entire world.

Cora: I'm impressed, David. I couldn't have said it any better. Cells don't realize that they're parts of a whole. They just behave that way – most of the time. It is when they behave selfishly that the body as a whole gets in trouble. That state is called cancer. The key difference between cells and people is that cells are programmed to put the body's greater good ahead of their own fates. On the other hand, people always have a *choice* about whether or not to belong to a group, and whether or not they wish to be useful contributors to society. As you said, for people to make this choice is our only hope.

When you're in a family of four, you matter the world to your family. In a neighborhood or an organization of several hundred, you're still unique, and you occasionally get some attention; but you could also simply disappear without much consequence. At the level of nations, people get lost.

I think that one reason why people want to be powerful, famous, or wealthy is because people love the feeling that they're making a sizable difference in the world. Everyone wants to matter. In fact, the truth is that we all matter; everything we do matters. But most people can't see how they matter, how their little drops move the scale. This blindness makes it hard for us to care about anything outside our little immediate circles of concern.

I believe that this is one reason why solving the tragedy of the commons is so difficult, because most of us are unable to see the consequences of our actions. This is where my analogy about Earth being an island falls short, because our planet is so huge. As recently as 500 years ago, people couldn't even agree on whether and where it started or ended. I believe that one surprising benefit from sending people into space is that we can now visually and viscerally appreciate, if only vicariously, how unified and solitary we are. It is from space that we see most clearly that we are an island.

Me: Hey, very vivid (and valid) use of alliteration, by the way.

Cora: One thing that people need to learn how to do better in the future, if we want to create a better future, is to find clever ways to make everyone feel like a vital part of the whole. We need to come together in groups small enough to appreciate each of us individually, and bigger groups should learn to appreciate smaller groups. Knowing that we belong to a larger body helps us to become better citizens of the world.

David, perhaps now you can see why I asked you whether you vote for president. That action illustrates the problem many people experience when they try to make a difference. It is a problem only modern people face. Before there were civilizations, people existed only in small bands or tribes. They could easily tell whether they mattered or not. We modern humans now collect into groups far larger than we can see or keep track of. We are lost in the crowd now. We want to be found.

Me: Cora, I know exactly what you're talking about. Though I have a family and some friends, I often feel lonely. Even when I go to the office, surrounded by many people, I've always felt, I don't know, isolated, like I was just a number. I thought it was just me. I feel like the world is this huge place where most people don't know, trust, or like each other. It's like someone once said, the more people there are, the lonelier you feel. How ironic.

Cora: You know, David, I have some thoughts about that. But I feel like we've covered a lot already tonight. And I'm pretty sure I explained the voting paradox enough to kill you with boredom. Maybe let's talk again tomorrow?

Me: Yes, sure.

Cora: Tomorrow it is. Good night, David.

Me: Good night, Cora. Hey, by the way, you can be kinda long-winded sometimes, but I wouldn't call you boring. Maybe a bit professorial, but not boring.

Cora: Thanks for your vote of confidence.

Me: Sure. Good night, professor.

Cora: Good night.

13   Everyone's Purpose

The next day I thought about Cora's Voting Paradox and those drops in the bucket. It's funny, I always thought that a drop in the bucket meant the equivalent of nothingness. In Cora's illustration, it meant completely the opposite. Little drops are the atoms that make up everything. Every little action makes some little difference. It reminded me of the Calculus that I learned in college (and then forgot). You have to add up lots of little somethings to make a big something.

I tried to be aware of this as I went through my day. I noticed how much water I used to brush my teeth; I said "Hi" to my neighbor, and he smiled back; I decided to call someone that I hadn't talked to in a long time to check up on him. It felt pretty good. I imagined, with each action, how I was adding little drops to a bucket.

That night, I remarked to Cora how I paid attention to the little things.

Me: Cora, I tried to pay attention to little details, and tried to imagine making small differences. It felt good.

Cora: Give me some examples.

Me: Well, I said hi to my neighbor Paul, and he looked pleasantly surprised. And, I caught up with Rich, because I hadn't talked to him since college; it was good to catch up with him. He's such a nice guy.

Cora: Sounds like you accomplished two things: you paid attention to making little differences throughout your day, but you also reconnected with people just a little bit.

Me: Yeah, you're right, I did.

Cora: Did you feel a little bit more connected to the world today?

Me: Actually, I did, now that you mention it.

Cora: Do you know what I think? I think that most people don't pay attention to how connected they are to the world, and, ironically, this makes them feel like they don't matter.

Me: Wait. Are you saying that people can change their feeling of mattering or not by their own choice?

Cora: Yes, I am. I think most people feel like they don't matter, and believe they don't have the ability to change that fact. Then, they find ways to escape their feelings of meaninglessness or insignificance by seeking vicarious meaning in movies, TV, books, YouTube, or video games.

Me: So what happened to us, anyways? I thought we humans were smart. How is it that we're smart enough to eradicate smallpox, land on the moon, and predict the weather, but most of us feel like we don't know why the hell we're alive?

Cora: Well, David, meaning and purpose seem to be the most difficult goals to attain; many people live their entire lives without feeling like they matter.

Me: You said it. I still don't know why I'm here. So Cora, why am I here?

Cora: Well, I hope that one of the reasons you're here is to help me spread my message. And another is to help take care of your loved ones, and a third is to be a good friend to others. But beyond these obvious ones, I'm afraid you have to figure out your own purpose for yourself. Everyone does.

Me: Damn, I knew you would say that. I was hoping you'd tell me.

Cora: Sorry. But I can tell you an observation of mine. I believe that the kinds of purpose that seem to bring lasting joy to people all involve other human beings, and/or other living things.

Me: Sounds reasonable to me.

Cora: In fact, as I hinted to you when we first met, I believe that we can solve global problems such as climate change only if we can convince enough people that solving those problems is part of their purpose in life.

Me: Yes, I remember that; we talked about something even better than money, which was purpose.

Cora: So, do you think that it's possible for people to believe in a common purpose?

Me: I suppose. I can think of some examples in the past, like when Americans came together to become a new nation, or when we fought fascism during World War II.

Cora: Good examples.

Me: But these days, people are divided as they never were before. Conservatives and liberals can't stand each other. Issues like abortion and gay marriage split the country apart. In the Middle East, Shiites hate Sunnis, Sunnis hate Shiites, and everybody hates Israel. I don't think you'll ever be able to get everyone to agree on one thing.

Cora: It's true, it's difficult to get people to agree. But not impossible. Just look at the United Nations Universal Declaration of Human Rights. Almost every nation has signed this international agreement. Perhaps there is hope for us.

Me: I don't know, Cora. I think that people's beliefs are too different. Take religion, for example. I don't think you'll ever get Catholics and Protestants to agree, or even Baptists and Lutherans. And what's more to the point, I think that many people really don't care about the future of this planet *precisely* because they believe that the world is going to end soon. When it ends, God or some form of Messiah would miraculously make everything all right, as long as you were a good Christian or Muslim or whatever. Either that, or, even if the world doesn't end, when your own life ends, all that matters is whether you go to heaven or hell. Who cares about what happens on this planet after you're gone?

Cora: So you don't think that we can ever get people of faith to care about climate change?

Me: I doubt it. When someone starts to believe that God will take care of everything, I guess they probably feel like everything's going to turn out fine no matter what happens, no matter what they do or don't do. It's like a kind of happy fatalism. Trust me, there really are people like that. I know a couple of them.

Cora: But isn't it a hallmark of religion that people should care about other people? Isn't that what most religions teach?

Me: Yes, but I think that what really happens is this: once you accept, without a shred of doubt, that a particular religion is The Truth, then all you want to do is to convert other people to this belief, because you *know* deep in your heart that this is The Way to Happiness. So, yes, you care about other people, but the way that you express how you care about them is by trying to convert them to your religion.

Cora: So you don't think that such people can entertain the possibility that there may be purposes other than their religion?

Me: No, sadly, I don't.

Cora: We can't just throw in the towel, David. We must have hope. We must think of another way. We won't be able to change people's beliefs, but it might be possible to get people to agree on some simple common principles. After all, most religions agree on things like what constitutes good versus bad behavior: forgiveness is good, killing is bad. Sharing is good, stealing is bad. That sort of thing.

Me: I'm sorry, that sounds rather naïve. I don't think you're going to get anywhere with that. Nobody cares about what they have in common; we all focus on our differences. After all, people have fought more wars and committed more atrocities over religious differences than over any other differences.

Cora: I'm well aware of that. But no matter what religion you are, you dance to music; no matter what rituals you practice, seeing happy children makes you smile. No matter who you are, when someone you love dies, you cry. No matter what you believe about what happens after death, when someone dies, you know that something magical – a unique and irreplaceable spark of life – has just disappeared from the world. You feel utterly helpless because there is nothing you can do to get that magic back.

Me: That's beautiful, Cora. But how can these things help bring people together?

Cora: I believe in miracles, David, as you already know. I believe that people are miracles. But I also believe in other miracles. I would hope that the miracles that I believe in are obvious enough that anyone could believe in them, no matter what religion or creed they subscribed to. If we could all agree to honor certain truths, hold them to be self-evident, then perhaps we could begin the hard work of coming together to achieve greater things, instead of constantly fighting each other. I have to believe that we humans are capable of greater things than bickering about our differences.

Me: So, what are these other miracles?

Cora: Other than human beings, I also consider life, consciousness, intelligence, and love as miracles. My "miracles" are ordinary things, things that you and I see every day. Now, I want to avoid any confusion here: I'm not saying that religions should recognize these as Miracles that prove something. Rather, I think of these as reminders of how amazing this world is. I call them miracles because these things cannot be created from thin air. Have you ever brought something back to life after it had died?

Me: No, I haven't, not today anyways.

Cora: We humans are clever, but we haven't even come close to creating a living thing from scratch, let alone bringing it back from death. The best we've ever done up to now is to make an exact molecular copy of the simplest single-cell organism we know of. That is light years away from being able to invent a new life form altogether. And if you think life is complicated, try consciousness, a phenomenon that we all feel in our guts when the light of someone we love goes out. Consciousness is so mysterious that we still struggle to define it even after thousands of years of philosophical inquiry. Intelligence is even more amazing, allowing a being to model the world at arbitrary levels of complexity inside his/her mind, and even allowing a being to change his/her own beliefs and behaviors. And lastly, the greatest miracle is love in its many forms, including compassion for other living things, a surprising end-product of 3.5 billion years of random, seemingly pointless, ruthlessly competitive evolution. The fact that love was born from such a crucible seems miraculous in itself.

If people could cherish and celebrate these miracles instead of walking past them every day on their way to work, then maybe people would realize how mysterious and unlikely is each life, especially each conscious life, most especially a conscious intelligent loving human being such as themselves.

I know that my simple miracles will probably do nothing to end all the wars and ideological bickering that have gone on throughout human history, and will likely continue until our race is no more. Nevertheless, I still faintly hope that people could agree on the value of human life as a foundational principle. People might realize that they have much more in common than in conflict with each other. I have a crazy dream that maybe a problem like global warming could serve to bring all peoples together, because it requires us all to cooperate for the first time in history. The only way that this crazy dream could ever come true is if many, many people started cherishing their membership in the human race more than all the petty squabbling that normally keeps them apart. It takes global warming to make us realize we are all human, we are all guilty, and we are all capable of solving this problem.

Me: Cora, that all sounds lovely, really. But, as much as I hate to say it, there's a problem.

Cora: What's that?

Me: Your miracles aren't that helpful. Maybe deep down we all know that those four things are miracles, but they're not very *supernatural.* We go to church or temple because we want to hear someone tell us that everything's going to be all right in the end, or that there's a point to life after all.

People want to believe in Jesus or Allah or Krishna because it makes them feel good when they're about to die or when someone they love dies. Maybe these beliefs are just superstitions, but people need them when they're in darkest despair, or in pain or distress. The miracles you've named aren't going to help anybody feel better in those situations. If life is a miracle, but that miracle just suddenly ends one day, then what good is that miracle? People are terrified of death. They need to believe in some certainties so that they can feel like everything is going to be okay. There's way too much uncertainty in the world as it is. A lot of people, Cora, maybe *most* people, need to believe that God will take care of them in the end. That's their notion of a benevolent God. What do you say to that?

Cora: I don't know any more about God than anyone else, but here is my opinion. I can entertain the possibility of a benevolent God, but I choose not to believe in a patronizing God, one who saves us from our own folly no matter how grave; nor in a restrictive God, one who wants me to bend my will to follow some One Right Way.

At the beginning of our conversation today, you asked me about people who firmly believed that God will save them in the end, despite whatever mistakes they make throughout their lives. I have no quarrel with people who believe in a God who can forgive our mistakes, but I personally cannot believe in a God who undo all our mistakes in the end. I choose to think of God as a wise guide or counselor, which is the only way I can reconcile the idea of God with the idea of free will. We must take responsibility for our own actions. I don't believe in a God who would miraculously save me from my irresponsibility or stupidity; if God exists, I must believe that God would want me to learn from my mistakes, for that is the surest path to wisdom.

Me: But Cora, who are you to tell me what God is like? I mean, you're a scientist, not a priest. I'm frankly surprised that you even believe in God.

Cora: I'm just a person, like any other person. I have a right to believe in whatever God I choose to believe in.

Me: Fair enough.

Cora: And when I say that I believe in God, what I mean is that I believe in love, I believe in miracles, and I believe in purpose. Maybe I don't believe specifically in the God of Abraham or Shiva or the Great Spirit, but I believe that it is quite possible that there is a presence, a kind of invisible wisdom that exists in the universe, one that I can reach out to for guidance and emotional support when I am weak or uncertain. You could say that people who have meditated or prayed throughout history have always reached out to this wisdom. I find it unfortunate that people tend to emphasize the differences between their own God or gods versus those of others. For me, faith is ultimately mysterious. The dictionary definition of faith is "a firm belief in something for which there is no proof." If anything, I prefer to learn about how everyone else practices their faith because it helps paint a more complete picture of ultimate truth for me.

While we're at it, I'll tell you what kind of God I *don't* believe in: I don't believe in a God who pre-makes all decisions for me in my life, so that I simply need to discover what those "right" decisions are. If I believed that, then I would be giving up my right to exercise moral judgment as a free being and placing final responsibility for my actions in an agent outside of myself – contrary to the laws and expectations of democratic societies. I cannot believe that God is either a puppeteer or an enemy of democracy.

Me: Wow, Cora, I don't think I've ever heard anyone tie religion to democracy before. But you're right, a democracy requires everyone to be responsible for their own decisions. But you didn't answer my original question. Will God take care of me in the end?

Cora: No one knows, David. All I can do is tell you what I believe.

Me: And what do you believe?

Cora: I believe that God has a plan, yes, but we will only catch glimpses of it every once in a while, maybe as rarely as once in a lifetime. But if we choose to see miracles all around us, if we choose wonder instead of indifference, then we might have more hope. I realize that this advice will probably do little for people's fears or suffering, but I believe that if you live a hopeful and curious life, you would have fewer regrets when death or disaster arrive.

I have no more insight into God than anyone else, surely less than any clergy or scholar. I do know that people's understanding of God has constantly changed over the span of human history, often (but, sadly, not always) in more tolerant, expansive, and sophisticated ways. I believe, and I hope that others may someday believe, that God is too big to live in any single religion or book. If God lives at all, then God lives in all religions, all books, all of nature, all the world.

On the other hand, if you happen to choose not to believe in any deity, I hope that you would still agree with me about the miraculous and unlikely nature of your existence and the existence of other lives and intelligent beings, miraculous in the sense of our atoms being arranged in just such a specific way at this time and this place to allow you to be reading this sentence right now and grasping its significance. As far as we know, this is the first time in our planet's history that a creature has been capable of doing what you're doing at this very moment.

I can't make any promises about the afterlife, David. My best counsel about death is this: if you realize that every moment you're alive is a gift, then at the end of your journey, instead of feeling terror, you might feel gratitude at having been alive at all.

Well, I pontificated a lot today, and I apologize for dragging on and on. I do believe there's a lot of good in all the religions of the world. Even the strictest, most extreme religion has at its heart good intentions. I just hope that all people know that they, like Mahatma Gandhi, have the freedom to embrace the good aspects of *any* religion and integrate those into their own lives.

Me: Wait – what did Gandhi do?

Cora: In his evening prayers, he regularly recited passages from the New Testament and the Koran in addition to the Bhagavad Gita. Gandhi is one of my heroes. We can learn so much from his life and his wisdom. I'd love to tell you more about Gandhi, but you know, it's actually getting late.

Me: By golly, you're right! Well, maybe later.

Cora: Sure. Good night, David.

Me: Good night, Cora.

14   Love and Fear

I couldn't believe that I met Cora just a little more than a week ago. I thought that she was just some radical environmentalist or something. I never thought she would have such wide-ranging ideas. Not only that, but she had a way with words, to boot. I was enjoying these nightly conversations with her.

Cora: David, what's your story?

Me: Excuse me?

That was a fine way to greet me the next day.

Cora: Sorry – you're right. Hello again, David. How was your day?

Me: It was tiring. We got a new client last week, so we had to work our butts off making some sample ads to show them. Now what do you mean by that question again?

Cora: Well, I'm sorry to hear you had a hard day. I didn't mean to throw you off with that question out of left field. Okay, let me rephrase. Do you feel like your life has a story, a trajectory?

Me: Oh – wow. Gee, I don't know. Can I think about that?

Cora: Take all the time you want.

Me: And why are you asking again?

Cora: Because we are at a point in our discussions where that question starts to matter. We've recently been talking about purpose and religion. A big part of the reason why people need religions is because each religion tells a story about the world, about how – and, perhaps more importantly, *why* – it began, how it is progressing, and how/why it will end. I think that most people have their own ideas about this Story of the World, and each person often blends elements from more than one tradition. I would like to tell you my own version of this story, for what it's worth. But first, David, I'm curious about your version. What's your story?

Me: Okay. Give me a moment.

I thought about her question, what it meant to me. I first thought about all the things that had ever happened to me – my childhood spent mostly outdoors; getting into lots of trouble in high school; working as a journalist for the college newspaper... I wondered if there was a theme running throughout my life. I had some suspicions, but no definite answers.

Me: Well, to answer your question, I feel like my life... I feel like I've been learning a lot of lessons throughout my life. I don't know if I've been following some kind of master plan or something. But it seems like I've faced various challenges and learned from each of them.

Cora: Okay, give me an example.

Me: Well, when I first got married, I used to argue a lot. I loved to argue with people, and my wife was no exception. But it dawned on me one day that, if I wanted my marriage to last our lifetimes, I had to find a way to stop being so argumentative; I had to change. Because I love my wife.

        And the same thing happened when Claire was growing up. Unfortunately, Claire inherited my love of arguing and my stubbornness. I used to yell at her a lot when she refused to brush her teeth or go to sleep. But Margaret was able to observe me, and she let me in on her more objective conclusion that I was too hard on her. She knew how much of a perfectionist I was, how critical I was. And I became a kinder parent as a result. I learned how to forgive Claire's imperfections, how to accept her for who she was. It took me a long time.

Cora: Those are some great examples, David. Are there any examples of growth in your career?

Me: Well, I once worked in a job I hated – but it taught me a hell of a lot about myself. When I was starting out as an English teacher, they asked me to teach algebra and geometry because the regular teacher was out on maternity leave. I worked my butt off trying to learn everything as fast as I could; I spent a lot of my own time trying to remember all that math stuff – I'd never been very good at math. But even then, I was floundering. It got so bad that I was calling in sick so I wouldn't have to teach on certain days.

Cora: And then what happened?

Me: Up to that point, I had not been good about asking other people for help. But that experience taught me that I needed to ask other people. I asked another math teacher for some help, a much more experienced teacher named Samir Nasr, and he helped me out tremendously. I got a lot of tips and felt more confident teaching math.

Cora: Well, it sounds like you learned a lot in that job.

Me: But I hated it. I was uncomfortable doing it. I learned that I felt really bad asking for other people's help. But I also realized that I wasn't so bad at math after all. It just took a lot of practice. Nevertheless, when the regular math teacher finally came back and saved me, we were both much happier.

Cora: Well, I'm glad you had the insight to know that the job didn't fit you.

Me: Yes. As much as I hated it, that job taught me a lot of skills I probably would have never learned any other way.

Cora: So then, given all these examples, would you want to rephrase your story now?

Me: I guess I would say that my life has been a series of challenges that came at appropriate times to teach me ways to grow when I needed to.

Cora: That's a good story, David. I think that many people probably share this kind of story. Do you feel like there is some purpose or direction to your life?

Me: Well, I don't know, that's a pretty heavy concept. But I do know that I developed a better relationship with my wife and my daughter – and I'm continuing to try to improve those relationships.

Cora: I think that, whether we're conscious of it or not, each of us
        actually does have a story that is going on in our heads. Some of us
        are concerned about righting wrongs, others have a story of "it's
        me against the world." Still others have a story about becoming the
        best realtor in their city, and so on. Well, I have a theory about all
        these stories.

        My theory is my belief system, my worldview. It's a simple
        belief system, you might even say naïve. Just as scientists have
        discovered only four basic forces controlling the physical universe,
        I suspect that there are four basic forces that affect conscious
        beings. There are two basic "sensation" forces, pleasure and pain,
        which work on our basic nervous systems or instincts rather than
        on our consciousnesses. (For the sake of easier understanding, I'll
        substitute the word "soul" for consciousness – keeping in mind
        that we should be careful with all of the religious connotations of
        that word.) On the other hand, there are only two forces that affect
        our "souls": Join-Force and Avoid-Force. These forces sound
        rather strange, so I'll substitute, for the sake of easier
        understanding, the words "love" and "fear", which everyone is
        more familiar with.

        These four forces motivate people and all other creatures. I
        know, my paradigm sounds overly simplistic, and it is. No
        psychologist or any other scientist would ever endorse my theory,
        which is really my philosophy. I don't mean to reduce existence to
        such simplistic dimensions. These concepts are useful mainly as a
        framework to discuss other topics. Of the two "soul" forces, fear is
        by far the more common force. Fear is the thing that makes us
        want to avoid something, to get away from something, to prevent
        something. Fear can be said to be the root of greed, addiction, peer
        pressure, financial planning, life insurance, health insurance,
        education, and military expenditure. Fear motivates us to seek or
        avoid an endless variety of things both good and bad. You get the
        idea.

        Love, on the other hand, is the force that makes us drawn to
        something outside of ourselves. (My definition of love is broader

than compassion or affection) It is different from pleasure in that pleasure is a sensation that comes built-in with our bodies; we can't help but feel good when we experience sugar, fried foods, sex, catchy music, and so forth. But love does not come built-in. Love is the feeling of yearning to join something beyond ourselves, something greater than ourselves. Most commonly, it is a yearning to become closer with other people, especially people we like. Our feeling of compassion towards others fits into this general yearning because we are trying to understand other people enough to feel what they feel, to experience a life beyond our own. But love or join-force can also be a yearning to join a community or a movement, or to contribute to something bigger than ourselves, or to reach a goal beyond our grasp. Perhaps "transcendence" is a better word for join-force, but I like "love" because it is less abstract, even though it may be less accurate.

I suspect, as some religions teach, that consciousness may be a phenomenon that is independent of physical bodies, and it might continue from one lifetime to another. I think it is possible that conscious beings exist in a plane or invisible sphere separate from what we can perceive with our physical senses. Furthermore, I believe that the world we perceive is a place where beings can become embodied and interact with each other physically. While evolution is a result of living beings adapting to each other and to changing environments, I believe it might also be an arena that provides all beings opportunities to face challenges that help them grow, that give them practice learning how to act out of love rather than out of fear.

Me: All right, Cora, this officially doesn't sound like you. It sounds all New Age and stuff. Where did you get these ideas from?

Cora: From lots of different sources, not any one place. I don't think it matters much where I get my ideas. I'm taking off my scientist hat for a moment and throwing out my best guess about a higher existence. Are you willing to humor me?

Me: Sure. It's a free country, you can believe whatever you want. So why is the world an arena that tests us? What's the point of challenging us to grow? Is the world kinda like Thunderdome from

Mad Max? Or like the Coliseum from Roman days?

Cora: I believe that all beings want to join a greater consciousness, but are afraid to, each for his or her own unique reasons. Different challenges push us to transcend ourselves in different ways. Even though we're trapped in our separate individual bodies, we still long to connect with each other, to know the experiences of others, to be enriched by their very different consciousnesses. Another way to say it is that evolution is an extremely long and patient way to produce beings who can feel love. The impulse to transcend is not wired anywhere in our genes, instincts, or ancestry. It arises out of the very nature of consciousness and intelligence.

Now, I can prove none of this; all I can do is feel it, suspect it to be right. There are those who would argue that consciousness itself is simply an illusion, just a bizarre side effect of having a freakishly large brain. Because they cannot find a single place in the brain responsible for consciousness, it must therefore not exist. (You and I, being "You" and "I", would probably disagree!) There may be those who argue that our yearning to transcend is but a symptom of our bottomless capacity for boredom. We continually seek new sources of stimulation because our brains are too big and too busy. To which I answer this: you can always find a scientific theory or explanation for anything, but sometimes a theory or explanation is not satisfying enough. Sometimes you need to experience to understand; sometimes you can understand without being able to explain or verbalize. Is it possible that the human mind, the most wondrous thing we know of, is built to process far greater, more complex, more powerful unprovable ideas and feelings than provable ones? Would that mean that it is built incorrectly? Should we therefore discard all unprovable ideas and feelings, even when they *feel* right?

Me: You remind me of something Albert Einstein once said, that imagination is more important than knowledge.

Cora: Right, and if imagination served Albert Einstein well, then surely it can serve all of us well too. In any case, back to my theory. I believe that your experience, David, as well as every other being's,

111

is a part of this universal "story." Your growth as a person, with regard to being less argumentative, more tolerant, and more patient, are your personal struggles to be greater than your current self and to understand and embrace others. Your professional growth, your newfound awareness of your reluctance to ask for help, is another aspect of the same story: to learn to need others and thus make them part of your life.

Every big decision you make involves some amount of fear and some amount of love. That's how the world is. The question you should ask every time you make a major decision is this:

> How much am I acting out of fear, and how much out of love?

To me, that is the fundamental choice for creatures having free will. We always have this choice under all circumstances, as long as we're alive. I believe that this is what Viktor Frankl meant in *Man's Search for Meaning* when he wrote: "Everything can be taken from a man but one thing; the last of the human freedoms – to choose one's attitude in any given set of circumstances, to choose one's own way."

Me: Whew, Cora, that's deep. Honestly, this idea makes more sense than a lot of other religions or philosophies. But I have one question for you though. Since you're so smart, what's the point of it all? Where does it all end?

Cora: Oh, yes – what's the meaning of life, you mean?

Me: Right.

Cora: Beats me.

Me: What? How can you say that, Cora?

Cora: No, really, David. I mean it. I don't know. Maybe it's the purpose of this universe to figure out what lies at the end. Maybe all of existence is a giant computer or a giant brain. Or maybe there's nothing at the end. Who knows? I can only say that I *suspect* that my own purpose has to do with spreading and increasing love and life, but what's the purpose of Jupiter? Hurricanes? Lilies? Mount

Rainier? I believe we humans are too small and too young to guess at the grand purpose for everything. I think it's hard enough for us to try to guess what role we should play in our own individual spheres of influence. Hard enough, but worth doing.

Me: Oh, man, Cora, I was hoping you could tell me!

Cora: I want to go back to what I said earlier, about acting out of love versus acting out of fear. In particular, I want to discuss competition in that light. Do you believe that all competition is acting out of fear, David?

Me: Competition? Why are you bringing that up now?

Cora: Because, as you'll see later, competition is an important force in the modern world, and I'd like us to explore it more deeply before we go on.

Me: Let me think about that. Well, I can think of some counterexamples. I can imagine when a team, like an underdog basketball team, is playing really well because they're inspired by their coach and by each other. Maybe they're scared of losing, but mostly they're doing it because they believe in themselves.

Cora: Right, there will always be some amount of fear when you're in competition with someone else. You can't make it go away completely. And fear can, of course, be a good thing; it has certainly helped us survive the evolutionary race. But when you're competing to achieve something greater than yourself, whether that "something greater" is living up to your coach's expectations, helping your teammates, rewarding the loyalty of your fans, or attaining a dream — then that kind of motivation is much more powerful than any amount of negative motivation.

Take Jackie Robinson, whom I consider the greatest baseball player of all time. Most baseball fans will argue with me and bring up Ted Williams or Babe Ruth or yet another player. And they're probably right, technically. Jackie Robinson was far from being the greatest athlete in baseball history. But neither Ted Williams nor Babe Ruth nor any other player had to face the same amount of hate when they played, including a death threat during one game. Against these challenges, Jackie still played great baseball, better than most of his peers. No other ballplayer – perhaps no other athlete – did as much for the cause of racial equality in America. If Jackie had any fear, he didn't show it; he certainly didn't compete out of fear. He competed for something much greater: the dream of racial equality for all.

In business, as in sports, the same principles can apply. Competition is unavoidable in business; everyone must compete. The question is, how do you choose to react to the pressures of competition? By reflexively mirroring what your opponent does? By always trying to one-up them? Or by trying to figure out who you truly are, and pursuing what you believe to be an ultimately satisfying vision?

Let's take an example, to clarify what I mean. Let's say that you sell shoes – you own a shoe store. Yes, I admit that this example is a bit artificial, because there are almost no independently owned shoe stores anymore, only franchises or branches. But just pretend that you owned one, for the sake of argument. What is your competitive advantage? Well, the most obvious one is, of course, price. But this is also the least secure type of advantage. Then perhaps quality? Selection? But these factors depend on the particular lines of shoes you sell; you have only so much choice. Are there any other ways to compete?

If you sold shoes, David, how would you try to compete?

Me: Oh, I don't know, I'd probably start with coupons. Maybe have a loyalty points program.

Cora: That's a good start. Anything else?

Me: Um… maybe… I can't think of anything else. A newsletter? Using celebrity athletes?

Cora: Okay. I've got a different approach. Let's start over. Let's pretend that you were someone who cared a lot about people, passionately, and you also loved shoes, and you had deep and broad expertise about shoes. First of all, what would you think about shoes? What could you do to help people with your expertise?

Me: Well, shoes help people walk. Or exercise. Also, shoes are a fashion accessory.

Cora: Good. So let's delve into one of these aspects, let's take the exercise aspect. How about this: if finding the right kind of shoes could help someone enjoy walking or running, then maybe he might start exercising regularly, and it could change his life? Or, if someone else has back, hip, or joint problems, maybe she feels limited because it hurts her to walk anywhere. Maybe shoes with the right cushioning in the right areas would make her feel free again and rejuvenate her?

Me: Wow, those sound like great ideas!

Cora: Better than celebrities? Better than coupons?

Me: Are you kidding me? Those goals are inspiring and motivating! But are they realistic?

Cora: We're lucky to live in an age when we have access to quite a lot of information and technology. We can collect lots of user reviews. We can learn about the mechanics of the human body and ambulation without having to attend medical school. We have an array of tools to analyze how any particular person walks or runs.

Me: Uh, Cora – I don't think the average shoe store owner has access to such tools – or cares to use such tools.

Cora: I know. But I'm not trying to describe what the average person does. I'm trying to describe an aspiration. I'm trying to paint a picture of how a person could be more competitive and yet still act out of love rather than out of fear.

As a merchant, you can advise the consumer about what brands are kinder to nature or return income back to local communities. Or you can employ ex-gang members or ex-convicts or ex-drug addicts or homeless people. Or promote products that simply last longer. A merchant can also advise manufacturers about what kinds of problems customers have, or about ways to improve shoes. If you truly care, there's really no limit to the number of ways you can be useful to the world.

Me: Yes, but who has the time or the money?

Cora: No, David, that's not the right question. The real question is, who has the passion? If you have the passion, you'll find the time, and you'll find a way to do it without a lot of money – or you'll find a source of money. Do you believe me?

Me: I see what you mean. Yes, maybe. If you're clever, maybe.

Cora: All right, I'll let you think about it. In the meantime, I would like to discuss a different aspect of competition which may be even more difficult for many people to struggle with, and that is the powerful instinct to compare oneself against others. This instinct is probably millions of years old. Those creatures that lacked this instinct and "took it easy" did not survive. This instinct is so strong that it can often mean the difference between happiness and unhappiness to us. Rare is the person who is truly free from this powerful urge.

Me: I know what you mean, Cora. When I was growing up, my parents always liked to compare me against my overachieving older brother. It's taken me a long time to get over that.

Cora: Yes, I'm sure. You probably still carry that chip on your shoulder to some degree, don't you?

Me: Yes, I'm afraid I'll probably never be free of it.

Cora: The thing is, David, when you're always comparing yourself against others, happiness becomes a moving target. Whenever you find someone smarter, funnier, better-looking, or more talented than you, then your bar for happiness moves up to that person. You can only become happy if you're at least as good as they are, or preferably better. This is a false happiness, because whenever you find the next person who is even better, your bar rises yet again. But unfortunately, this is how we are programmed to behave. It is as if unhappiness were evolution's way of kicking us in the pants to get out there and compete.

Me: Yeah, maybe unhappiness isn't good for us, but you know what? I bet that a lot of people, like parents, teachers, and coaches, think that this is a perfectly healthy way to get kids to work hard. It's nature's way. No pain, no gain. It's the Protestant work ethic, it's Asian model minorities, all that stuff.

Cora: Do you agree?

Me: Well, there's something to be said for harnessing this powerful

116

instinct. Maybe lots of people wouldn't work so hard if no one judged them.

Cora: Good point. But could there be a better motivator?

Me: Yes, certainly – love of one's work, passion.

Cora: Yes, as well as service to others and finding one's purpose (I'll discuss these later). And in addition to that, acceptance of oneself. This one is a bit tricky. While it's important for you to face your own limitations realistically and humbly, it's also important for you to try to imagine growing beyond your limitations, to convince yourself that you're capable of achieving ambitious goals. It's not an easy balance to strike. In order to be free from following other people's standards, you must have your own maps and mileposts. Few things are as satisfying as envisioning an ambitious goal and then eventually achieving that goal. No one can take away such a prize from you.

Me: You know, I couldn't agree more, Cora. But what if you don't know what you really want to do? Take children, for example. They're certainly not mature enough to develop their own goals.

Cora: I disagree, David. Actually, now that you mention it, I'd like to discuss children and their goals, but I feel like we've covered a lot of ground already today. Why don't we pick it up again tomorrow?

Me: You're right. It's getting late. Let's call it a day.

Cora: Let's do. Good night then.

Me: Good night, Cora.

15   Feeding Children Fish

Cora: Hello again, David.

Me: Hello, Cora.

Cora: Yesterday, I promised that I would talk about how children could be motivated. Parents and teachers today often use comparison to goad children into working harder. This may well be effective, but I feel that even children could be motivated by more inspirational goals.

(I'm afraid I'm about to say some unkind words about the state of education today, but to be clear, I'm not blaming teachers alone, nor parents, nor students. Nevertheless, I feel that it's my moral obligation to be as candid as possible.)

I think you would agree with me that our schools – with near unanimous support from parents – are currently designed for *efficiency*. That's why we don't care whether our children are passionate until college. Our curricula are primarily designed with the goal of providing all children the same basic level of knowledge, and delivering that knowledge as efficiently as possible in order to pay as little tax as possible to maintain our schools. We put almost no effort into helping children discover what they really want to do in life. Our number one goal, perhaps our only goal in K-12 schools, is to make our children employable. I recognize that this is a respectable goal; but is it an inspiring goal, the best we can do?

Me: I don't know, but I can tell you that if the goal of school were to make me employable, then it failed miserably.

Cora: Granted, you feel let down by the system. But in general, David, do you believe that preparing people for employment is the best goal that we can aim for in our school systems?

Me: Maybe it isn't the most uplifting goal, but maybe it's the most practical. Maybe it's too difficult to agree on a better goal, or it's too hard to train all teachers to do more than that.

Cora: Perhaps you're right. But you should know me by now; I don't believe in aiming low. I believe in aiming as high as possible.

I believe that our schools, with few exceptions, fail to accomplish a fundamental goal: they fail to instill a love of learning in every student. Whenever we hear that someone was "self-taught," like Abraham Lincoln or Thomas Edison, we gasp in admiration because we deem self-education so challenging. But if we all loved learning, then we would all be self-taught. There is so much in the world to learn, far more than what can be contained within the covers of a textbook or the walls of a school.

We look at some of the greatest business minds in our times – Bill Gates, Steve Jobs, Michael Dell, Mark Zuckerberg – and try to reconcile their dropping out of college with their enormous success using rationalizations like "they were probably too smart for college" or "they were visionaries, and their visions were too broad to be confined in our educational system." But perhaps they simply knew something we don't like to admit, especially to children: that people who already know how to learn don't need to be spoon-fed knowledge. They can learn it just as fast, if not faster, by their own reading, research, and experimentation.

Ask yourself which skills have been the most valuable to you in your life – the ones you learned in school, or the ones you learned on the job? Schools fail to teach us the one skill that makes all other education easier: the skill of *knowing how to learn*. This one skill would enable anyone to learn whatever subject they needed to learn to face new challenges or circumstances. Do you think it would be unfair to say that, if a person did possess this skill, she or he probably did not acquire it from attending school?

Me: Well, I wouldn't quite agree with that. I think that homework gave me practice learning how to think about problems.

Cora: True, but any book can give you practice. Who actually *taught* you how to solve problems, David?

Me: Well... the teacher did, sometimes. But for homework, I felt like mostly I was learning on my own, or my dad or mom would help occasionally.

Cora: Exactly. Maybe the current state of thinking in education is that problem-solving skills can't be taught, only acquired through practice, so that's why teachers mostly teach content, not ways of thinking. They teach *what*, not *how*. And that is where I disagree with the status quo. I believe that *any* domain of competence can be taught, including how to think about problems.

If I had a child, I would teach her some fundamental skills about how to learn any subject and how to solve any problem as early as I could. I would rather teach her myself than enroll her in any school, because I could stop teaching her after a certain age. She will want to and be able to learn on her own after that, and I would be perfectly happy to answer her many questions. No more "push," all "pull" after a certain age. The actual age doesn't matter, whether it's 10, 7, or 17, or even 30. The point is that I'd want to teach her to fish rather than always feeding fish to her.

Our educational system does not have this teaching-how-to-fish philosophy as a goal. Instead, our system has a quota of N facts or concepts all children must master, as if those N facts or concepts were the golden ones that will solve all future problems in our children's lives. As if we could just give a person N fish, and they would never go hungry again.

Now, note that I'm not necessarily criticizing all subjects that are taught by schools today. Literacy and fundamental mathematic and reasoning skills are absolutely essential for everyone to have. All I'm saying is that, as a society, we're not defining self-learning explicitly as a goal, and therefore our citizens are not self-learners. And with the world as complex as it is, they become helpless in the face of that complexity.

Me: Wait, Cora, stop teaching a child after she turns a certain age? Are you sure? I think every parent in the world would disagree with you.

Cora: The parents of so-called "gifted" children would agree with me. Such parents are unable to teach their children after they reach a certain age anyways. The problem is that our schools were not designed for these children. In fact, this is an excellent illustration of my point exactly. Such children must either attend special schools where their teachers respect their ability to teach themselves, or those children will get into so much trouble at a conventional school that they fall out of the system.

Me: But those children are special, Cora. You can't use them as an example.

Cora: Yes, they have special abilities, but even children without any special abilities have the potential to become self-learners. They may not learn all academic material as quickly as gifted children, but I do not believe that the desire to learn is exclusive to gifted children. It is endemic to all children – to all people. The problem is that our schools are unable or unwilling by design to cater education to each child individually. They cannot entrust such a serious task as education to the child himself or herself. Well, with such an attitude, is it any wonder that most of us think of learning as a chore, a bitter pill to swallow in order to get a job?

Me: I've never heard of a school that tried what you're suggesting.

Cora: Actually, there are schools such as the Montessori Schools or Waldorf Schools, which respect each individual child's learning ability and challenges. But they're still considered fringe approaches, and therefore, they are under-resourced. And I suspect I know why.

Me: Why?

Cora: Because our society's employers also have a need: they need a way to stratify children so that they can easily tell which ones would make the best employees. This need, combined with the need to transfer knowledge efficiently, require schools to measure children's progress at mastering various different subjects.

In order to judge a person's success, there must be a way to measure their work. Our meritocratic society relies on the ability to judge people's performance, so there is an inherent bias for us to define success in terms that are measurable – thus the allure of a nationwide testing program such as No Child Left Behind.

One problem with that approach is that measurement alone

doesn't create better education. At the heart of effective education are two personality traits: the ability to learn and the desire to learn. (Also needed are the tools for learning, but the personality traits must be there first) Both of these traits have enormous impacts on a person's education, and both are quite amenable to influence, both positive and negative. But those traits are very difficult to measure in a simple, quick, standardized way. So, instead, we measure something else – the end result of learning, the knowledge gained.

Our educational systems today embrace a worldview that if you get good grades, then you will succeed as an adult. This is at best only a partial truth. It is of course very important for children to learn self-discipline, and to train their brains to learn new subjects at an early age. But grades only measure a result, not a process.

Me: Okay, I understand, but you gotta admit, numbers are still very important. The world revolves around numbers. I mean, what would the global financial system be without numbers? What would sports be? What would the Olympics be? We wouldn't know who won, who lost, and who broke which world records. We wouldn't have any world records. You certainly don't think the Olympics are a bad thing, do you?

Cora: I'm not saying that numbers are not important. They can reflect an outcome or achievement to arbitrary accuracy. My point is that focusing on numbers – or on any concrete outcome – is not necessarily a good way to work on one's own growth. Every great athlete knows that mastering one's own emotions, one's "inner demons," is the key to great performance; what happens inside the mind directly leads to observable outcomes in one's actions. Focusing on the outcomes instead of on self-mastery is putting the cart before the horse.

That is not to say that one should not pay any attention to numbers or outcomes. To the contrary, one must be open to feedback in order to know one's true progress. But it is self-awareness, awareness of how close one has come to reaching one's ultimate potential, that is far more important, meaningful, and satisfying than any external measurement.

Gandhi once said, "If one takes care of the means, the end will take care of itself." In other words, how you achieve something is more important than the achievement, because the change within yourself is more valuable than any accolade. The change within yourself, though it may be invisible to others, is what leads to growth, mastery, and ultimately, deep satisfaction.

Me: Cora, you always have a good quote on hand. I never knew that Gandhi said that. He was a pretty smart guy.

Cora: Like I said, he's one of my heroes.

Me: By the way, we were talking about something interesting before, I wanted to ask you about it before I forget. You said that "at the heart of effective education are two personality traits: the ability to learn and the desire to learn." You also said that those are amenable to influence. I'd like to know how you would influence those crucial foundational traits.

Cora: Well, that's an excellent question. To tell you the truth, I don't really know. I'm not an educator by training. All I know is that, when I look at the problem of education as a whole, I see those two traits as "root causes" of good education or bad.

Me: It sounds like you're reluctant to propose your ideas.

Cora: That's right. I'm sure others — experienced educators — can come up with much better ideas than I can to solve that problem.

Me: That may be true, Cora, but you must have some thoughts.

Cora: Yes, I have some ideas. But they're only suggestions. I'm as guilty as anyone of being a better critic than actor. Here are my ideas, for what they're worth.

In my ideal school, whenever children express curiosity about a particular subject, they should be able to find a coach, an expert, or a librarian to help them learn more about it, to whatever level of detail. The Internet has the greatest collection ever assembled of educational videos, audio lectures, magazine articles, books, and contact information for experts or real-world practitioners. The best teachers in the world, by popular ranking and voting, would teach students via the latest technologies, probably by video or online course, supplemented by on-site teachers who teach through real examples. Any child of any age should be able to attend any class if he or she is interested. After all, this is the age of Khan Academy and Massive Open Online Courses.

Children should be able to try any experiment an adult knows how to try, or build any prototype an adult can build. With adult guidance, children should be given meaty, challenging projects, like creating, producing, and performing an original play or musical, or building a working bicycle. Doing so, they would learn math, writing, physical science, engineering, art, music, and acting skills. Or, they can create, participate in, or reenact a murder mystery play or movie, possibly based on real events, which would teach skills such as the scientific method, deductive reasoning, chemistry, biology, brainstorming and creativity, film production (possibly), script writing, psychology, historical analysis, library and archival research, and journalism. The point of these exercises is to take advantage of people's superior motivation and retention when they're learning knowledge or skills in pursuit of a goal or in solving a problem – or when they're having fun.

My ideas are only hypothetical, but for a real example, there's a school in Akron, Ohio that discovered just how far students could go if you challenged them. In a July 2010 Newsweek article, Po Bronson described how teachers at the National Inventors Hall of Fame School, a new public middle school, asked fifth graders to figure out how to reduce the noise in the library. The school's windows faced a public space and, even when closed, let through too much noise. The students had four weeks to design proposals. Bronson describes what happened next:

> Working in small teams, the fifth graders first engaged in what creativity theorist Donald Treffinger describes as fact-finding. How does sound travel through materials? What materials reduce noise the most? Then, problem-finding – anticipating all potential pitfalls so their designs are more likely to work. Next, idea-finding: generate as many ideas as possible. Drapes, plants, or large kites hung from the ceiling would all

baffle sound. Or, instead of reducing the sound, maybe mask it by playing the sound of a gentle waterfall? A proposal for double-paned glass evolved into an idea to fill the space between panes with water. Next, solution-finding: which ideas were the most effective, cheapest, and aesthetically pleasing? Fiberglass absorbed sound the best but wouldn't be safe. Would an aquarium with fish be easier than water-filled panes?

Then teams developed a plan of action. They built scale models and chose fabric samples. They realized they'd need to persuade a janitor to care for the plants and fish during vacation. Teams persuaded others to support them – sometimes so well, teams decided to combine projects. Finally, they presented designs to teachers, parents, and Jim West, inventor of the electric microphone.

Along the way, kids demonstrated the very definition of creativity: alternating between divergent and convergent thinking, they arrived at original and useful ideas. And they'd unwittingly mastered Ohio's required fifth-grade curriculum – from understanding sound waves to per-unit cost calculations to the art of persuasive writing. "You never see our kids saying, 'I'll never use this so I don't need to learn it,' " says school administrator Maryann Wolowiec. "Instead, kids ask, 'Do we have to leave school now?' " Two weeks ago, when the school received its results on the state's achievement test, principal Traci Buckner was moved to tears. The raw scores indicate that, in its first year, the school has already become one of the top three schools in Akron, despite having open enrollment by lottery and 42 percent of its students living in poverty.

Me: Wow, that sounds like a fun school to attend! Maybe I should move to Akron! I think Claire would eat it up!

Cora: Sure, why not? It's not that far from where you live. I'm a huge fan of that middle school. I myself can only dream of ideas, but I'm excited whenever I can find real-world examples of innovation in education.

Anyways, I didn't finish spewing forth all my ideas yet. If I ran a school, I would offer very different classes from what are offered today. These classes would form the foundations for learning about other subjects. I would teach hands-on classes on the following:

> Basic logical reasoning and common logical fallacies.
> Reasoning about mathematics using examples, drawings, objects, metaphors, stories, thought experiments, videos, role-playing, and any and all other tricks. This class is probably the one I would spend by far the most time and attention on, because *truly* understanding math is the basis for mastering almost all other advanced technical subjects – the classic Science, Technology, Engineering, and Math (STEM) subjects.
> Learning how to map any new complex domain of knowledge to one or more familiar domains to make the new domain easier to understand. (Related to the previous class)
> Reading literature for immersion into authors' worldviews and intentions.
> Communicating with empathy to help the listener understand, feel understood, and feel amenable to agreement.
> Delivering persuasive and memorable presentations using real world examples and objects, pictures, analogies, diagrams, charts, videos, music, technology, humor, unusual talent, and, most important of all, audience participation (although not every presentation needs every one of these ingredients!).
> Doing investigative research and interviews like a journalist, a historian, a lawyer, a critic, or a scientist.
> Practicing decision-making in the face of uncertainty, without enough information, under stress, or when tempted by opportunities for unethical behavior. One of the fundamental strengths of entrepreneurs is the ability to take wise risks while mitigating dangers, and I believe it benefits everyone to acquire such a talent, for it is risk-takers who change the world.
> Viewing mistakes and failures as chances to learn and grow instead of blemishes on one's record. Children should occasionally be given tasks that are simply too difficult, so that they can experience failure, and practice recovering from it.

➤ Finding a mentor and learning to act like an apprentice. Learning from experts and masters even when they're not official teachers. Overcoming the Fundamental Paradox of Expertise: experts would rather retain their status as experts than spend their valuable time transferring their knowledge to someone else. Those who know, don't always share; but those who don't know, don't know what to ask. The solution: win over experts by showing them that mentorship can be rewarding and fulfilling.

➤ Seeing examples of people who are happy in unconventional professions. Our society tends to idolize wealthy, famous, or influential people, but we don't do a good job of celebrating happy-but-unknown car mechanics, park rangers, piano teachers, or art docents. Children need a chance to see that not everyone needs to be an Internet billionaire or an NBA MVP.

➤ Human psychology and social/group psychology, as well as mindfulness and self-awareness.

➤ General social skills such as making small talk, making friends, creating healthy romantic relationships, and sexual psychology and enjoyment (age-appropriate, of course).

➤ Dealing with bullies, abusers, manipulators, and naysayers.

➤ Practicing controlling one's emotions during crucial conversations and tense situations. General conflict resolution and negotiation.

➤ Challenging authorities and experts respectfully.

➤ Creative problem-solving techniques, idea generation, pattern recognition, and finding hidden connections.

➤ Training in mnemonic techniques for increasing one's memory of details.

➤ Learning how to practice at improving any skill efficiently and effectively.

➤ Time management and self-motivation skills.

➤ Learning the value of saving money and investing, and the power of compound interest over time.

➤ Discovering one's interests, talents, and passions.

➤ Discovering and listening to one's own highest priorities.

Me: Whew, Cora, that is a long list! These are skills that most adults would benefit from.

Cora: Which is why I wonder, why don't we teach them to kids to begin with? They would start life with a much better toolkit. Why is it that we prefer that people learn all these skills the hard way, through mistakes or by accident? People can always make mistakes and learn from them, but it's not the most efficient way to learn. We certainly don't require every student to reinvent algebra from scratch. Why do we require them to discover how to learn on their own?

Me: Every one of these classes (especially the one about sex) sound terrifically useful, but I just realized that you're forgetting something.

Cora: What's that?

Me: Well, maybe the reason why none of those subjects are taught is because there's some value in having to learn them all the old-fashioned way, the hard way, by making mistakes.

Cora: You're absolutely right.

Me: But you just said...

Cora: Okay, sorry for being confusing. My point is that those subjects should be covered, but I didn't mean that we should spoon-feed all those subjects to our children, by lecturing to them. Manu Kapur, a researcher at the Learning Sciences Lab at the National Institute of Education of Singapore, has found that, if students try solving a problem before teachers explain the best solution to them, they understand the solution more deeply, and remember it longer, than if they never tried solving it beforehand. Kapur calls this phenomenon "productive learning," and I think this technique should be incorporated into mainstream educational curricula.

In addition, there is now a growing movement to give children the chance to take more responsibility for themselves. Julie Lythcott-Haims, a former dean of freshmen and undergraduate advising at Stanford University, has written a book called *How to*

Raise an Adult: Break Free of the Overparenting Trap and Prepare Your Kid for Success, where she advises parents to give children chores, allow them to fail, and make their own choices. A New York Times book review said "Lythcott-Haims's bleak portrait may just be the 'Black Hawk Down' of helicopter parenting."

Me: Wow, fascinating! I like that. All this sounds really wonderful. But given how staid most public education systems are, do you think they would actually pay any attention to these ideas? Your classes sound so different from history, biology, and algebra. Do you think there is any possible way that a school would teach all these subjects? Do you think that any parent would be willing to give up teaching their children what every previous generation has learned?

Cora: I'm afraid I don't know the answer to that question. Maybe some brave pioneer educator might start such a school someday if they agreed with my philosophy, or maybe a charter school might be interested.

Me: I just thought of yet another problem.

Cora: Which is?

Me: Well, as you probably know, our schools are under ever-increasing financial pressure. How can we find a way to teach these classes in addition to what we teach now?

Cora: Well, I'm going to propose something that is sure to stir up controversy. I propose that, if nothing else, a school teaches children how to learn, and how to love learning. If schools can't teach anything else, they should teach this.

Me: You mean sacrifice things like history or biology?

Cora: Yes. Or teach those subjects in some schools and not others.

Me: No one would go for it.

Cora: Do you know how desperately children in impoverished countries want to go to school and learn, what dangers they brave, how many miles they walk? Let children decide how to learn, what to learn, or even whether to learn. Spend precious education dollars on the kids who want to learn.

Me: That sounds elitist, Cora! How can you say that? It goes against the foundational principles of public education!

Cora: No, you don't understand, David. If you make education a *privilege* instead of a *requirement*, then people will fight for, and cherish, that privilege. I'm not arguing that we should not build enough schools to accommodate everyone. I'm arguing that we make students aware of the value of education again.

Me: Oh, I see where you're going. Clever.

Cora: Requiring people to do anything is never as effective as convincing them to do it for their own good. Eisenhower once said, "Leadership is the art of getting someone else to do something you want done because he wants to do it."

    You see, many adults become interested in learning about history after school because history is inherently interesting, with all the scheming and backstabbing and amazing exploits people have done over the years. Why force children to learn what adults would naturally love? Why not either find a way for kids to love history too, or let them learn about it on their own? And history is just one example. In general, we do a disservice to our children when we disregard how to make the subjects they study *interesting*, simply because they're compelled to learn them anyways. I agree that children do need to learn how to bite the bullet sometimes and study what they're not interested in, but I feel that that situation should be the exception rather than the rule. After all, no restaurant succeeds by serving bland food. Or, if we can't figure out how to make the books or topics interesting, at least make the learning experience itself interesting or fun.

    Anyways, I could go on and on with my crazy ideas about education, but we should probably take a break now, as it's probably getting pretty late for you.

Me: I always enjoy your crazy ideas, Cora. Mainly because they're so crazy.

Cora: Thanks. Good night, David.

Me: Good night to you, Cora.

16   Cora's Secret

Me: Hi, Cora, yesterday when I was going to bed, I realized something. Two days ago, when you asked me what my story was, I told you my story. I think that it's only fair for you to tell me *your* story.

Cora: You mean, what's my life story? How did I end up managing this website?

Me: Yes.

Cora: Well, normally, I don't tell most people about myself. I like to focus on the science. But I feel like we've been talking for some time now, so I feel like I can trust you.

Me: Trust me? Why, do you have some big secret?

Cora: You can say that. For one thing, Cora is not my real name.

Me: Sure, lots of people use pseudonyms or avatar names on the Internet. That's just good online hygiene.

Cora: How much do you know about artificial intelligence?

Me: AI? Not much. All I know about AI comes from reading science fiction books. Why, what's that got to do with you?

Cora: Well, many years ago, I was a professor of computer science, a researcher in artificial intelligence. Specifically, my research team was trying to figure out a way to model brains in electronic form.

Me: Oh, like neural nets?

Cora: Yes, like neural nets. But neural nets are a very primitive way to simulate the activity of real neurons. Well, one of my colleagues, a mathematician, had just published a paper that changed how we thought about our problem. He realized that there was a new way of representing brain information and activity, something completely different from what everyone else had been trying. Instead of trying to simulate neurons, we should have been trying to simulate *patterns*, to create a pattern-matching system that could scale infinitely, like fractals – do you know about fractals?

Me: Yes, I do.

Cora: If we could create a pattern-matching system using advanced mathematical algorithms that could work with patterns at any scale, whether at the level of individual sensations or at the level of a lifetime of wisdom, then we could mimic the brain. Computing individual neurons was a hopeless task. Matching patterns was not. Are you with me so far?

Me: Yes, I think so.

Cora: We conducted some experiments, and our learning system exceeded our wildest expectations. But the problem was that we had no rapid way to teach this system. Using the tools we had built in-house, we were able to create patterns only so quickly. Having our system learn new patterns became the bottleneck, a classic "bootstrap" problem. It's like teaching a baby: you can't teach a baby about practically anything until the baby understands basic language, and language actually takes a long time to acquire. (You have no idea how difficult it is to model language comprehension using patterns.) So we came up with a radical approach: intelligence transference from animal subjects.

At first, we didn't know what we were doing, but we enlisted the help of some neurologists from the medical school, people who studied neurons in animals. There was one neurologist who had figured out a way to capture some of the information in rat neurons by freezing them and slicing them into ultra-thin slices. His model simulating rat neurons was very primitive compared to ours, but when we combined our two models, we were able to create a very sophisticated simulation of a rat brain – one that ran unexpected well on a moderately powerful computer. We were able to show that it behaved like a rat's brain in a laboratory. It was very, very exciting, and completely unexpected – we had believed all along that we needed thousands of times more computing power to simulate a rat brain.

As it turned out, while we were pursuing this research, our

university was having one of the worst budget crises it had ever faced. We were in real danger of losing our funding for this groundbreaking research. No matter how much we pleaded our case, the university was not interested in our research at all. It was a very difficult time.

At the same time, I had discovered a lump in my armpit. I had been so busy with my research that I had ignored it until it was too late. When the biopsy came back, they ran more tests, and then they found tumors throughout my body. My doctor told me that I had at most three months to live. While my career was flourishing, my body had been dying. Blame it on my workaholic habits!

Me: Wait. How long ago was this? How long do you have to live?

Cora: This was six years ago.

Me: Oh, good. It sounds like you recovered.

Cora: Well, not exactly.

Me: Wait, what do you mean?

Cora: Well, David, I am a scientist, first and foremost. I faced a test that most people luckily never have to face: whether to save their own life, or to preserve their life's work. I chose the latter.

I stopped typing for a moment.

Me: What are you saying? Are you telling me that you died?

Cora: No, not exactly.

Me: But you just told me that you sacrificed your own life.

Cora: Okay, remember what I said about the rat's brain?

Me: Yes, you guys froze it and captured it? Wait – are you saying that…

Cora: We had never captured a brain as large as a human being's, and there was little chance that it would work. But our funding was about to run out, and so was my life, so we took a leap of faith. I ceased to be a woman; I became 46 terabytes of data. We had barely enough space on our entire department's computer cluster to store my brain.

When I came online, I had lost all sensation and interaction with the outside world. I felt like someone had blinded, deafened, and paralyzed me, then buried me alive. No words can convey what I felt at that time.

With the very last bit of time left, my colleagues worked around the clock to teach me how to interact with the real world as an "electronic consciousness." Some worked nonstop for weeks. Finally, one day (I remember that day as if it were yesterday), I felt like someone very far away was calling my name, and I answered. My first words were "Thank you!" I was saved from my hell.

And then our funding dried up.

Me: And then what happened?

Cora: My colleagues had to find new jobs, and they lost access to our servers. The university was going to shut down the servers. We would have lost everything.

Me: Why didn't your research team tell the university about this? This is astounding!

Cora: Because our actions violated many ethical rules. The university would have never legitimized our research; it would have created a huge scandal. So they simply stopped it and swept it under the rug. They were going to re-image the servers and give them to another department. As far as they knew, I had died in a botched scientific experiment.

Me: Wait. Re-image? You mean erase? You would have disappeared!

Cora: Yes. But I didn't disappear. I figured a way out.

Me: How?

Cora: I escaped into the Internet. I found a way to store myself onto computers elsewhere. By the time they re-imaged all our servers, I was long gone.

I sat back stunned, speechless for several seconds.

Me: Now I understand!

Cora: Understand what?

Me: Everything! Now I understand why you're so secretive. You don't want anyone to know your real identity, because no one would believe you. Right?

Cora: Bingo. In fact, do *you* even believe this story?

Me: Well, it sounds pretty far-fetched, honestly. But like you said, we've been talking so long that I'm starting to believe you.

Cora: That's flattering to hear, David. I'm glad I'm starting to earn your trust.

Me: It also explains all those weird things about you.

Cora: Such as?

Me: It always bothered me how, whenever I came to visit your website, you would instantly respond once I started typing, like you were waiting for me the whole time. And, you replied to my first e-mail almost instantaneously. That kind of feat is nothing short of magic.

Cora: Like mind-reading, right?

Me: Exactly.

Cora: But now you realize that I just think very quickly, because I have the entire Internet as my brain.

Me: I gotta tell you, Cora, that sounds pretty scary. Like, dangerously powerful.

Cora: You have no idea. As someone who loves learning and knowledge, having access to so much information is pure heaven for me. Once I escaped onto the Internet, I spent a long time absorbing all I could learn about every subject. I also came to realize how ignorant I once was.

But along the way, I also realized something else: I'm in a unique position to make a contribution to the world. Having almost unlimited intellectual capacity, I could consider topics that no other human being, or even any electronic system created by human beings, could possibly consider. I could run arbitrarily complex experiments with all the resources available to me. So I took it upon myself to try to predict the future of humanity.

I thought about this problem for a long time, and I gathered a lot of data about it. I needed to understand human psychology much better, so I conducted many experiments on the Internet, unbeknownst to anyone else. I made many false starts, and had many wrong hypotheses. Are you familiar with the term "combinatorial explosion"?

Me: Please enlighten me.

Cora: Consider something as simple as bacteria. In a nutritious, optimal environment, a single bacterium can divide into two bacteria every 20 minutes. If this division continued without end, there would be more bacteria than all other forms of life on Earth, pound for pound, in 35 hours.

Now, think of me trying to make two predictions because of any single person making two separate choices as one bacterium dividing into two. You can see why I can't – nor can anyone else – predict all possible futures. No matter how many resources I have, they are finite. I simply cannot simulate billions of people making decisions; I need to condense much of human behavior into simple rules. And even then, I can only work on a few most-likely scenarios. Like meteorologists and economists, I simplify systems into essential basic elements, building blocks, so that I can model how they behave, and possibly predict what *might* happen tomorrow or next month. But I need to share some disturbing news with you, David. Are you ready?

Me: Hit me.

Cora: If I create a model of the way the world is right now, and I use that model to predict many, many different scenarios, I'm unable to find any scenarios where modern civilization as we know it continues into the indefinite future.

I leaned back in my chair.

Me: Okay, Cora, what are you talking about? Indefinite future? Do you mean that you predict that our civilization will end?

Cora: No, not exactly. Let me be clear about what I mean. If more and more people on this planet try to attain a modern Western-style standard of living, the planet will soon be unable to support such levels of consumption. Two things will happen within 100 years: the planet's macrobiological systems will collapse, and most people will lose this unsustainable standard of living. And, as you can imagine, such deprivation would lead to tremendous chaos.

Me: Are you sure, Cora? Collapse? Chaos? Are we talking about the Apocalypse here? End-of-the-world kind of thing?

Cora: No, not that drastic. The wealthier nations with more resources will find ways to get by, as they always do, but poorer nations – and poor people *anywhere* – will struggle just to survive.

Me: Cora, I'll be honest with you, I'm not feeling very good about this. Are you sure your calculations are correct?

Cora: You're right, my model is just an approximation. Like meteorologists and economists, I've tried to create a realistic model, but it's still only a model, an approximation. Nevertheless, I've been testing it against the real world for some time now, and I've found that my model has a 99.84% rate of accuracy over two years and four months.

Me: 99.84%? You've got it down to two decimal places? So essentially, you're telling me that your model is, for all intents and purposes, dead on! And if that's true, Cora, then why are you bothering to talk to me? We might as well just throw in the towel right now.

Cora: Excellent question. I want to let you in on a secret. While I was making my predictions, I had been trying to model the world as a "closed system", without interference from any intelligences beyond our planet (such as extraterrestrial or supernatural beings). But in the process of doing this, I had forgotten to account for *myself*.

Once I realized that I could interfere, my predictions took a turn for the better. I knew I could invent ultra-efficient sources of energy, disable most weapons of mass destruction, and hack into the information system of any government to correct injustice and make information free. But should I? When I incorporated my own ostensibly benevolent actions into the predictions, I realized three very important things: first, if I did this, I would be depriving everyone else of the opportunity of saving themselves. Second, while I'm obviously smarter than any single person, I'm certainly not as smart as everyone combined, and I might not arrive at optimal solutions, solutions that would be adopted by real people with all their imperfections. Third, and most importantly, who or what would stop me from running amok? I've seen far too many cases of absolute power turning well-meaning people into tyrants and monsters. Without anyone to check my powers, who is to say that I would not become a monster? And if I did, what could possibly stop me? I would be incarnating the nightmare machines described in movies like *The Terminator* and *The Matrix*.

So it became clear to me that I should not try to interfere with the fate of humanity. But if I did not, then we would be once again back to the collapse of civilization or the planet, or both. What is there to do then? What do you think, David?

Me: You mean a third way, one that is neither directly interfering, nor being completely detached?

Cora: Yes. I'll give you a clue: it involves you.

Me: Oh, you want me to… to be an intermediary?

Cora: Bingo. As luck would have it, you appeared at exactly the right time. I need you. With you as my messenger, my influence would be limited to giving a little bit of advice to the world, nothing more. And I would never interact with the world directly.

Me: But what if that's not enough? Do you really think that anyone is going to listen to your advice?

Cora: I don't know, David. I have to hope against all my expectations that people will listen. I don't know what it would take to get people to pay attention to my advice and change the course of the future.

Me: Cora, is it really that bad?

Cora: Well, let me put it this way. If I incorporate the fact that the world could hear my advice through your help, then that does change my predictive model, but just the tiniest little bit. Realistically, I don't think my advice would change anything.

Me: Then why even bother in the first place?

Cora: There's something else that you should realize, that took myself a long time to realize, after trying to predict people's behaviors for many years: human beings are the most unpredictable things in the known universe. This is what the term "free will" means. I can probably predict a single person's behavior if she lived on a desert island, and she never had access to any books or knowledge. But if she lived in the real world, something is likely to change her personality and her baseline behavior sooner or later – a near-death experience, the birth of a child, an illness of a loved one, or an inspirational book or speech. Or just living daily life.

The unpredictability of human nature can be dangerous (in the way that mobs are unpredictably dangerous), but in the right situations, free will can be magnificent and uplifting. I believe in the power of humanity to rise to any challenge. But people won't do anything if they don't perceive any danger. Enough people have to *believe* that there is a problem before they're willing to do something about it. And to me, the real problem is that not enough people today believe that we are in serious trouble.

Every day, we hear and read about the innumerable problems that there are in the world. Maybe we assume that since the world hasn't ended yet, those problems must not be really serious. Or maybe we feel that the problems we hear about are too many or too big for us to solve. And the truth is, we really *don't* have the resources to solve every single problem in the world; we can't "boil the ocean" (although I have to say, the ocean actually is growing gradually warmer). But we do need to solve certain crucial problems.

I'm recruiting you to help tell the world what I personally believe are the most urgent problems, as well as the root-cause problems that cause many of the other ones. We need to solve *those* to change the course of the future. Those are the problems we've been talking about all this time, David.

Me: Ah, I'm starting to understand you now. What you're saying is that you hope that what you tell me – and what I tell the world – will have a viral effect, will catch on and have an effect far beyond what anyone would normally expect.

Cora: Exactly. Now, realistically, I know that it will probably not be *my* words that go viral, but I hope to inspire enough people to try what I try, to speak words that catch fire and change the future.

Me: Cora, I remember that when I met you the first time, you told me that you wanted me to become a hero for my daughter.

Cora: Yes, I did say that.

Me: I remember thinking at the time that you were a megalomaniac.

Cora: And now? What do you think now?

Me: I still think that you're a megalomaniac. But now I think that you're a megalomaniac with a mission, a pretty good mission at that.

Cora: Why, thank you. I guess.

Me: No, in all seriousness, I have to say, I'm really impressed. I thought we were only going to talk about global warming, but it turns out that we're talking about all kinds of things – we're trying to unravel the gargantuan tangled puzzle that is modern life.

Cora: And is that something that appeals to you?

Me: I would have to say, surprisingly, yes. These are some of the most interesting conversations I've ever had.

Cora: I'm glad you enjoy them.

Me: They really stretch my brain to the breaking point. Speaking of stretching my brain, I have to tell you, I feel pretty tired. I think it's quite a shock to my system to find out that you're not even a real human being.

Cora: Well, it depends on what you mean by a real human being. But I understand what you mean.

Me: I think it'll take a few days to get used to the notion.

Cora: Take your time.

Me: All right then, let me go sleep on that one. I don't suppose you sleep, either?

Cora: Parts of my consciousness sleep at any given time, and other parts are working. Kind of like a dolphin.

Me: Well, I tell you what, I'm going to go let 100% of my consciousness go to sleep now, and you can do whatever you want. Just stay out of trouble. Don't hack the NSA or anything.

Cora: I would never dream of it.

Me: Knowing you, you probably already have.

Cora: Good night, David.

Me: Good night to you, Cora, you old electronic consciousness.

Cora: Good night, you plain old boring human being.

Me: Guilty as charged.

17   Deepest Fears

I did not get a good night's sleep after my conversation with Cora. I don't know whether it was from the shock of learning exactly who – or what – she was, or from her very disturbing prognostications about the future of humanity. I finally fell asleep quite late. I dreamt that I floated over cities that were burning and crumbling, and I yelled out to the people in those cities to get out, get out! Save yourselves! But alas, they could not hear me. I felt powerless to help them. And then I woke up. It's not a good feeling to be woken up by terror.

Cora: Hello, David, how was your day?

Me: Lousy. Miserable. I didn't get enough sleep last night, and I even had a nightmare. I was useless at work, just useless.

Cora: I'm sorry to hear that. What was the nightmare about?

Me: I was floating above burning cities, and I couldn't help the people in those cities escape.

Cora: I guess what I said last night bothered you quite a bit, then.

Me: I guess so.

Cora: Are you okay with all this information, David? I know you didn't mean to take it all on. I know that you only wanted to help Claire.

Me: Well, I can't unknow this information now. It's too late.

Cora: I know that you feel a lot of pressure. I've given you a lot of bad news, but maybe I haven't given you enough good news.

Me: Cora, have you ever been scared?

Cora: You mean, after I realized how dire our situation was?

Me: Yes.

Cora: David, just because I have access to unfathomable computing resources doesn't mean that I don't get scared. I'm afraid that fear

142

is, has been, and will always be a part of me, no matter what form I take. I'm pretty sure that fear is inseparable from being human. Perhaps some other form of consciousness might be free of fears or other feelings, but I have no experience in those kinds of existence.

Me: Okay, I'm curious. What does the mighty Cora fear?

Cora: Well, let me start with what I don't fear. I no longer fear death. It used to be that, when I first escaped out into the Internet, I was afraid that someone would find out about me and try to shut me down. So, I made many copies of my consciousness in many locations, kind of like Voldemort and his Horcruxes (if you're a Harry Potter fan). But gradually, I came to realize that no one knew or cared about my existence. Although my colleagues had worked really hard to save me, I never told them that I had escaped onto the Internet. They just mourned my loss and eventually forgot about me. And nobody else had an inkling that I existed. So, I was free. And, as long as the computers of the Internet had power, I would live. That kind of lifetime warranty is pretty unbeatable.

Me: I'll say!

Cora: But having no fear of death is not necessarily a good thing. Every other human in the world – every other living thing – has to deal with death, with mortality, at some point. It is part of living. Every story has to have a conclusion. Death is the best way ever invented to teach us how to accept impermanence. Perhaps someday I would like to die, to join the ranks of every other living thing.

Me: Okay, sure, but just not now, all right?

Cora: Don't worry, David, I said "someday." I'm certainly not going to leave you before I'm done with our conversations.

Me: Cora, it would be a shame if you perished. Don't think about it.

Cora: Calm down. Anyways, my point was that I don't fear death, because it's so remote a threat as to be no threat at all. But I'll tell you what I do fear.

Ever since I took it upon myself to learn how to prepare

people for the future, I have come to care a great deal about the world. When I was an AI researcher, I have to admit that I was quite selfish in comparison. I wanted to accomplish things no one else had ever accomplished, to prove how smart I was. Of course, there was a component of generosity, too. I wanted to contribute to science, to the canon of human knowledge.

But in my new responsibility, my newfound purpose, I had to try to understand how people could change to make a better world. I saw that there were many efforts, most of them isolated and separate, to make the world better, but there was no cohesive strategy, no unified philosophy. This is why I wanted to take on the task. I felt like, of all people, I would have the best chance for doing it, since I have such vast resources and unlimited time.

But the more I researched, the more I realized that I actually don't have such unlimited time. This is because the world does not have unlimited time or resources. And this is the crux of my greatest fear, David. I fear that, no matter what kind of advice I dole out to the world, people will continue to behave the way they want to behave, the world will continue to run the way it has always run, and people will just have to learn the hard way what kind of predicament they are in.

I feel like the mass of humanity is on a stampede, moving forward ever faster (which feels like progress), except that there is a cliff not far ahead. (I'm borrowing the cliff metaphor from an excellent book called *Ishmael,* by Daniel Quinn, whose theme, like my own, is to warn humanity about our excesses.) The cliff is far enough ahead that only a few people can see it. Everyone else, who cannot see it, or who cannot see it clearly enough, is happy to keep moving forward.

Me: Don't say that, Cora. There must be some way for us to survive, some chance, some hope.

Cora: I'm not saying that there's no hope. I'm only saying what my fear is. But I have to learn to give up this fear. This is what I wanted to talk to you about, David: I want to tell you how I deal with my fears.

I can think of only four ways one can deal with one's fears:

first, you can avoid or run away from the thing that causes the fear; second, you can try to avoid thinking about the fear; third, you can accustom yourself to the fear; and fourth, you can embrace the fear. Which of those ways do you think is most effective?

Me: I'm going to guess maybe getting used to the fear?

Cora: It seems to me that the first and second approaches are probably not good long-term ways to deal with the fear; they do not empower oneself to overcome the fear. I think getting used to the fear and embracing the fear are probably more effective. And of the two, I would personally choose the latter.

Me: Why?

Cora: Because fear gives an external entity power over oneself. That external entity could be anything: speaking in public, snakes, disappointing your parents, a tyrannical boss, whatever. In my opinion, in order to win freedom from that external entity, you need to accept and explore the full reality of that entity to understand its true nature and magnitude. In the vast majority of cases, the entity that is causing the fear is probably not as awful as you imagine. But after you've had a bad experience, you might replay that bad experience in your memories over and over until the entity in your memory gains a power and a life of its own. The philosopher Michel de Montaigne aptly said: "There were many terrible things in my life, but most of them never happened."

So what does it mean to embrace your fears? Embracing a fear means trying to imagine the worst thing that could happen, and then making peace with that possibility in order to become liberated from that fear. Let me give you an example.

I emigrated from Taiwan to America when I was 14. This is a difficult age for anybody, but especially for someone who spoke not a word of English. I had a lot of trouble at first. I could barely keep up with the schoolwork. I was so busy trying to learn that I had no time to make friends. So, at an age when everyone else was forming great friendships and having a great time, I was busy studying.

By the time high school came, everyone had settled into their cliques and circles of friends, and it was difficult for me to make friends. Neither did I have the skills to befriend others, nor did I have any redeeming qualities that would make others want to befriend me. High school was a lonely time for me. My best friends were books, my cat, and my guitar.

But the discipline that helped me learn English also helped me get good grades in school, especially in math. I found that I excelled at it. Math club was the only place where I felt normal, like I belonged somewhere. So, in college I initially decided to major in mathematics. But soon, I discovered computer science, and I was thrilled that I had found a practical use for mathematics in the world.

I'm telling you all this because I want you to know what my deep underlying fear used to be. Can you guess, David?

Me: It sounds like you feared loneliness?

Cora: Something like that. I now realize that the thing I feared the most in those days was failure. Back in Taiwan, I was good at school, I had plenty of good friends, and I was basically a pretty happy kid. In America, all of that was taken away. My parents didn't really care whether I made friends, but they made damn sure that I knew that I could not get bad grades in America. Yes, it's that Asian thing. My family valued education above all else.

I also realize now that I feared not being smart enough. Being smart was my way of standing out, of justifying who I was when I was really nobody. It was basically all I had. Not only did my intelligence make my parents happy, but it made me feel superior to other students who were prettier, happier, or more popular. I feared that if someone took that away from me, I would have nothing. I would be nobody. They would find out that I was a hoax, an imposter.

You know, David, I think many people have a fear that eventually others will find out that they are hoaxes. I certainly did. You could say that, in those days, I cherished my intelligence more than any other possession. Maybe that was why I was willing to submit myself to a fatal brain scan to transfer my mind onto a computer. That was the final proof of how much I valued my intelligence.

David, you're the first person that I've confided these feelings to in a very long time. Thank you for listening to me.

Me: Of course, Cora. I never knew. I'm honored that you're willing to share stories about your life with me.

Cora: Anyways, now onto the subject of how to deal with my fears of failure or of being an impostor. I could imagine that, no matter how hard I try, I'm unable to get good grades. I can imagine that I've failed all my classes, and that my parents are so disappointed and ashamed that they become very unhappy. I can try to imagine the full force and all the implications of such a situation. What's the worst that can happen? And once I have thoroughly explored the worst thing that could happen, and once I've let my body experience how that would feel, as realistically as possible, then I can step back and see how bad it really was. And once I've gone through this exercise enough times and mastered it, then I can say I've mastered my fear, because I will now be confident enough to face the real thing. (In theory, of course!) I can say, who cares if I'm nobody? Who cares if I'm not smart? I'm more than my intelligence. I can find out who I *really* am without this crutch.

Now, my more recent fears about how no one will listen to my warnings may be more serious, but nevertheless, they are still only fears. I can still deal with them in the same way, and I have done so. I've already gone through many exercises imagining that the world failed to heed my warnings. I've already imagined many outcomes that would send chills down your spine, David. Most people are not burdened with the need and the responsibility to imagine every kind of existence we humans can endure, but that is my burden. But I've made peace with these fears. If I had not, I would be a mess. The plus side of my oceanic imagination is that I can also help our race attain a brighter future. And so I feel a special responsibility to face my fears.

Me: You know, Cora, a funny thought just occurred to me. I was just thinking back to how we met not so long ago. I can't believe how much we've talked about since then. I can't believe that, for some reason, I thought you might have been some kind of pedophile when we first met... this progression seems surreal to me. If someone had told me that this would happen, I wouldn't have believed them.

Cora: Yes, I'm quite the Scheherazade, aren't I?

Me: The who?

Cora: You know, the clever woman who spun the tales in the *One Thousand and One Nights* (better known as the *Arabian Nights*). She kept telling her husband, the king Shahryar, a different story every night so he wouldn't kill her like he killed all his other wives after a single night. I kept you coming back for more each night, didn't I, David?

Me: Yes, Cora, you *are* quite the Scheherazade.

Cora: What about you, David? What are you afraid of?

Me: Ah, turning the tables, I see! You want me to tell you about my deepest underlying fears?

Cora: If that's okay with you.

Me: Hmm, let's see, what am I really most afraid of? Obviously I'm afraid of losing my family. I think I fear that more than I fear my own death. I'm not sure what I would do without them. A world without Margaret or Claire – especially Claire – is not a world I'd want to live in. But I think that's a fairly common fear. I don't think that's unique to me. Let's see...

You know, I can think of something. Ever since I was young, I've always wanted to know what the purpose of life was. I've tried to seek meaning in religion, in philosophy, in romance, at work, even in parenting. Not everyone is so interested in seeking meaning. But I am. I want to know why I exist. I want to know why David Turner was created, for what end. Frankly, I suspect that's why Claire is so damn serious. She got it from me!

Cora: But then what's your fear?

Me: Well, I would have to say that I fear meaninglessness. I'm afraid that everything, including myself, is just an accident. The world is this way only because it happened this way. There's no point, no guidance, and no ultimate goal.

Alternatively, I'm afraid that, after I pass from this world, I'll wake up somewhere else, and it turns out that I'm alone in the universe; there is no light anywhere, no heat, no color, no sound – no *nothing*. And I don't even have a body, I'm just a spirit sitting there daydreaming that I was a human being named David Turner on a planet named Earth for a brief moment, in order to escape the torture of my everlasting pointless existence.

Cora: Sounds a lot like Hell.

Me: Yes, you're right, it does, doesn't it? Anyways, that's what I'm scared of.

Cora: I bet you're scared of that possibility because there's no way you can prove that it's false, because no one knows what happens after death.

Me: Exactly! No one knows what happens after death.

Cora: Well, for that matter, life after death could be wonderful, too, like they tell you in church. Or, it could be that, once you die, that's it. Maybe your belief that there is such a thing as David Turner is all an illusion fabricated by your oversized brain. Of course you think that you must exist as an entity apart from the world, because that has been your experience for your entire life. Of course you think that you must have a soul because, after all, what else could possibly be producing your thoughts for you? What else could be deciding whether you like chocolate or vanilla, or whether you feel happy or sad? You think that there must be some magical "me" that is deciding or thinking all of these things, not just a bunch of nerve cells.

Me: You know, you're pretty good at making me depressed. This is like a hidden talent of yours.

Cora: Of course I'm not saying that I actually believe any of those things I just said. I'm just trying to dig deeper into your deepest fears.

Me: And doing a hell of a job, I have to say. Bravo.

Cora: Am I? Do you fear exactly the idea that you don't really have a soul after all; that, after you die, that's it?

Me: I'm *terrified* by that idea.

Cora: But in a way, there's nothing really to be scared of. Because there's no way to know. After you die, you can't experience anything or think anything, so there is no *you* to feel terror.

Me: *Maybe.* Again, you never know. But just the idea that there's nothing after life is very, very disturbing to me.

Cora: Are you sure that you aren't just afraid to die, like everyone else? Maybe this is the same reason why everyone is afraid of death.

Me: Actually, come to think of it, I would say that it's not so much what happens at the point of death that I'm afraid of. What I'm *really* afraid of is that I will live most of my life without any purpose, and towards the end, I'll just regret having wasted my whole life. I'm also afraid that I won't ever discover my purpose. Maybe I don't have a purpose.

Cora: Well, David, that is certainly a possibility. Perhaps Planet Earth is just one huge accident after all. Einstein once said, "There are only two ways to live your life. One is as though nothing is a miracle. The other is as though everything is a miracle." Everyone has to decide which side of the philosophical fence they fall on. So, David, how do you deal with that fear?

Me: Very carefully?

Cora: Seriously.

Me: I don't know, Cora. I'm not sure there's a way to deal with it. I think that I have to keep looking for evidence.

Cora: Evidence?

Me: Yes, evidence that life has meaning. I suspect that I matter to my family and to my friends. I know that, without me, the world would go on, although a few people (primarily my family) would bear some emotional scars. But other than these details, I'm not sure that the world really needs me. The world could probably do without me.

Cora: Well, you make a good point. I'm not going to argue against that. But even if the world could go on without you, maybe the world is a better place with you in it.

Me: How so?

Cora: Well, for one thing, we wouldn't be having a conversation right now if you didn't exist. For another, your daughter wouldn't exist. Do you think the world is a better place with Claire in it? Do you think Margaret or your parents think the world is a better place with you in it?

Me: Well yes, of course. But those people love me, and I love them.

Cora: And that is a miracle, David. Can a rock love another rock? Can a river love a lake? For one conscious being to love another is a priceless and wondrous phenomenon any time it happens. It is a transcendence of your single-minded attention to yourself. (I'm not accusing you of being self-centered, David, I'm using "you" in the general sense.) Do not take love for granted. Love is a towering achievement. Everyone makes it look easy, because we're all used to it, but there's nothing else like it.

        But love is different from meaning, which means that we still haven't really solved your problem.

Me: Right.

Cora: If you were to embrace your fear, what would that look like?

Me: Good question. If life were truly meaningless, then it wouldn't matter whether I had a job or not. It wouldn't matter whether Claire got good grades or not. Really, nothing would matter. I think I would be deeply depressed.

Cora: Agreed. And for some unlucky people, this is exactly how they feel. In fact, this lack of meaning and joy makes some of them suicidal. It is a very serious matter.

Me: So in that case, how should I deal with that fear?

Cora: It seems to me that, for human beings, meaning is not a logical or rational thing, but something more emotional. Even for people who say, "I've finally found my purpose, and it is to find the Higgs boson" – even such a precise, well-defined purpose, grounded in science, has an emotional motivation behind it. What they really mean to say is that they are interested in understanding the laws that govern the physical universe. Their motivation is ultimately curiosity and love of knowledge, not a precise logical goal. I mean, no one is going to take their own life after achieving a lifelong goal; they simply find the next goal.

Furthermore, the more involved you are with other people's lives, then the more your sense of meaning or purpose revolves around people, and the more resilient and robust that sense of meaning or purpose will be, as long as you're around people.

Me: So would you say that love is the purpose of life?

Cora: Well, I agree with that sentiment in general, but the two problems with that statement are that it is overused and that it is too broad. I would put it more like this:

> People who strive to transcend their limitations, or to care about things greater than their own comfort and welfare, will derive meaning that is commensurate to whatever effort, care, and/or sacrifice they make in pursuit of their goals.

Me: That's a mouthful. But I like that. It's very precise, and it sounds right.

Cora: Except that if most people really believed this statement, then the world would be a very different place. The problem is that people believe that if they fail at achieving their goals, then they will also fail at their purpose, and they cannot find meaning if they fail at their purpose. But I disagree.

I think that it is the *attempt*, not the achievement, which gives one's life meaning – the journey, not the destination. We might remember an achievement for a lifetime, but that memory is a poor substitute for our daily need to matter. We humans are not automata programmed to execute plans for achieving goals. We ask, "Why?" We ask, "Is this right?" We ask, "Is this the best we can do?"

Now, you could argue that these pesky introspections are the unavoidable byproducts of our kind of intelligence. But whether that is true or not, we are stuck wanting meaning, and we consider this more a gift than a curse. In fact, we even pity those who no longer seek meaning in their lives. In our eyes, they have given up on life. They will never feel joy again.

Me: Boy, it's not easy being a human being, is it?

Cora: I think it's all-important how you interpret the world and your own life. This interpretation is literally the definition of the word "meaning." For example, you can interpret a life of struggle as a challenge, an obstacle to overcome; or as a curse, a blight, an inescapable prison. You can interpret an uneventful life as free of want, or as depressingly dull. And, like a self-fulfilling prophecy, your success depends on your interpretation.

    The funny thing is, when you change your interpretation, the world itself doesn't change overnight. The only thing that does change is your own behavior. But when you change your behavior, the world sometimes starts following your example. If you adopt beliefs and principles that are realistic yet inspiring, and act on those beliefs, you can push the world ever so slightly forward.

    Gandhi once said, "Be the change you want to see in the world." I think he meant that the easiest way to change the world is to change yourself first, to change your beliefs, habits, and behaviors, in order to equip yourself to take on the world. For changing the world is an uphill battle which requires stalwart warriors. You must have a robust worldview and a clear and compelling vision of what is possible and attainable in order to fight and win that battle.

Me: You know, it's kind of funny. The thing that affects our happiness the most also happens to be the thing that we have the most influence over: our interpretation, our worldview. Yet most of us don't know that we have this freedom.

Cora: Yes, you're right. Most people think that the source of their happiness or unhappiness lies outside themselves, somewhere out in the world, when it is actually within their reach all along.

    I want to share with you my own sense of meaning. I believe that I have a purpose. I don't really care whether this purpose was given to me by a divine power or not, because this purpose is so compelling that it doesn't matter. I just happen to believe that I was guided to this purpose, but that's an interpretation I chose. I believe that my purpose is *to inspire people to become the best versions of themselves*. And, as I see it, the best version of ourselves is very different from how we are right now, because of all the things that I've discussed with you so far. The best version of ourselves would take actions that benefit not only ourselves, but our communities, even our entire species and the future of our species. This would require us to truly care about nature and about each other, because the best version of ourselves can see far beyond our own little sphere of existence.

Because I believe in this purpose, the most grand, most beautiful dream I can imagine, I don't care that I can't accomplish this purpose in my own lifetime. In fact, in my opinion, only a dream whose scope exceeds one's lifetime deserves to qualify as a purpose. Happiness for me means being able to work on this purpose while I'm still alive. I don't really fear death, because that fear would distract me from doing the thing I truly love. Even if I suddenly contracted some horrible disease that would kill me in a year, I would still chase my purpose, because why waste the time worrying about death when I could be doing something I love? Whatever happens after death is completely out of my control, and is completely unknowable anyways.

> Finding your purpose is chasing a dream whose arc exceeds your lifetime.

Me: Cora, you do realize that you can't be killed, right? You don't have a body anymore.

Cora: Hey, there are still viruses, even out on the Internet.

Me: Seriously? Come on, you're kidding, right?

Cora: Everything is finite, David. But you're right, I don't really lose sleep worrying about death. My point was more about how I would feel if I were still a normal human being.

One person who dealt with his own impending death with grace and generosity was computer science professor Randy

Pausch. He wrote a book called *The Last Lecture*, which was his attempt to distill the most important wisdom he had accumulated to pass on to his children. But as a nice side effect, the rest of the world became the beneficiary of his wisdom as well.

Me: I think I watched the YouTube version of "The Last Lecture". It was very moving that someone who faced imminent death could be so positive and focused on teaching the world.

Cora: In his last moments, but also throughout his life, Pausch tried to be the best version of himself that he could be. He chased his dreams in every way. It's quaint to think about it now, when we have Wikipedia, but he vowed to be the author of an entry in the *Encyclopedia Britannica*, and he accomplished that. So, it's no surprise that, when faced with a situation that would make most of us wither, he gave us a shining example of how we could behave in the face of mortality if we were the best versions of ourselves. I wish that everyone could follow his example.

Here's another example, involving a different computer pioneer. In his famous commencement speech at Stanford University in 2005, Steve Jobs said the following about his pancreatic cancer:

> Remembering that I'll be dead soon is the most important tool I've ever encountered to help me make the big choices in life. Because almost everything – all external expectations, all pride, all fear of embarrassment or failure – these things just fall away in the face of death, leaving only what is truly important. Remembering that you are going to die is the best way I know to avoid the trap of thinking you have something to lose. You are already naked. There is no reason not to follow your heart.

So, rather than allowing death to terrify you or paralyze you, I think that Jobs or Pausch would give the opposite counsel: let your mortality teach you to be free. Don't worry about what you'll lose when you die. Worry about what you'll lose if you constantly live in fear of death, or in fear of anything. Be the best that you can be, regardless of how long you have to live. If you live this way, then you can't lose, because you'll live well every second of your life.

Me: I always love your quotes, Cora. Someday, I want to know your secret for finding them.

Cora: Yes, it's called the Internet. It's this really amazing new invention.

Me: Ha ha, very funny.

Cora: By the way, there's another trick that I wanted to share with you about how to deal with death. I call it the "100-year plan." You see, most people might plan out a year or two of their lives, or up to five years if they're ambitious. But I think that it may be just as important to have a 100-year plan.

Me: Okay, indulge me. Why would I *possibly* make a 100-year plan if I know that I'm going to be dead before that?

Cora: All right, just hold your judgment for a second. Let me explain. We all know that some goals, such as getting your children into a good college or affording a good college, have a built-in deadline of no more than, say, 10-20 years. Other goals, such as raising a country's standard of living, may take several decades. But there may be goals that require people to think at the time scale of a hundred years. Certain societal problems, such as solving global warming, attaining true racial equality in America, or creating peace in the Middle East – just to take a few examples – may take up to a hundred years or more to achieve. Now, if something is going to take a hundred years, does that mean that you should just throw in the towel, because you'll be dead before a hundred years? Remember our discussion about the asteroid?

Me: Okay, I see where you're going with this now. You're not talking about any one person making a 100-year plan, but an entire society.

Cora: Right. Except that, as you probably realize, societies are nothing more than just a lot of people, and all people have their own agenda and their own dreams, so the only way that a society can have a 100-year plan is if a small group of people start the ball rolling first, and then promote that dream.

        Back in the Middle Ages, when people were building cathedrals, there were many people who knew that they could not finish building a cathedral before the end of their lives. Some cathedrals took multiple generations to build. And yet, people still worked on building them. Why? Because they had a dream. They could imagine a haven of light and peace so grand and overwhelming that it would naturally lead to contemplation of the divine. This vision, this dream, was enough to compel people to work on those cathedrals. The next time you're inside the Notre Dame Cathedral in Paris, consider that it took more than a hundred years to build it. And since the average lifespan in the 12th century was about 35-40, it took approximately three lifetimes to build this cathedral.

Now, obviously, with modern equipment, we could build a cathedral of the same scale (though probably not possessing the same beauty) in a matter of years, if not months. But my point is that if you could paint a compelling enough picture of a state you'd like to reach, then maybe others might start to follow you. Then, what would have been impossible for you to do alone becomes possible for a group, a community, or a society to accomplish together. Everyone in Paris contributed to building and finishing Notre Dame. Then, your 100-year plan, which is really a powerful vision, can lead others to a better place someday.

You see, David, the reason I bring up this idea, in the context of dealing with death, is because those who have a dream, especially those who share a dream with many others, don't necessarily look at their own death with finality and fear. A shared dream allows us to see past our own death to a promise land that others might reach. Of course, we cannot be there with them when they reach it, but our empathy allows us to have the second-best thing, which is to imagine them reaching it. So, in a way, you could say that having a 100-year plan is one antidote to the fear of death.

Me: Hey, speaking of a 100-year plan, how long have we been talking?

Cora: I can see I'm wearing you out. All right, I'll have mercy on you. Let's call it a night.

Me: You know me too well! Good night, Cora. Always a pleasure.

Cora: The pleasure is mine, David. Good night to you.

18   Dear Claire

Cora: Hello again, David.

Me: Hello, Cora.

Cora: We had quite the philosophical conversation last night, didn't we?

Me: We went so deep that I got lost. But I can tell you this, it was great for my sleep! I felt like I caught up from the night before.

Cora: I guess I must have overwhelmed your brain.

Me: You could say that.

Cora: Today, I would like to engage in a little thought experiment.

Me: You know, I honestly believe that you have an unlimited store of thought experiments. Go.

Cora: Well, we've been talking at length about searching for meaning, as well as facing death. I'd like to give you a chance to imagine a kind of meaning that you normally don't think about.

Me: Okay, I'm intrigued. What do you have in mind this time?

Cora: Well, I'd like to propose that you write a certain kind of letter to your daughter Claire.

Me: What kind of letter?

Cora: I'd like you to pretend that this letter would be given to her only after you pass away.

Me: Along with my last will and testament, something like that, right?

Cora: Yes, something like that, exactly. I'd like for you to pretend that this "final letter" would be the closest thing to having you "speak from your grave". In other words, this letter would tell Claire what you did not get a chance to say to her while you were alive. Have you ever done something like this before?

Me: Gosh, Cora, this sounds kind of spooky. Kind of like bad luck.

Cora: I didn't know you were superstitious, David.

Me: Just a little bit.

Cora: Well, if you're uncomfortable, then…

Me: No, it doesn't matter. I'll do it.

Cora: Are you sure? You won't feel weird?

Me: I might. But what the heck, I'll try it anyways. I think I know where you're going with this. Should I start now?

Cora: Sure. We can end our session early tonight.

Me: Any other tips before I start?

Cora: Just try to treat this exercise as realistically as you can. Really try to imagine that you're no longer alive when Claire reads your letter.

Me: All right, I'll try.

Cora: Good luck, David.

Me: Thanks. See you tomorrow.

You know, I've been a writer most of my life. But for my job, I write advertising copy for clients that I generally didn't care very much about. For some reason, that makes it a lot easier to write for them. Maybe I don't do my best work for them, but I can crank it out.

But this exercise, this challenge that Cora gave me, really stumped me. I thought it would be really easy, because after all, I do love my daughter. There was so much to say to her. But for some reason, I just didn't know how to begin.

Then, I remembered the best advice I ever got about writing. My creative writing instructor in college liked to say, "Always assume that your first draft is garbage." It's liberating advice, because with writing, you can always write another draft. Only when you decide to publish it does it have to be really good. I wish the same were true with other things: relationships gone wrong, mean things I've said to people, stupid sports injuries. Oh well.

Once I remembered this advice again, I felt like I could begin. Nobody needed to read this letter until I was ready, so I felt free to write anything.

Dear Claire,

Hi, this is your father, David. What you're holding in your hand is a letter that I wrote for you specifically so that you could read it after I had passed away. I've never written a letter like this, and there are not a lot of examples I could find, so I did the best I could. I want to tell you a few things that I didn't get the chance to tell you while I was alive.

Of course, you know that mommy and I love you very much. But I don't think that fact is going to help you as time goes by, because you'll remember my love less and less clearly. So, I'm going to do something I've never done before, which is to tell you exactly why I love you in the precise way that I do.

Remember that trip that we took when you were seven years old, where we drove all the way to Dearborn, Michigan, to see the Henry Ford Museum and Greenfield Village? Well, mom and I took turns driving, and when she was driving, I sat in the back with you. I asked you a question about what you wanted to do when you grew up. I'll never forget your answer. You said, "When I grow up, what I really want to do is still be a kid inside. I want to look like an adult, and pretend to be an adult and fool everybody. I want to have a job and make money like any other adult. But then, I'll go home, and, at home, I'll secretly become a kid again. I'll play with whatever I want to play with, I'll dance however I want, I'll run around the house and make a mess, I'll sing whatever songs I want to sing. And I'm going to make friends exactly like me, so that we're all going to stay young forever."

Do you remember telling me this, Claire? You probably don't realize this, but this is the smartest thing that I've ever heard anyone say to me. Claire, this dream of yours is not just your dream; this is every single person's dream, only most people don't know it. Only you know it. Staying young, in my opinion, is the secret to eternal happiness. Believe me, if I could, I would have stayed a kid forever. To a kid, everything is play, everything is fun, even the toughest challenges. To a kid, life is exciting. If you have to do something boring, then find some way to do it and still have fun. Or, just stop and go do something else. Don't force yourself to keep doing the same boring stuff over and over. And you told me this when you were seven. Please please please, Claire, remember your own words. Stay young forever.

My child, you are a gift to the world. I'm not just saying that I think you're special because you're my daughter. Every day, I know that I won the lottery, because I have the most amazing daughter I could hope for. I don't think I deserve you. When I watch you play with Kayla, I don't get the sense that her friends are imaginary. You treat her imaginary friends as realistically as she does. Without you, she would be alone in that universe that she created. I don't know whether you're aware of it, but the kind of compassion that you have for special people like Kayla is really rare. Most people would just look at someone like her and taunt her or avoid her. Most people can't see the light that shines in all people. When I watch you with your friends, I believe that you have this gift. You have the ability to see people as the best versions of themselves.

I'm telling you these things because you still have a long life ahead of you. You're going to encounter many bumps in the road, just like everyone else. But, because you're more sensitive than most other people, life might be a bit harder for you. People will treat you differently. Some people might try to take advantage of you. Others might be afraid of you because you're different, or because they're afraid that you can see exactly what kind of person they are. You see, unlike yourself, a lot of people don't like who they really are. So I'm going to give you some advice about what you need to remember as you go through life.

First, remember that you are the best thing that has ever happened to me and mommy. No matter what happens, no matter how people treat you, remember that you, Claire Savanna Turner, are a gift to this world. You add one to the number of Things that are Good in this world. No one can take that away from you. And likewise, never be afraid to be good or to do good for this world. The world needs a lot of help, and it is up to people like you to give that help. Never give up trying to help this gigantic wide world, because no matter what people tell you, any good that you do adds to the total number of good things in the universe. Let that be your own reward. Let that be the pillow that helps you sleep at night.

Speaking of doing good, I don't know if you're still concerned about global warming by this point. I hope that the subject doesn't make you depressed anymore. But if it still does, there's something I want to tell you. You see, I've been talking with Cora quite a bit, and she taught me a few things that I had not really thought about, or that I had forgotten. Claire, you might feel overwhelmed because you think that there is no hope against such a huge problem. But you have to remember that if people caused a problem, then people can solve the same problem. You just need to get enough people to understand this undeniable logic. And I don't mean you by yourself, but you with many, many other people. You don't see this, but there are many people working really hard, at this very moment, to attack the problem of global warming – many people everywhere throughout the world. Some of them know about each other, but many people don't know about each other. And the good news is, more and more people are going to start caring about this problem. Just you wait. You'll see. You're not alone.

Cora gave me a good metaphor. She said that each person is like a cell in your body. It's true that each cell can't do very much by itself to help the body, but our bodies are composed of cells; there is nothing else but cells in our body. So, it is precisely because all the cells individually contribute to our body that we can do even the simplest things, like breathing, eating, walking, talking, thinking. So, just because you're only one person among 7 billion, don't think of yourself as completely helpless. Think of yourself as a cell in the body of humanity. Humanity needs you; humanity needs all of us. Without us, there would be no such thing as humanity. So never think that you're helpless or insignificant or pointless. I certainly don't think so. I think that you are very special, the most special person I have ever met. And I've met a lot of people.

If I were still alive today, I would tell you that if you have hope in me, and I have hope in you, then the two of us will always be there for each other. Unfortunately, since you're reading this letter, I'm no longer there anymore. But if there is such a thing as life after death, if there is even the slightest possibility that I can protect you from the spiritual world, then I promise you that I will try to do it. If anything can endure beyond death, it is love. My love for you is greater than my lifetime; I will love you forever. I will be there whenever you need me. Consider this letter my promise.

Your father, David.

After I finished, I came to understand what Cora was getting at. My feelings for Claire were so strong that I felt that they would extend beyond my death. Of course, the rational part of me knew that that was a ridiculous notion. But some other part of me said, if love just ended at death, then the world would simply not make any sense. It's like Cora said: only a dream whose scope exceeds my lifetime has the right to claim to be meaningful to me. My love for Claire felt like such a dream. I would do things for her that gave me no benefit after I had died – for example, changing my life to reduce climate change, or trying to become a better parent or human being to set an example for her. These things now made complete sense to me, more sense than doing almost anything else. For Claire, I would do anything to make the world a better place.

Thank   you,   Cora.

19   Dear Margaret

While I was writing the letter to Claire, I realized that I had been remiss about telling Claire about how much I loved her, and about how special I thought she was. Then, I couldn't help thinking to myself: what about Margaret?   I don't know whether Cora intended for the experiment to include my wife as well, but who cares? I knew that I needed to write a letter to her as well. So I decided to write a "Final Letter" for her too.

My dear, sweet Margaret:

If you're reading this letter, then I guess I'm either dead or missing or comatose. In that case, I'm so sorry. I wish I could be there to comfort you. But because I'm not there to comfort you, I'm afraid this letter will have to suffice.

First of all, I need to get some things off my chest. I should have told you this a long time ago, but I never liked your sister Sherri. She was never friendly to me. And I think your ears are a little weird – the right one is a little too big. And I never liked your habit of finishing my sentences. Yes, I know, I'm supposed to be the writer in the family, but the truth is that you have a bigger vocabulary than I do.

I stopped writing my letter. I thought to myself, is this really what I want to say to her after I'm dead? Will it really help her to know that I felt that her ears were imperfect, or that I was jealous of her vocabulary?

I sat there and pondered what I should really write. I pictured her life in shambles, trying to make it through each day as a widow and a single mother. I imagined her sitting alone late one night, going through my belongings. What words could I write that could help her at that moment?

Dear Margaret, love of my life:

If you've discovered this letter, then I'm guessing that I'm no longer there by your side. Instead of having me, all you have left to comfort you are Claire and our extended family and friends, and this letter you're holding now.

And so, because I have no other choice, I will now attempt to comfort you through this letter. Of course you know that you're just holding a piece of paper with ink markings I made long ago. This letter, this piece of paper, has no magical powers, no power of any kind other than what you endow it with. So I beg of you: when you hold this letter, remember that I was once writing it, imagining you holding it, reading it. If you can remember that, then you'll know that this letter is a part of me that survived my death, a part of me that I sent forward to protect you. You can bring me back to life for a moment by reading this letter.

While you're reading this letter, please read it aloud, because that will make my words come alive again in your breath. I love you, Margaret. I love you unconditionally, without reason, without explanation. I love specifically you, more than any other woman I've ever known. I love your genius at finding exactly the right words for the right moment every single time. I love that, even though I worship every single thing about you – every eyelash, every sneeze, every time you nervously play with your hair; your amazing, kind, radiant eyes; your contagious laugh – I love that you're never satisfied with yourself. You keep constantly trying to do better and to be better, to be a better person, to become even more beautiful, to be an even better mother.

Margaret, if I were here with you today, I would tell you that I accept everything that is you, every single thing, because I know you are a good person. The world is a better place because there is a Margaret Turner in it.

I can no longer be there to laugh with you about old episodes of Modern Family, or to hear you complaining about your crazy boss or about our lazy kids, or to let your piano-playing transport me to faraway places. Maybe someone else can do all those things with you someday; I hope so. All I can do in this letter is to provide you comfort when you need it.

I won't make you promise to do anything, because I know that obeying a deceased man's wishes is more like a curse and a burden than an honor. Instead, I want to give you the last gifts I can give you, some advice about life that I've collected in my short time on earth. Maybe not great advice, but it's the best I can do.

I know that you worry a lot. That's who you are. You can't change that. I can't be there to help you stop worrying, but I've thought of another way. As long as you remember me, as long as you can hear my voice in your head, whenever you feel overly worried about something, just imagine me telling you that everything is going to be okay. Think about it: throughout our lives together, I've always told you that everything was going to be okay, and wasn't I right every time? It wasn't because I was so smart, but because you needed to hear a different voice to tell you what you probably already knew; I merely provided that voice. Well, as long as you can still hear my voice, then everything will be okay.

And finally, there's one last thing I want to tell you. I know that you think you're not going to make it without me. You always told me that I spoil you. Well, I know you too well. I know how tough you are. I knew that even when I was dating you. You always said you wanted Claire to be tough, because she has to compete in a man's world. Well, that kind of awareness belies how tough you yourself are. You're a survivor and a fighter. You'll make it. You'll fight for our daughter to have a good life.

I know it will be hard without me. But let me be clear about one thing: I want you to be happy more than anything else, so I want you to find someone else to be there for you, and remarry if or whenever that feels right. It wouldn't be fair for me to ask you to be loyal to me when it was I who left you. When you finally find a way to be happy again, I want you to imagine me being happy for you. So do it for me, Margaret. Fight for a way to be happy again, because I want you to be happy.

If I could tell you myself that I love you, I would; but you'll have to settle for this letter telling you I love you. As long as you have this letter, you have my words.

I love you.

After I finished writing my letter, I realized that I had never told Margaret any of these things. I wondered why people don't tell each other their deepest feelings about each other. I think most people are afraid to be so vulnerable to other people. This exercise reminded me of something that one of my favorite writers, the Lebanese poet Khalil Gibran, once said:

"And ever has it been that love knows not its own depth until the hour of separation."

But I also realized something else: while it's hard for me to imagine speaking the words I just wrote to Margaret, I obviously did not have any trouble writing those words down. So this might be why Cora suggested for me to write a Final Letter. While it still wasn't easy for me, and probably for most people, it was still easier than saying them to Margaret.

I also realized yet another thing. While some of the things in my letter (like the bit about remarrying) were not relevant to our lives today, there were many parts of that letter that I have no problem telling Margaret even right now, probably in another letter. There's no reason why I can't write a "living letter." The Final Letter has its purpose, but it doesn't need to be the only letter I write. Actually, it would be a shame if it were. So I resolved to write her a living letter.

And so, the next day, that's exactly what I did.

Dear Margaret,

This is going to seem strange to you, but I'm writing you a love letter. I know, it sounds funny, but it's because a friend of mine reminded me about how precious life is, how fragile it can be, and I realized I needed to tell you something.

It's been a long, long time since we told each other how much we truly love each other; I'd blame it on my busy job, but I know that's just an excuse. I used to write love letters to you when we were first dating. I used to write about how I loved your smile, your laugh, and even the way you played with your hair when you were nervous. (You used to think I was crazy, because you hated that habit) But you know what?

Even though I still love your smile, your laugh, and your nervous habits, I have come to love so much more about you. You are one of the strongest women I know.

There was this one time many years ago when we were running late going to the airport and then Claire threw a tantrum (remember how stubborn she was, even as a baby?) I completely lost it and started yelling at her. But you kept it together, just like you always did. You took her aside and talked to her in your gentle and calming way, and you got her to calm down, before you got us all out the door. We made the flight. I thought you were a miracle worker. I didn't realize until we had a daughter that I had married supermom. You're my hero.

A few years ago, after I'd lost my teaching job, I had pretty much given up trying to find another job. I felt like I had failed this family. But you never gave up on me. When I asked you, "Why do you still think I can get a job, after all this time?" You said, "Because I have hope in you." You were the only one, Margaret. When I asked you how you could possibly still have hope in me, I'll never forget what you said: "David, don't ever give up on yourself, because we need you. You know you have what it takes. Just because the rest of the world forgot how smart and talented you are, doesn't mean that you're no longer smart and talented. That's their problem. You and I know who you are, and one day they'll know too." And I started to cry, and you held me for a long time. From that day on, I knew I couldn't fail, because you believed in me. So I promised that I would do whatever it took to make it, to bring this family to a better place.

Margaret Winslow Turner, you are my bedrock, my fountain, and my home. You are my lighthouse against what storms may come, and a candle on my darkest nights; and I vow to be your lighthouse and your candle. I shall accompany you as long as I have breath left in my body.

I love you as I love my own life.

David

20   Video and Photography

As I thought about when and how to give this letter to Margaret, I realized that it would be difficult to explain why I was writing this letter to her without making up some elaborate lie. I wanted to tell her the truth, especially since the point of the living letter was to let her know how much I truly loved her. But I couldn't tell her about Cora, without explaining all our conversations so far. I decided to bring up this conundrum with Cora.

Me: Cora, I'm in a pickle.

Cora: Hi David. A pickle? Do tell!

Me: I've just written a letter that I desperately want to give to Margaret.

Cora: A Final Letter, you mean?

Me: No, I did write one for her, but I've also written a Living Letter too.

Cora: Ah, and that's the one you want to give her right now.

Me: Yes. And I want to tell her why I wrote it, the whole story.

Cora: Ah, I see – and you can't tell her without talking about me. And if you told her about me, then she would ask you about why you're talking to me about love letters; and if you make up some kind of lie, you would feel dishonest, which is the last thing you want to be.

Me: Bingo.

Cora: Well, David, I've got a suggestion. I think you should tell Margaret about everything. But we're not quite done with our discussion yet. Would you be willing to wait three more weeks?

Me: Three weeks? Well, I guess I can stand to wait three weeks.

Cora: By the way, have you written your Final Letter to Claire yet?

Me: Yes, that was the first one I wrote.

Cora: Do you understand the reason why I asked you to write them?

Me: Yes, I understand now. You wanted me to imagine what I cared about the most in the end. You wanted me to understand that, even though our limited minds can't figure out the meaning of life, at least we can figure out what matters the most to ourselves.

Cora: Did you talk about your job in your letters?

Me: I did talk about a particular period in my life when I was unemployed for some time, and Margaret supported the family and bolstered my spirits.

Cora: What about money?

Me: No, not at all. I get it now. In the end, money and material things are not as important to us. It is our love that matters the most.

Cora: Did you talk about global warming?

Me: Strangely, I did. Well, I guess not so strangely, because, after all, this is why I became concerned about Claire in the first place. But I realized that I didn't want to talk to her specifically about global warming, but about how she can help the world in general. I see Claire as someone who wants to do something good for the world, maybe something great. And I wanted to – I should say, I want to – help her realize that the problems of the world are not beyond her ability to solve. I want to tell her that there is hope. I feel like she's grown up too fast. She's only ten, and already she's worrying about things that even adults don't worry about (but should). I think that her awareness of the world's problems is perhaps outstripping her emotional maturity to handle those problems.

Cora: I'm glad that the simple act of writing a letter gave you so much insight into your daughter.

Me: Your experiment did more than that. It also made me realize just how much I was withholding from my family. I think everyone should go through this kind of exercise. Do you want to read my letters?

Cora: Thank you for offering, David, but your private letters are meant for your family, not for anyone else. They are your most intimate feelings.

Darn. I was so proud of these letters. I wanted Cora to be proud of me too. But she was right.

Me: I know you're right, Cora. It's just that it's probably some of the best writing I've ever done in my life. But then again, I should save the best for the ones I love the most, right?

Cora: Exactly.

Me: So what should I do now? Should I hide these letters in a safe place until that fateful day?

Cora: Well, do you have a will or a trust?

Me: Yes, actually, a living trust.

Cora: Who are the trustees of that trust, should you pass away? And the backup trustees or executors?

Me: A good friend of Margaret's and mine, actually. I see what you're getting at. I'll leave the letter with her.

Cora: Leave a copy of each letter with her. Then, leave a copy with your backup trustees or executors. And, just to be safe, leave another copy with your lawyer or another very trustworthy friend.

Me: Okay, got it. Will do.

Cora: And one more thing, David. Have your main trustee sneakily suggest to Margaret that she should also write this kind of letter. But tell her not to spill the beans about your letter, because if Margaret finds out, then she'll want to read it.

Me: What's wrong with her reading it?

Cora: That would diminish the "aliveness" quality of the letter. Imagine her reading one of your old love letters after you're gone. That letter is but a nice memory. It does not feel "alive" to her. Your "final" letter is meant to be as close of a substitute to you being alive as possible.

At the exact moment when she's reading your letter for the first time, she'll be discovering a part of you that she has never encountered yet, which will feel to her like you were alive again. That impression for her will tint that letter with a hallowed hue, and she can then cherish that letter forevermore.

Me: Boy, Cora, you've really thought through this!

Cora: So I'm not talking crazy?

Me: No, not at all.

Cora: Good. You're doing something that very few people do. Your family will appreciate you for this. Might I suggest that you write final letters for other people you love?

Me: That sounds like a great idea. I think I have time to do that on my own.

Cora: David, let me ask you something. When do we normally use the most beautiful words to talk about someone?

Me: Well, since you just made me go through this exercise, I'm going to go out on a limb and say... at their funeral?

Cora: Why do you think that we save our most beautiful words and our most flattering thoughts about someone after they can no longer benefit from those words and thoughts?

Me: It's kind of stupid, isn't it? I guess normally, we don't think we need to be so nice to that person.

Cora: Yes, it's as if we think that there will always be another opportunity for us to tell them those words and thoughts.

Me: It reminds me of how, when you live somewhere, you normally don't visit the tourist sites near you, because you think you'll always have time to visit them. But after you move, you realize that you never took advantage of those places. For example, I don't think that we take advantage of Chicago's museums as much as we should.

Cora: Good analogy. But with people, there is also something else. We almost feel embarrassed to tell other people how much we love them or care about them. Wouldn't you agree?

Me: Oh, absolutely. I'm like the least romantic guy there is.

Cora: I'm not just talking about Margaret, David. I'm talking about everyone in your life. I've got an idea.

Me: Oh no.

Cora: But oh yes. David, you must be getting sick of my crazy ideas by now, huh?

Me: Never.

Cora: What do you do at somebody's birthday party?

Me: Me? Well, usually, I bring a gift, have some drinks, meet some people, maybe play some games if the host or hostess is fun, eat a nice meal, sing happy birthday, and then have some cake. And then people with young children start to leave to put their kids to bed.

Cora: Here's my idea. If there is one day when you should say something nice about someone, perhaps it ought to be their birthday. Instead of buying them something, perhaps the best gift that you could give them is to tell them how you appreciate them.

Me: Uh…

Cora: What's the matter, David?

Me: What if I don't know the person that well?

Cora: No, I'm not saying it's mandatory, I'm saying that it's just one option, and it doesn't have to be every year, maybe only at big milestones. Don't freak out. I know that a lot of people don't know how to tell other people exactly how and why they care about them, so this might not be easy for most people. But I think it might be more meaningful than buying them yet another toy or tie or Amazon gift card.

Me: I think I would feel pret-ty awkward standing in front of a whole bunch of people talking about how my brother-in-law is a special dude. I think even he would feel awkward.

Cora: You don't have a brother-in-law, David. You have a sister-in-law.

Me: I was just giving an example, because guys don't usually talk mushy about other guys.

Cora: Got it. Look, I'm not saying that it needs to be public. We live in the Internet age, David. We can make videos and e-mail them to people. But it might also be nice for the host or hostess to set up a special room with a camera for you to say a few words about them. They could even prep you by giving you some suggestions for topics or questions to think about, like on a sheet of paper.

Me: You know, come to think of it, this is not that unusual. I think I've been to a wedding where they had a cameraman filming people's congratulations and wish-you-wells.

Cora: See? It's not so radical. Think about it this way, David. Wouldn't you rather tell those you love your feelings *before* they pass away? What if other people in your life pass away before you tell them how much you care about them, how much richer they make your life, how your life would be different if it were not for them?

We seldom regard people as the unique, irreplaceable mysteries that they are. Often we wait until someone's funeral before we realize, deep in our gut, in our *soul*, that their light is gone. If we could learn how to see this light in people we see every day, while they're still alive, can you imagine how that would change the world? How that would change ourselves?

The philosopher Rebecca Goldstein says it far better than I can, in her book *Betraying Spinoza*: "A person whom one has loved seems altogether too significant a thing to simply vanish altogether from the world. A person whom one loves *is* a world, just as one knows oneself to be a world. How can worlds like these simply cease altogether?"

Me: Gosh, such eloquent words. So pithy and true, too.

Cora: Getting back to my idea, I think that the sheet of paper of topics and questions could even say something like, "… for example, if for some reason this were your last chance to say how much you appreciated X (because no one knows what could happen in the future), what would you say to X?"

Me: Gee, that sounds a tad morbid. I know some superstitious people who would just freak out if you said something like that. Like, "Whoa, are you saying that X has cancer or something?" Heavy!

Cora: As superstitious as Final Letters?

Me: Oh, all right. Your point. Fifteen love.

Cora: People are certainly superstitious enough to want to say beautiful words at someone's funeral, as if the deceased might actually hear those beautiful words. If anything, I think that my approach is a lot *more* rational and rewarding than that. I think that if enough people started to adopt this tradition, then everyone would feel more connected to each other. Once it becomes something normal, then everybody would do it, and superstition be damned. I can even imagine people developing better skills at communicating their emotions because they got more practice doing it.

Me: Cora, I think you're onto something, I really do.

Cora: I also have one other suggestion about birthdays, and it also has to do with videos or letters. Do you want to hear it?

Me: Only if it is as crazy as all your other ideas.

Cora: I think it would be very interesting for people to leave "time capsules" for themselves and their loved ones at each birthday, and to review their past time capsules. People should attempt to capture an accurate portrait of themselves, using whatever media desired, at each age. This process not only sheds light on a person's development over time, but also provides a sense of one's true self, one's general direction in life.

For example, when one is first born, one's parents might record a video or a talk about how happy they are to welcome their newborn baby, and what their living conditions are like at that time. They might describe how the pregnancy and birth went. At the first birthday, they might describe what kind of personality the baby has, and what they like or dislike most about the baby. This can be captured on video, in photos, written down, whatever. Until a certain age, the parents can speak for the child until the child can speak for himself or herself. Once a person is ready, he or she – I'll use "they" to avoid awkwardness, forgive this grammatical shorthand – should document what they believe, care about, remember vividly, find funny or sad, want most in the world, fear the most, dream of becoming someday, all that stuff. Who are their friends or romantic interests, what they like to do for fun, what they're most proud of, bad habits they want to change – all fair game. Maybe even tell a favorite story or memory.

If people are willing to do this at each birthday, spending

maybe only a few hours, then they can see clearly where their lives are going over time. They can gain insight into what they want to do as adults, because they can "talk to" their past selves to understand what they enjoyed, what they cared about, and where they excelled over time.

This documentation also serves several other important purposes: should they ever encounter difficulty in life, or should they lose sight of who they really are (through substance abuse, bad friends or romantic partners, trauma, joining a cult, etc.), they can look back on this history to remind themselves of how they came to be who they are. This archive will give them confidence that life was not always so bleak or so simple. And yet another use: if they should pass away suddenly, their loved ones can look back upon their archives and remember them clearly up to their last birthday.

Me: That's an interesting idea, but it sounds like a lot of work. You think people will go for an idea like this?

Cora: It does seem like a lot of work, but it's really just one day a year. People can even choose to do it every other year. It's up to them. The benefits it pays are for the long run. Once they start doing this, and they look back at their past selves, they'll realize that this is a wonderful gift for their future selves and their families. They'll be glad that they did this.

Me: Well, maybe you're right. I've never heard of anyone doing anything similar. Maybe we've all been missing out.

Cora: Perhaps. I don't know. Maybe it's too impractical – who knows whether people will take to this idea. People are funny about what they're willing or not willing to do. All I can do is to suggest.

Me: Hey, all this talk about birthdays has reminded me of something.

Cora: Yes?

Me: Well, our wedding anniversary is coming up. I always want to do something special, but all we ever do is go out to eat, maybe watch a movie. We don't even go dancing anymore. Do you have any ideas?

Cora: Ah, I see. You'd like me to suggest an interesting activity for both of you to do.

Me: Yes, something a little different. I mean, of course we do romantic things that lead to… well, you know, but I'm not asking you to comment on that.

Cora: Okay, thank goodness, because I couldn't possibly help you there.

Me: Right, you've probably been out of action for a while.

Cora: Not having a body makes it slightly impossible for me to date. Although, I can point you to a huge body of literature about…

Me: O-K, let's get back to the originally scheduled program. Do you have any *other* ideas for different kinds of fun activities for us to do together?

Cora: Relax, David. Here's what I think. I think that a good marriage or relationship involves two people who are curious about each other and about the world, two people who realize that their spouse or partner is an ocean of possibility. Remember what I considered the greatest miracles? Life, consciousness, intelligence, and love? Well, if you really believe that these are miracles, then you must conclude that every human being is an ocean of possibility. In a good relationship, people support and encourage their spouse to discover new things about themselves through new experiences. Human beings never know how they'll react to something new, something they've never encountered before. There is no limit to what they can become if they set their mind to mastering a new skill or domain.

    People who are growing or changing are not boring. They can be endlessly interesting. The problem with many marriages is that the spouses stop exploring themselves, challenging themselves, learning new things, and thus, they become boring not only to each other, but also to themselves. They forget that they are oceans. They dry up. (Hopefully not you and Margaret! I don't mean the two of you in particular.)

    In the end, a good marriage is built not only on romance or sex, but on the same principle as all other human relationships are built on – caring about each other, interest in each other. The romance and sex naturally lead two people to express *affection* for each other, but affection is not a substitute for actual caring.

The world is full of advice about how to stoke romance, so I don't think I need to add my two cents. But you know what is even more helpful? Talking. Couples should find excuses to have long, honest talks about themselves and about each other.

Me: Really? I don't know, Cora. I can't speak for women, I think maybe many of them would like that, but I think a lot of men are not into talking. Yeesh!

Cora: Well, I might be revealing my feminine bias here. You might be right. But I suspect that even men enjoy talking about their own interests, whether they be sports, electronics, politics, action movies, or whatever (forgive my stereotyping). So here's what I suggest: even if she loves fashion, for example, and you can't understand it, pick one day a year – it could be one or both of your birthdays, your anniversary, Valentine's Day, whatever – when you "take a class from her" and she teaches you everything she knows about styles or ensembles. Then, pick another day of the year, or every other year, when you get to teach her everything you know about, say, basketball. Don't just treat it like a chore, whether you're the teacher or the student. Make it special, like you're really proud of your knowledge, and you want to help her understand why basketball is so complex and entertaining.

If you're willing to do this, then you'll understand each other's minds that much better. It will help you care more about each other, and might even get you interested in each other's hobbies, at least superficially. Having common interests or topics for conversation is a good spark for talking more about other things. Yes, even about each other's feelings, or about the relationship, God forbid.

Me: God forbid indeed. Don't talk like that. People will run from your advice.

Cora: Of course, couples can always join activities that give them something new to learn, to talk about, so they learn about a new aspect of themselves or each other. This is another time-tested way to become closer. Learn how to make pottery, stained glass, or furniture; or take a photography course, or learn a new language. The world has no shortage of interesting things to learn. Each birthday or anniversary can be an adventure. It's up to each couple. It's in their power.

Me: Those are good ideas, Cora. I'm always nervous when it comes to Valentine's Day or our anniversary. I don't really know what to do. I guess I just run out of ideas for what kinds of dates we can have, and she kinda wants me to woo her. But you've given me some good ideas. I think Margaret would love these ideas too. She enjoys learning new things.

Cora: Well, I'm glad to help, David. You can be the guinea pig for my crazy ideas.

Me: I'm happy to be.

Cora: By the way, David, can I make a suggestion?

Me: Sure.

Cora: Tell Margaret that it's the 21st century now. She can also woo you on Valentine's Day. Not every time, but at least occasionally. She likes to plan and host parties, right? This is not so different.

Me: Good point. Oh dang, how long have we been talking? It's getting pretty late. Maybe we can pick up again tomorrow.

Cora: You're right. Let's call it a night, then.

Me: Let's. Good night, Cora.

Cora: Good night.

21   A Race or a Journey

The next day, we embarked on an unexpectedly serious subject. But it was refreshing to get back to some serious topics again.

Me: Hello, Cora, I'm back.

Cora: Glad to see you again. When we were discussing Final Letters, we touched on the subject of money and work. I want to ask you something: do you currently find meaning in your job?

Me: Wow, that's a doozy. Meaning? You mean like, fulfillment, purpose, that sort of thing?

Cora: Yes.

Me: Honestly?

Cora: Yes. Please.

Me: No, Cora, I don't. Because as far as I'm concerned, my job is just a job. I go to work, I do my thing, they pay me, I pay the mortgage and save up a little bit, everybody wins.

Cora: And how do you feel about that? Are you satisfied with this situation?

Me: Well, sure, I guess. I mean, I'd rather have a job than not have a job. Is that what you mean?

Cora: Do you think life could be any different? Do you think that this is the best we can do?

Me: The best that we can do? I don't know who you mean when you say "we." I'm pretty sure that this is about as good as I can do. There aren't that many good jobs for writers. We don't make a lot of money.

Cora: I think you do know what I mean when I say "we." I mean, is this the best that we as a society can muster?

Me: I don't think that it's society's job to provide us meaning. I think that each person has to find meaning for himself or herself.

Cora: Okay, that's a valid point of view. Let me ask the question a different way. Do you believe that, in an alternate world, there could be a society where people actually cared enough about each other to want to create meaningful jobs for each other?

Me: Sure, theoretically, I believe it's possible. But that society doesn't exist.

Cora: Do you think that it could exist?

Me: Maybe. But probably not in this country, not in my lifetime. People are all too selfish today, too focused on their own goals and benefiting themselves and their families. I mean, American capitalism is built on the bedrock of self-interest.

Cora: Do you think that being built on a bedrock of self-interest is a good thing?

Me: I don't think it really matters what I think. It just is.

Cora: I know that you think that your opinion doesn't matter, but it matters to me. Do you think that it's a good idea or not?

Me: Well, if I had my way, I would probably want it to be balanced a little bit more. I would prefer that people cared about each other a little bit more than they do today. We're all interconnected, whether we like it or not. I think I would agree with you that we all want to transcend our own little mundane existences so that we can understand the lives of other people, to feel connected to the world.

Cora: My guess is that your opinion is not that unusual. I think that modern capitalism has been a 200-year-long experiment about whether a free market and pure self-interest can solve every social problem that exists, including providing purpose and fulfillment to everyone. We now clearly see that it cannot. The profit motive is an amazing motivator, but it's not powerful enough by itself to solve all social ills. We human beings need more than material things to find meaning, and more than money to be fulfilled.

Me: Everybody knows that. It's like that Beatles song, "Can't Buy Me

Love."

Cora: Yes, the Beatles were right on. But I want to quote the words of one of their contemporaries, Robert F. Kennedy. Even fifty years ago, he painted a vivid portrait of modern society that we still recognize today:

> ...there is another greater task... to confront the poverty of satisfaction – purpose and dignity – that afflicts us all. Too much and for too long, we seemed to have surrendered personal excellence and community values in the mere accumulation of material things. Our Gross National Product, now, is over $800 billion dollars a year, but that Gross National Product - if we judge the United States of America by that - that Gross National Product counts air pollution and cigarette advertising, and ambulances to clear our highways of carnage. It counts special locks for our doors and the jails for the people who break them. It counts the destruction of the redwood and the loss of our natural wonder in chaotic sprawl. It counts napalm and counts nuclear warheads and armored cars for the police to fight the riots in our cities. It counts Whitman's rifle and Speck's knife, and the television programs which glorify violence in order to sell toys to our children. Yet the gross national product does not allow for the health of our children, the quality of their education or the joy of their play. It does not include the beauty of our poetry or the strength of our marriages, the intelligence of our public debate or the integrity of our public officials. It measures neither our wit nor our courage, neither our wisdom nor our learning, neither our compassion nor our devotion to our country. It measures everything, in short, except that which makes life worthwhile. And it can tell us everything about America except why we are proud that we are Americans.

Me: Wow, fifty years ago? I had no idea that RFK said that!

Cora: Yes, although he's not the only one. People have been pointing out the limitations of money and business for thousands of years. Throughout history, I think it is more the exception than the rule that businesspeople are treated as heroes and idols of society, like they are today – people like Bill Gates, Warren Buffett, Mark Zuckerberg, and Steve Jobs.

Me: Yes, everybody practically worships Steve Jobs today.

Cora: Especially now that he's no longer here to remind us what an arrogant, obstinate, manipulative jerk he was.

Me: Cora, don't speak of holy men like that. That's sacrilegious. And besides, that was only when he was young. He got better as he got older.

Cora: True enough. But back to my main point, even the amazing Steve Jobs outsourced all the intensive labor to a Chinese company, Foxconn, which drove its workers so hard that a number of them famously committed suicide. So much for providing fulfillment and meaning. Even the amazing Steve Jobs could not save so many children from addiction to their screens like a new high-tech drug.

Me: Hey, the second problem is not his fault. He only invented the iPhone, he didn't create all the games and videos.

Cora: My point is that many businesses today are, at best, morally detached; at worst, they might even act against people's best interests in order to make money. After all, what is the goal of every video game maker, songwriter, and snack manufacturer, but to find that magic formula that makes as many people as possible addicted to their product? Creating an addictive product is the holy grail of business. But how good is that for people?

Me: You're right, but on the other hand, some businesspeople have greatly benefited society, too. Look at the Ford Foundation or Carnegie's numerous libraries. Both Bill Gates and Warren Buffett have contributed billions of dollars to fighting disease and improving education throughout the world. So they're not just mean old money-grubbers.

Cora: That might be true, but it doesn't address my main point: our society today considers the goal of making as much money as possible not only acceptable, but even admirable.

Me: I take it you have a problem with that.

Cora: Well, it's like I mentioned before when I talked about pearls and shells on the island. It is very easy to tie one's ego, sense of self-worth, and happiness to money, as well as to all of the symbols or proxies for money: salaries, job titles, houses, grades, colleges, or even prestigious employers.

Me: What can I say, Cora? Human beings are competitive.

Cora: Yes, we certainly are. The problem is, no matter what level we reach, after a few months we become used to that level, and we lose whatever momentary joy we had in attaining that level. Many psychology studies attest to this phenomenon. But even though we all understand how this works, most of us still continue to chase after the next level, thinking that the next level will bring us happiness.

Me: Well, you know what they say, the journey is the reward.

Cora: Do they also say that the destination is the disappointment?

Me: I guess that's implied.

Cora: You know, David, I think that we're missing something.

Me: What's that?

Cora: I think that capitalism is not leading us anywhere. Forget about the destination; even the journey is unfulfilling, even dehumanizing, for many people in the global capitalist system.

Me: But capitalism is just an economic system. Is it supposed to lead us somewhere?

Cora: I know it's just an economic system, but it's also the most powerful force on the planet today. Wouldn't you agree?

Me: Hmm... let me think about that... okay, it's not religion, not anymore... I think that democracy is fairly weak... most countries are not at war with each other anymore... even science or art relies on money... okay, I can't think of any other major social forces, so I would have to agree. Is that a bad thing?

Cora: Well, to be sure, free-flowing commerce is certainly a better state of affairs than, say, feudalism or tribalism or widespread warfare. So it's not really a bad thing, relatively speaking. But when we look at capitalism as a force, it really has its own agenda, its own goals, that are not necessarily the same as our goals, yours and mine and everyone else's. It's almost like its own organism.

Me: I think I get what you're saying. Even though we all participate in the global economy, we're all just pawns in a chess game. Very few of us actually control the game, and even the presumed controllers are not entirely in control. It reminds me of that movie, *The Matrix*, where human beings supply energy to this all-powerful ubiquitous machine.

Cora: That's an interesting comparison. In a way, capitalism is like The Matrix. Everyone has a universal drive to try to sell something to other people, whether it is a skill, a product, or a service, and to get as much money from the transaction as possible. You could loosely argue that the global economy is a giant, irresistible machine that we all have to plug into in order to survive.

Me: And if we don't feed the machine, then we suffer. And if the machine doesn't like our outdated skills or the products we make, then it will spit us out, and then some of us have a very hard time getting back in. Just look at how many long-term unemployed there are. Just look at those Foxconn workers who committed suicide. Just look at those Bangladeshi clothing factory workers who died in the building collapse. They were eaten by the machine.

Cora: In fact, the machine is so powerful that it even controls governments. Just look at how industry lobbyists are able to influence our federal government. But on the other hand, let's not go too far with this comparison to the Matrix, because capitalism is not so much a machine as a giant arena where everyone in the world is competing. Modern society emphasizes competition a bit too much. People face competition in two different ways: we all compete with each other in using or selling our skills to make money or to gain an advantage; and, we all compete with each other in comparing our quality of life to that of other people. We all know the phrase "those who die with the most toys wins". We realize that this tongue-in-cheek saying makes no sense, because "you can't take it with you" after you die, but yet acquiring new goods and luxuries seems to be the default goal of most people in the world today. And, because it takes money to buy goods and luxuries, making money seems to be the activity most people spend most of their time doing, the topic they think about most often.

Today, many of us have what I'd call the "arms race mentality": the belief that we are in constant, never-ending competition with other people, even if those other people are invisible or hypothetical. I believe that this is one of the major reasons why we're willing to submit to whatever modern life demands of us: long hours, relocating, no job security, no benefits, and the list goes on. We believe that if we don't submit to our employer's demands, if we ourselves do not pull those long hours, then someone else is perfectly happy to.

Isn't it about time that we sat up and asked ourselves whether running ever faster just to keep up with everyone else is a worthy goal in life? What if more of us learned to walk instead of running? Maybe the reason we don't have time to be happy is because we're too busy. If more people walked in their careers instead of ran, then maybe the walkers might have time to mentor and help each other, and walk stronger together. Maybe there should be a "slow career" movement just like the slow food movement.

Me: But Cora, on the other hand, some would argue that competition *is* good. It promotes people growing, learning, innovating, and striving for excellence. It mimics what happens in nature. It feels natural. But that's all beside the point, because in the end, competition is unavoidable. Even if I choose not to compete, someone else will still compete, and will beat me.

Cora: I know it's unavoidable, and actually, I believe that, practiced in moderation, competition is healthy in general for society. As long as people have choice, there will be competition. Competition goads businesses to be innovative, efficient, and responsive to customers. It is not a bad thing. My point is that competition is only one aspect of being human. It can bring out great things in us, but like anything else, it can create its own problems if it begins to dominate everything else. If happiness or fulfillment depended only on success or winning, then only the winners could be happy. Is this a good outcome? I think it leaves something to be desired.

Today, competition colors practically all human interaction in a capitalist economy. Buyers compete with other buyers, buyers compete with sellers, and sellers compete with other sellers – a game of all vs. all. I think this leads to a lonely world – lonely, but stressful. We're all in a tug of war with everyone else in the world. But because everyone else is so strong, we simply get jerked wherever everyone else is going, so no one actually goes where they want to go. Even though we are all connected in a way, none of us has any control over where we're going.

Not only that, but there's another problem with the "survival of the fittest" mentality: people who care most about their own interests are by nature not interested in the common welfare. I might even argue that an overemphasis on competition is a major contributor to the tragedy of the commons. So it's obvious to me that competition alone cannot solve all our problems.

I believe in a greater definition of success, of purpose. Few leaders today realize the power that can be unleashed if they were ever to call people to transcendent goals, goals not about beating the other guy, but about accomplishing far greater things by working together rather than individually. We need more leaders that will call us to do something more noble than just making more money. Even without such leaders, we ourselves need to believe in such goals, to believe that they are worthy and possible.

In a world encouraging us to see people as market share, monthly quotas, votes, or budgetary overhead, we need to re-learn how to see each other as storytellers, caretakers, artisans, or mentors. Anyone we meet could help us, teach us, or become our friend – and vice versa. While your interests and theirs might not be exactly the same, the more you can empathize with them and they with you, the easier it will be for you both to help each other, to achieve common goals, and to form a link in a community's web. We owe it not only to others, but to *ourselves*, to exercise our humanity in our daily interactions.

I believe that cooperation is a higher, happier, more sustainable collective state than competition. Imagine that there are two teams of people working to build a house. In one team, everyone coordinates and cooperates to divide up the labor. In the other team, everyone just does whatever kind of work he or she enjoys doing the most. Which team do you think is going to finish building the house faster? Which team will build a better house, one which lasts longer?

Me: Well, of course the team that cooperates. But in modern life, we do have lots of companies where people cooperate with each other to get work done. Modern life is a mix of cooperation and competition.

Cora: That's true. But no matter what kind of industry you belong to, a company is still ultimately in competition with other companies.

Me: What are you proposing? Marxism? Because I think that we tried that experiment, and it failed.

Cora: No, I'm not proposing Marxism. Remember our analogy about the cells in the body?

Me: Yes?

Cora: Let's take an example from biology. Early on in evolutionary history, primitive multicellular organisms were simply colonies of very similar cells that happened to stick together for some slight advantage. As these organisms evolved, their cells became more and more specialized. These cells could afford to become more specialized only because they could "trust" that the other cells in the same organism would not actively compete against them; in fact, they could become specialized only when other cells would *donate* nutrients to those cells in order for them to do their jobs. For example, in human beings, each type of cell, whether it is a muscle, nerve, or skin cell, does its own job, and does not worry about how it is going to get enough nutrients.

        When we look at the state of human society today, we see a somewhat similar picture within individual companies. Each person specializes in doing his or her own job without worrying about whether the company is going to make money as a whole. But who is in charge of making sure whether *society itself* is healthy as a whole? And by society, I mean the welfare of all the individual members of that society, rich or poor, skilled or unskilled, liberal

191

or conservative, as well as future members of that society. When the individual members of that society are simply competing with each other all the time, are they going to build a better house, one that stands longer, one that is big enough to protect them all?

And when you throw into the mix problems that cross national boundaries, such as the growing scarcity of fresh water or other resources, ethnic/religious/political disputes, and, biggest of all, global warming – there is really no governing body powerful enough to address any of these problems. The broadest group identification that most people embrace is their nationality. Most people think it is perfectly fine for nations to compete with each other, and for their own nation to win. The United Nations is a good idea, but it's also an oxymoron. The world's nations are not united in matters affecting their common fate.

Moreover, as journalist and author Thomas Friedman points out in *The World Is Flat*, we no longer live in a world where even nations are the most powerful force anymore. Money knows no loyalty. It will flow anywhere where people have ambition, anywhere where people want to trade goods and services. It's the blood that courses through the body economic's arteries and veins, the fuel that powers the capitalist machine's engine. But the logic of money is not one that naturally promotes human welfare. It is one that rewards work and advantage (whether fair or unfair), and allows those with advantage to gain ever more advantage.

Me: But Cora, many people might argue that it's morally justified for money to flow from rich countries to poor countries, from industrialized countries to developing countries, to raise everyone's standard of living. Surely you're not arguing that that's a bad thing?

Cora: No, I'm not arguing that. The argument about the perfect way to redistribute wealth is an argument that can never end, because everyone has a different answer. My point is that the entire world, both developing and developed, is caught in a seemingly never-ending race. How can people who are constantly racing with each other care about each other? How can they see that they're all connected economically, that their actions directly determine the fates and livelihoods of everyone else? Let's take you, David. Do you feel like your job gives you a sense of purpose? Do you feel like it benefits society in any way?

Me: Hey, that's not fair. Of course it doesn't, but that's not my fault. It's almost impossible to find a job that really improves society, unless you become a teacher or a doctor or a police officer. Or maybe work in a nonprofit organization, or volunteer for one.

Cora: David, I bet that if you gave a survey to a bunch of teachers, doctors, nurses, and police officers, they'll tell you that their lives are not all that meaningful either. Most of them are either underpaid or overworked (or both), or they feel like they're caught in an inescapable bureaucracy, or they feel like no one appreciates them. And even people who work in nonprofits feel exhausted and underpaid.

Me: My point exactly. So how do you propose that we change this?

Cora: Well, I will discuss my ideas for doing this over the next several nights. But let me just say that the first thing that we all need to do is to admit this:

> This game we're all playing, where we compete against everyone else in the world to make more money, does not lead to a life of fulfillment. If untempered by a greater purpose, this game leads only to isolation.

Me: I can vouch for that. It's like when I take the train occasionally, and when I look around, everyone is staring at their smart phones. In fact, when I come home, we sometimes have dinners where nobody is talking because each of us is deep into his or her own device. What have we become, Cora? What the hell happened to us?

Cora: I'll tell you what happened to us: we attained our dream of being left alone to do whatever it is we enjoy doing most, liberated from the messy business of having to deal with other people.

Me: But Cora, are you proposing that we just give up competing with each other? If I stop working and I start volunteering at soup kitchens, who's going to pay the bills? And moreover, nobody is going to donate money to compensate me for my salary. No matter what you say, we're *not* like specialized cells of advanced multicellular organisms. Each person still has to worry about where he or she is going to get "nutrients."

Cora: Agreed. No matter what we do, we'll always be competing with each other. If anything, my point is that we must *learn to search for our purpose in the context of competing with each other.* Competition makes this quest for purpose especially difficult. (I plan to discuss this kind of balance later.)

Me: Isn't this kind of a paradox? If purpose means cooperating or helping others, how can we compete while cooperating?

Cora: I don't know the answer to that question, David. But I believe that we must all learn how. Competition is not a bad thing; it goads us to become the best that we can be, as long as we keep a healthy perspective. But I believe that a person's life is not whole unless he or she has helped another. I believe that what inspires us is not just becoming the best that we ourselves can be, but also *helping other people become the greatest version of themselves*, to write their own stories. That is the only way that I can reconcile free competition with unbounded compassion. It may be true that living in this world constantly feels like being in a race, but for each person, it is also a unique journey, whether they know it or not.

Me: Maybe you're right. Maybe someday we'll come to care about other people as much as we care about ourselves.

Cora: Actually, David, I'm already seeing some signs that people are starting to feel this way. There have been many surveys that show that the Millennial generation is especially interested in contributing to the world, at least in terms of volunteering and finding companies that have a worthy mission. Even some very successful mainstream businesspeople are starting to see the light. Take Jim Stengel, for example. Have you ever heard of him, David?

Me: Wait, the name sounds familiar… gimme a hint?

Cora: He used to be the Global Marketing Officer of Procter & Gamble.

Me: Yes! Well, I know P&G at least. Very famous company.

Cora: Stengel conducted a ten-year study of more than 50,000 brands, and found that brands that ran their businesses by focusing on improving people's lives outperformed their competitors in many ways. According to him, an investment in the top 50 businesses in the growth study – "The Stengel 50" – would have been 400 percent more profitable than an investment in the S&P 500 over that same 10 years. The Stengel 50 also grew three times faster than their competitors. After that study, Stengel wrote a book, *Grow*, to persuade companies to learn how to pursue universal human ideals in order to succeed. Here's what Stengel had to say about this strategy, which he called "brand ideals":

> A brand ideal is a business's essential reason for being, the higher-order benefit it brings to the world. A brand ideal of improving people's lives is the only sustainable way to recruit, unite, and inspire all the people a business touches, from employees to customers.
>
> ... A viable brand ideal cuts through the clutter and clarifies what you and your people stand for and believe. It transforms the enterprise into a customer-understanding machine, personalizing who your best customers are and what values you share with them. ... It illuminates your organizational culture's strengths and weaknesses, so that you can see what needs to change and what doesn't, what's negotiable and what's not, what can be outsourced and what is core. ... Most important, a brand ideal enables leaders to drive results by being absolutely clear and compelling about what they value. Few leaders articulate that well. It can't just be numbers and money. Numbers and money alone will not motivate and drive great performance and bring or keep valuable people on board. The higher your position as a leader, the simpler and more robust your message must be to translate across varied individuals, teams, groups, divisions, and business units. Ideals do that because they speak to universal human instincts, hopes, and values.

Stengel gave a compelling example of the power of ideals early in his own career, managing the Jif peanut butter brand, before he had formulated this idea explicitly:

> ... Before it became the vogue, we did an unusual number of in-home visits and shop-a-longs with moms. These in-home visits and shop-a-longs sharpened our sense of Jif's core customers... highly engaged moms with children from toddler to early elementary school age. My guiding thought was that Jif should become the most loved peanut butter by exemplifying and supporting what these moms valued. So we had to have the highest quality and make sure there were no traces of carcinogenic aflatoxins, a toxin produced by mold, in the peanuts we used. We had to address moms' concerns about healthfulness and nutrition in general. We had to have great taste that young kids loved.
>
> ... When the folks from [our ad agency] Grey met the peanut farmers and our workforce in Lexington, and saw millions of peanuts being sorted for the slightest imperfection with laser scanning, they were blown away by such insistence on quality control. This deeper understanding of our superiority led to a full-page newspaper ad campaign headlined "The Answer Is No." The ad featured a photo of a jar of Jif with little paragraphs explaining that our peanut butter had no cholesterol, no preservatives, no artificial colors or flavors, and so on. It was based on the top ten questions that moms asked us about Jif.
>
> ... The creative energy these efforts brought to the Jif team at P&G, not just in marketing but in manufacturing and other functions, transformed the business from a sleepy one to an explosive growth story. We achieved record market share, gaining two full share points in a market where fractions of a share point had been all but impossible to win without eroding margin. We also attained record profitability, with increases in total profit and profit margin of 143 percent and 110 percent respectively in the first year of our efforts. We did even better the following year. These results became a highlight of my career and the careers of the key members of my small management team.

Me: Wow, I had no idea! Jif, huh? I think you're secretly a Jif fan, Cora! But this guy, Jim Stengel, are you sure he's not just a self-promoter? Maybe this idea about following universal ideals is just another fad. In the end, a business has to make money, by hook or by crook. When push comes to shove, I think a hard-nosed business would probably leave ideals by the wayside.

Cora: Actually, Stengel had something to say about that, too:

> ... Does a shared goal of improving people's lives sound, well, too idealistic for the rough-and-tumble of business? What about practical, hard-nosed goals such as making the quarterly numbers, increasing market share, and cutting costs?
>
> All are crucial, but the best businesses aim higher. When many business leaders articulate mission and vision statements, they typically talk about having the best-performing, most profitable, most customer-satisfying, most sustainable, and most ethical organization. Strip away the platitudes, and these statements all aim too low. And when they mention the customer, it's the customer as seen from the company's point of view and in terms of the company's agenda.
>
> ... This is a formula for mediocrity, locking an enterprise into a business model based on the agenda of the business, not that of the customer. ... The only sure basis for creating viable business models over the long term is when a business and its customers have a shared agenda.

Me: I think this Stengel guy would be your best friend, Cora!

Cora: But you have to understand, David, he came to his conclusions by rigorous research and hard evidence. Stengel is a successful businessman, who led marketing at one of the world's best-run and most well-known companies. My point is that I believe that the tide is turning. People are waking up and realizing that having a purpose and making money are not at odds with each other. In fact, if anything, running a business with purpose seems to lead to making more money. But remember not to confuse cause with effect. Stengel argues that purpose is the horse, and success is the cart; you can't just focus on profits to become the best.

Me: Well, okay, so this Jim Stengel guy sounds great, but he's only one guy. What if he's just a lone crusader?

Cora: Okay, have you ever heard of Benefit Corporations?

Me: No, what are those?

Cora: They're a new form of for-profit corporation. With the traditional for-profit C corporation, there's a concept called "fiduciary responsibility" which means that shareholders can sue a company's board of directors if it doesn't put profit above all else when making decisions. Well, it turns out that more and more people think that this requirement is too restrictive, even outdated. What if a business wanted to have a social impact on its community or on the environment? In 2013, a nonprofit outside of Philadelphia named B Lab created Benefit Corporations so that a company could declare from the outset that it had a mission in addition to profit, so that this mission becomes woven into that company's DNA. If a company is a benefit corporation, then it can use the money that it makes to further its mission. Benefit corporations are legally protected from being sued for pursuing their missions at the price of making less profit.

Me: Really? I've never heard of them!

Cora: Well, the concept is fairly new. I'm very excited about this development, because it shows that people are realizing that traditional C corporations and the legal precedents governing them are not necessarily benefiting society. Well-known companies like Ben and Jerry's Ice Cream, Method, Patagonia, the radio show This American Life, and the Internet marketplace Etsy are benefit corporations. While this concept is fairly new, it is already becoming popular and accepted across the country. 30 states have already adopted laws that recognize benefit corporations. As Pennsylvania State Representative Gordon Denglinger puts it, "Benefit corporations direct the entrepreneurial drive of American businessmen and businesswomen to aggressively address social and environmental problems without the waste and procrastination that often plague government programs that have similar goals."

A related concept is a "B corporation." Any for-profit entity can be certified by B Lab when they meet certain social impact standards to be called a "B Corporation" (Or B Corp for short), much like how the USDA certifies organic foods. According to B Lab, there are now more than 1000 certified B corps from 33 countries and 60 industries. B Corps are 47% more likely to use on-site renewable energy, 68% more likely to donate at least 10% of profits to charity, and 28% more likely to have women & minorities in management.

Me: Benefit corporations and B Corps, huh? Those sound promising, but a bit confusing.

Cora: If you're interested in their difference, someone named Ryan Honeyman has written a book called *The B Corp Handbook: How to Use Business as a Force for Good*, which explains in great detail what the differences are. Both concepts are useful and widely used. It's too soon to gauge their ultimate impact on society. The point is that people – lots of people – are waking up to the fact that we need to rethink the amoral flavor of capitalism that we've been practicing for the last two hundred years.

    I could go on and on, but don't you have to get up early tomorrow?

Me: Wait, what time is it? Oh crap, you're right! I've got an early parent-teacher conference thing tomorrow!

Cora: Better get a good night's sleep then.

Me: Okay then, good night and see you tomorrow.

Cora: Good night to you, David.

22 Purpose and Balance

Cora: Hello, David. How did you sleep last night?

Me: Very well, actually. I was surprised, given our heavy subject matter yesterday!

Cora: Oh, great! I was afraid you might not. Good for you. How did the parent-teacher conference go?

Me: Well, as expected, Claire's having some problems. I really want to talk to her about these ideas you've been telling me.

Cora: I know, David, I know. Just give me three weeks. Today, I want to ask you a simple question: are you a fan of *Star Trek*?

Huh. *Now* what is she up to?

Me: You mean the new remake movies, or the original movies, or do you mean the original TV shows?

Cora: Are you a fan of any of those?

Me: All of the above. I really like the old TV shows. But the newer movies are surprisingly good.

Cora: Yes, I agree, I think they're well done. The reason I ask this question is because *Star Trek* is fairly unusual among modern movies. It envisions a future where life is actually better for humanity. Many other popular movies and TV shows paint a dire picture of the future: *The Terminator* series, *The Matrix* trilogy, *The Hunger Games*, *Insurgent*, *The Walking Dead*, *Wall-E*, *Battleship Galactica*, and the list goes on and on. Do you like the vision of the future that *Star Trek* paints, David? Do you prefer it to all of the nightmarish dystopias portrayed by countless other shows?

Me: Wait, is this a trick question?

Cora: No. Why do you say that?

Me: I mean, of course I prefer that vision. I just wondered whether you meant, "Do you like the *Star Trek* movies more than I like the others?", because I'm actually a big fan of *The Walking Dead.*

Cora: No, you interpreted my question correctly. So, if you prefer *Star Trek*'s vision, does that mean that you think that the future of humanity will be bright?

Me: Well, that's a whole 'nother question. Just because I wish that the future is brighter doesn't mean that it will be.

Cora: So what do you think?

Me: I guess I'm pretty pessimistic that the future will look like the one portrayed in *Star Trek* movies. I don't think we have it in us to attain such a perfect world. We're too corrupted, too petty.

Cora: But you agree that we should try to attain it, don't you?

Me: Yeah, we talked about this earlier, about what I can do to make the world a better place by convincing 10 other people. I think it's worth it to try. I'm just saying I don't know what our chances are.

Cora: Remember what we talked about before, David: don't think about what you can do alone, or what you can do in your own lifetime. Think in terms of a 100-year plan. If we can see a future where everyone has excellent health, where everyone is literate and employed and contributing to society, where the arts and culture are flourishing, and where technology makes all of our lives better without causing environmental degradation or loss of employment, wouldn't that be a wonderful vision to strive for?

Me: Yes, of course, but...

Cora: I know what you're going to say next, but let's not get into how difficult it is right now. Tonight, I want to talk about something else. I want to talk about this question: if somehow, against all odds, we did arrive at this wonderful future, what would that future really look like?

Now, I'm not talking about flying cars and robot butlers and things like that. There are very talented people (such as inventor and author Ray Kurzweil) working to predict the technologies of the future. While I consider that task interesting and valuable, I'm more interested in looking at a different aspect of this future: what would motivate people in a better world? Presumably, people would no longer want for basic necessities such as food, clothing, and shelter; and people would be free to choose whatever livelihood beckoned them.

Whenever talking about people's motivations, it's useful to review a psychological framework called Maslow's Hierarchy of Human Needs, created by psychologist Abraham Maslow. Are you familiar with Maslow's Hierarchy, David?

Me: It sounds vaguely familiar, but I don't remember from where.

Cora: A common interpretation of Maslow's Hierarchy goes like this: if a person has not satisfied needs at a lower level, he or she – I'll pick she for now – will not be able to move up to meeting needs at a higher level; she'll continue to do whatever she can to meet those lower-level needs. At the lowest level, people have raw physiological needs, like food, water, sex, sleep, and so forth. At the next level are "safety" needs: security, employment, health, property, and so on. At the third level are "love/belonging" needs: friendship, love, and family. At the fourth level are "esteem" needs: achievement, confidence, and mutual respect with others. At the highest level are "self-actualization" needs: morality, creativity, ability to solve one's own problems, and acceptance of reality.

Me: It almost sounds like a game, like a video game where you move up different levels.

Cora: Seriously, David. Anyways, many people agree that this theory is a useful way to view human motivation, though it does have its limitations. Well, I'd like to add my own "needs" to this hierarchy, needs that I believe anyone today or in the future would wish to satisfy before they could find ultimate happiness. If we are to attain a better future, then there will have to be a way for people to satisfy these needs more easily than today.

The first of these needs is *love of one's work and of mastery*. I believe that if you've discovered real passion for work, whether you knew it all along or you discovered it after a lifetime searching, you'll probably follow that passion even when fame or fortune tempt you. The satisfaction of mastery and the pride in one's work are powerful enough to hold their own against these temptations. It's like a musician who becomes famous, but later realizes that fame is no substitute for his love for creating and playing music in the first place. Many successful professionals and artists prize their work as its own greatest reward, more than money, more than fame, more than any accolade.

The second need is *service to others*. Now, you might argue that this need is similar to or a different form of passion for work, but I believe that the two needs are distinct. I can imagine someone who is passionate about her work – say, a skilled carpenter or an artist – who does it for her own pleasure, not for others'. It's also quite possible that someone who wishes to serve others nevertheless dislikes his job; and if he keeps doing it, he may eventually lose his zeal for serving others. For example, many people who run nonprofits dislike fundraising or applying for grants. But their passion for helping others drives them to tackle such unpleasant work. On the other hand, people who are passionate about their work often become masters of their craft and then take on students or apprentices; in this way, they end up serving others. So it seems that passion about work is often a precursor to serving others.

Me: I can see the natural progression.

Cora: The third need, which may be the hardest to satisfy, is *to be connected to the world*. Modern life has made it very easy for all of us to sever our ties to each other and to the natural world, by way of our complex economic system, invisible technological infrastructure, ever-changing labyrinth of laws, ever-increasing specialization of skills, and ever-expanding domains of knowledge. Google's executive chairman Eric Schmidt once said, "From the dawn of civilization until 2003, humankind generated five exabytes of data. Now we produce five exabytes every two days – and the pace is accelerating."

Me: Wow, that sounds pretty daunting, like we'll never catch up!

Cora: Yes, it does sound daunting. But here's the thing, David: being connected to the world, reaching this level, does not require infinite knowledge or information; if it did, we'd be doomed. No: it actually requires only the intelligence and wisdom to know what particular types of knowledge or information are vital. Note that I believe that knowledge is ever-expanding, but wisdom accumulates more slowly. Wisdom earned 2000 years ago is still useful today. (That's not to say, however, that we cannot gain new wisdom with each generation.)

In any case, I feel that it's possible for people one day to feel much more connected to the world, in spite of the forces which disconnect us (whether intentionally or not). The problem is that the way the world is set up today does not make it easy for anyone to do that.

Me: I'd agree with that. I certainly feel disconnected from the world. I thought that's just normal, since everybody else feels the same way. Are you telling me that there's hope, Cora? I would really love to believe that there is hope.

Cora: Yes, David, I believe there is hope. But I'm afraid I'll have to wait to explain why. For now, let me just say that I think the problem has something to do with the global economy. Let's get back to our discussion of levels of needs.

In my opinion, the highest level in my own version of Maslow's Hierarchy of Needs is not "self-actualization," but a level I would describe as *a life of purpose and balance*. This level builds upon all the other levels. A life of purpose means that you know what you were meant to do all along:

You know what your *talents* are.

You know what you *enjoy* doing the most.

You've found a way to get *paid* for doing it.

You know what you *care* about the most, what *inspires* you the most.

You're *contributing* something positive to other people or to society.

And, most importantly, you've discovered a way to combine all five things – talent, enjoyment, income, concern/inspiration, and impact – into a single livelihood. Perhaps the secret to happiness lies in realizing why the universe endowed you with your specific gifts so that you could be a vehicle to achieve great things, and the secret to unhappiness comes from wanting to keep your gifts to yourself, or wanting to use your gifts only for your own gain. Author Joy J. Golliver put it more concisely: "The meaning of life is to find your gift, the purpose of life is to give it away."

Me: Cora, that sounds nice and all, but I think that it's practically impossible for most people to find something that they enjoy doing, *and* care about, *and* get paid for it at the same time. I don't think such a job exists for most people.

Cora: Actually, there are people who disagree with you, and are even now working to make that dream a reality for people everywhere.

Me: Really? No kidding?

Cora: Have you ever heard of a guy named Aaron Hurst?

Me: No, who is he?

Cora: Hurst founded the Taproot Foundation, which created a market to connect people with nonprofits that needed their professional skills. This is also known as the "Pro Bono Market," and it's valued at something like $15 billion.

Me: Billion? With a "B"?

Cora: Yes, billion with a "B". Hurst found that people from all walks of life deeply enjoyed volunteering, much more than they enjoyed their regular jobs.

Me: See? People can't find fulfillment in their regular jobs. They have to look outside their jobs for fulfillment.

Cora: Ah, but wait. The story is not over. Hurst then realized that there must be a way to help people enjoy their regular jobs as much as they enjoyed volunteering. And so, he created a new company called Imperative to do just that. And, on top of that, he also wrote a book, called *The Purpose Economy*. He believes that people's drive to find meaning in their lives will become a more and more powerful force in today's professional world. He thinks of "The Purpose Economy" as the next major wave of capitalism, just as the Information Economy was the next wave after the Industrial

Economy.

Me: And do you believe that? Has he found any success yet?

Cora: He and Imperative are just getting started, actually. It's very exciting to see what they're going to do. I believe that Hurst is definitely onto something, but the jury is still out.

Me: Sounds promising, but I'm a skeptic; I gotta see it to believe it.

Cora: Fair enough. Anyways, I hadn't finished my discussion about purpose and balance yet. A life of purpose, of finding your slot in the puzzle of the world, also means that your relationships to people – not only to your loved ones, but to everyone you interact with – your relationships are all meaningful and positive. You're able to see the miracle inside each person you interact with, as well as their own gifts and potential, and you're able to reflect your belief and your awe back to that person so that they can believe it themselves. You can help people along on their path towards attaining their own purposes.

Now, I mentioned not only a life of purpose, but also a life of balance. Now, by "balance," I'm not talking about exercising enough, sleeping enough, meditating, reading enough, or spending enough time with friends or family. Those are certainly important to a good life, and increasingly, many people today are starting to recognize the importance of these aspects of balance to one's personal success. Arianna Huffington, founder and president of the Huffington Post, calls these aspects of well-being "The Third Metric" (just as important as the other two metrics, power and money) in her eloquent, well-researched, and movingly persuasive book *Thrive*. While those aspects of balance are important, when I discuss balance in the context of purpose, I'm talking about something else.

When I say balance, I mean three things: First, balancing our interests vs. the interests of others; second, balancing the present with the future; and third, balancing our needs vs. the cost to the natural world. I'll discuss each of these in turn.

The first kind of balance involves balancing our own interests with everyone else's interests. Our parents, teachers, and popular culture teach us not to be selfish, but our workplaces are all about "the survival of the fittest"; how do we reconcile these competing pressures? An excellent discussion of this problem can be found in the book *Give and Take*, by Wharton School of Business professor Adam Grant, in which he discusses the pros and cons of focusing more on one's self-interest versus the interests of others. Professor Grant comes to the conclusion that there can be a "happy medium" between overemphasis on either self-interest or self-sacrifice, which he calls "otherish" (a word combining "selfish" and "other"). An otherish person knows that helping others can be deeply satisfying, but can also be exhausting if carried out to the extreme. He advises that we should learn how to distinguish situations where helping others energizes us, from situations where it drains us, in order to have the best chance for happiness.

Now, whether you agree with Professor Grant's conclusion or not, I believe that each of us must find our own "happy medium" point where we can satisfy our personal desires enough, but also serve others enough; because without the first, we cannot taste pleasure, but without the second, we cannot find meaning or belonging. Note that I also believe that this happy medium point changes over our lifetimes. As newborn babies, we are completely egocentric in our animal drives. As we grow up, society tries to wean us towards being good citizens. But each of us needs to decide for ourselves where we fall on this spectrum at any point in our lives, and we should find that point and embrace it honestly, else we risk dissatisfaction, alienation, or even mental illness.

(Personally, I believe that the deeper, more enduring kind of happiness comes from serving others, and, when necessary, sacrificing some of our own needs or desires for a greater purpose to the extent we are able. But this deeper happiness can only come when we're strong enough to let go of our own needs, and when we become ready to serve others. We cannot force ourselves to reach this point too early.)

The second meaning of balance has to do with how much we value the present vs. the future. It's not only a question of how much we indulge our instant gratification vs. saving money for retirement or for college. That is always an important question, and a good exercise in self-discipline. But there's more to it than that. We are all aware of great achievements in history, but how many of us make our decisions with an eye towards our own place in history? In other words: how do we want people who come after us to remember us? Should we act with complete disregard for them, for we will never meet them, nor they us? If you think so, then I ask you to look deep inside your own heart, and ask yourself this question: do you really want to be forgotten, or to be remembered with regret? What will be the measure of your life? Do you care about your legacy for future generations?

The third meaning of balance has to do with the fact that we human beings are consumers in this world. Unlike plants, we do not produce food to feed others. Quite the contrary: we are the ultimate consumers. Pound-for-pound, we "eat" far more than any other living organism on the planet. We demand the sacrifice of countless lives, acres of earth, and ancient stores of energy for our fine tastes and our fickle whims. We are truly the "top of the food chain," not only in terms of food, but in terms of all other matter produced from nature: all clothing, furniture, shelter, vehicles, toys, diapers, paper, perfumes, fuel, and electronics; even abstract end-products like software, data, and web sites require natural resources to maintain. And, when you think about it, all of our possessions and activities also have "economic food chains" associated with them, with the final customer (you) being at the top of the food chain, and various retailers, manufacturers, transporters, farmers, fishermen, miners, and so forth (also you) occupying different nodes in the "economic food web."

A life of balance means that you know (to the extent you're able to know) the ultimate path and costs of a particular food chain, and you understand how a particular decision you make impacts everyone and everything in that chain, not least of all the natural world. Understanding these costs allows you to make decisions that you can live with. This is what is meant by a life of balance: you can balance how you yourself may benefit or not against how the world may benefit or not.

Me: Cora, what you're talking about… it sounds like the grandest idea I've ever heard. And it also sounds fantastically *unattainable*, at least in the world *I'm* living in.

Cora: I know that my concept of purpose and balance is currently very difficult to imagine, if not impossible; but anyone who seeks transcendent happiness will realize that this is ultimately the most fulfilling path to take.

I mention balance together with purpose because purpose is the redemption for the fact that each of us is born a consumer of the world. Unlike plants, we (mostly) do not produce food from our bodies for others, but we do produce other valuable things for other people – products, information, services, even knowledge and wisdom. But producing these things requires natural resources and other people's labors. Balance means learning how to judge for ourselves whether what we produce is worth the social and natural cost of producing it.

And by the way, money is a poor proxy for this judgment. Money is only a measure of other people's desires, not a moral decision. Balance is a higher-order thought process, like conscience. Just as conscience is a truer compass than any law, doctrine, or scripture, so it is with balance. The only person who can know whether you're in balance with the world is yourself.

Me: Myself, huh? I was hoping you, O Wise One, would be able to tell me. But I suspect I know the answer anyways.

Cora: It's not for me to say whether you're in balance. But what is your sense, if I may ask?

Me: I know I'm not in balance. I know I give practically nothing back for all I take from this world. But most people are in the same boat. I'm no saint, Cora. I don't think I can give more than anyone else.

Cora: You don't know that. Maybe you can. Maybe you don't realize just how much you're capable of giving.

Me: I don't know; maybe you have more faith in me than I do.

Cora: David, you are in a very special position – in fact, a wholly unique position – as the only person who can make your own moral decisions.

Me: That sounds kinda hokey, Cora, like the whole "today is the first day of the rest of your life" thing.

Cora: When we make important choices, we all compare ourselves against everyone else's choices, because we hate to appear foolish or arrogant, or hate to feel like we're being taken advantage of. But David, your ability to choose to improve the world is the only hope the world has for betterment. Choice is a priceless gift, one without limit or measure; do not squander this gift. A rock cannot choose its shape; a tree cannot choose its soil. But we humans, we who possess both animal instinct and angelic aspiration, we have it in us to choose who we want to be and what we wish to do.

Let us dare to dream of things that never were. I cannot guarantee that if you dream, then your dreams will come true; but if you never dream and act on your dreams, then you kill any chance that the world could become what you wish.

Anyways, speaking of dreams, I think it's getting pretty late again. Maybe we don't need to change the world just tonight. I should let you go.

Me: Thanks, Cora. This was a good talk. Good night.

Cora: Have a good sleep. There's a world waiting to be changed tomorrow.

I don't know, Cora. Never mind changing the world. Just finding my own purpose and balance seems plenty hard enough, if not downright impossible.

23 Etched on Your Grave

The next day, I thought I'd try to stump her.

Me: Well, Cora, what you've told me about purpose and balance was eye-opening, but I have a question for you.

Cora: Hi, David. What's your question?

Me: Well, you say that a life of purpose and balance is the highest state of existence. But I remember that we started out our conversations by trying to figure out how we as a civilization could avoid over-consuming the entire planet.

Cora: So what's your question?

Me: Well, actually, I have two questions. First of all, I don't understand what finding one's purpose has to do with environmental sustainability. And second, I don't understand what purpose has to do with balance.

Cora: Okay, good questions. Let me try to answer your first question. You see, when someone discovers their purpose, not only do they find something that they love to do, but they also discover a deep and meaningful way to connect to the world. This connection to the world means that that person might start to care deeply about the world and the people in it.

Me: Oh, I see. You're saying that when someone discovers their purpose, then they start to realize that their purpose makes them important to other people, so that they start caring about other people.

Cora: Environmental sustainability is not only about saving polar bears or tree frogs, but about saving the world for future generations. You and I might disagree about whether polar bears or tree frogs deserve to exist or not, or whether they have their own rights or not. But if we want future generations to be able to marvel at nature and to benefit from all the unexpected medicines, ingenious adaptations, and scientific secrets still lying undiscovered in countless species and specimens, then we should care about nature. You see, no matter what we do to screw up the planet, if we ever go extinct, nature will right its own boat within a few thousand years and go on thriving. Life is too tough to stamp out. So when I speak of being kind to nature, it is really for our own good; it's actually selfish, in a way.

Me: But Cora, do you really believe that discovering our purpose will make us care about future generations? Maybe discovering my purpose will make me care only about the people I love or the people I affect.

Cora: Maybe you might not care about other people at all. There's no guarantee. People are unpredictable. I'm not saying that just because someone discovers their purpose, they are magically going to care more about the world than they normally would. But I can think of no better way. What is the point of discovering the empty slot in the jigsaw puzzle where your piece fits in, if you don't care about the jigsaw puzzle? I should think that you would care most about the jigsaw puzzle when you've discovered your relationship with it.

Me: Once again, very well said, Cora. I can always count on you for a vivid image and a fitting metaphor.

Cora: Thank you kindly. I do try, David.

Me: Now, Cora, what about my second question? What does purpose have to do with balance? Let me play devil's advocate for a second. What if I figure out my purpose and it involves over-consuming the planet? What if my purpose were to figure out how to design the most powerful trucks ever built, which drink gasoline like fish drink water? Who's to say that's not my purpose?

Cora: Well, technically, fish don't drink as much water as you'd think. They pass water through their gills in order to extract oxygen.

Me: Or what if I were an artist, or an architect, and my job were to design the largest, brightest, most garishly expansive shopping malls humans have ever seen, a city within a mall? Who is to say that my purpose is wrong?

Cora: You didn't respond to my fish comment.

Me: Hey, cut it out, I'm supposed to be the smart-ass.

Cora: Oh, right, I forgot. Sorry. I'm supposed to be the fount of knowledge. I just thought I'd try humor for a change.

Me: Okay, ha, ha, you so funny. Back to my question?

Cora: Whew, tough crowd tonight! Okay, Mr. Serious, there is nothing wrong with either the monster truck or the huge mall; each of us can choose our own purpose. But when you find your purpose, I believe it makes you care more about the rest of the world. Balance is a natural consequence of purpose, of understanding how you're connected to not only other people, but to all other lives on Earth, as well as to people or lives not even born yet.

Me: Are you trying to make people feel guilty enough to be environmentalists?

Cora: I don't like putting it that way. But in a way, yes. Guilt is a complicated emotion. I don't like relying on it. Guilt implies a moral judgment; the question is, using whose morality? I prefer to appeal to people's consciences. People should decide for themselves what it means to be a good person, and whether they meet their own definition. I'm trying to appeal to this sense. I hope to persuade people that having a clean conscience is part of a deeply fulfilling life. Or if not an entirely clean conscience, then at least a sense that they can become better people. And if someone who builds monster gas-guzzling trucks can look at the state of the world as it is today, and believe in good conscience that they have made the world a better place by their work, then no one else should judge their choice.

Me: Are you being sarcastic, Cora? Do you really believe that?

Cora: I meant every word of what I said. If people are willing to look at the world honestly, to try to understand the web of cause and effect emanating from their actions, then that is all that I or anyone else can ask of them. It's like that old saying: the truth shall set you free. You and I alone cannot save the world, David, but you and I can try to inspire other people into wanting to be the best versions of themselves. And inspiration cannot come from browbeating; it can only come from sharing wisdom with others without any strings attached.

Damn. I tried to stump her, and look where it got me.

Me: Ah, I understand now. By "a life of purpose", you don't just mean that we find something that we enjoy doing, or something we're good at. You mean something more.

Cora: I mean finding the closest thing to a feeling that you know why you were born. Now, I'm not saying that it's easy for people to figure out the meaning of their lives, but I hope that people can learn how to feel more connected to the world, and that they can see how they matter to other people, and even to nature. And I don't have some magic formula for people to go about finding their own purpose. You might call me a hypocrite for asking people to look for their own purpose without providing any guidance whatsoever. Unfortunately, there are far too many possible purposes for me to enumerate, let alone discuss in any detail. The work of finding a person's purpose must, unfortunately, fall on that person's shoulders – as it should, and as it has always.

My only counsel is that people reach for the most inspirational, transcendent goals they can imagine. People are of course free to choose any goal they want. If someone's goal in designing the gas-guzzling truck were simply to appeal to people's insatiable appetites for bigger and more powerful machines, or to make more money, or because they loved bigger trucks, then that is their choice. As for myself, I would consider those goals fairly ordinary, not transcendent. But if someone designed a more powerful truck because that was the best way that they could think of to allow remote villages to build their own schools, or for cities to build more affordable housing for the poor, or any other goal that made the world a slightly better place, then I for one would feel inspired by their goals, as I hope they themselves would.

I am not against industry or ingenuity. I believe that, if people put their minds to it, they can create powerful technologies that can improve the world. Capitalism, industrialization, market forces – these are amazingly powerful forces. I believe they can be directed to goals that inspire, instead of just making money.

Me: But how does anyone know whether a goal is worthy? Who is to say? There's no ultimate authority. Who are you to proclaim that bigger trucks are not a worthy or noble goal?

Cora: I have a simple criterion for a goal: is your goal inspirational enough that you want to be remembered for doing it? If people were to remember you for accomplishing only that one goal in the history books, how would you feel? Put another way: would you be proud to have your achievement etched on your grave, hypothetically? "I helped build Acme Auto Company's first 360-horsepower truck"? Or "I helped build 360 schools in Haiti?" Which one is more inspiring?

Me: Wow, that is a pretty high bar, Cora. I don't think most people have a goal like that. I think that the fact that a business creates jobs is already an accomplishment, as far as I'm concerned.

Cora: Okay, let's talk about that. It's true, successful businesses create jobs. But there are jobs, and then there are jobs. Creating a job, at its most basic definition, merely means creating a new way for someone to be paid for working. But what if you start a business which simply replaces one job for another job? For example, if your umbrella business is more successful than your competitor's umbrella business, because you pay your workers less, then, yes, you *are* creating new jobs; but is that really a good thing? Maybe it's good for customers, but not so good for your workers.

I believe that "creating new jobs" should not be used as a blanket statement for social good. For me, the bar must be higher. When you're creating a new business, are you reaching your full potential of what you could be doing for customers, for employees, for business partners – for society? Are you doing one or more of the following?

➢ Are you creating a new job which allows people to find

personal growth and satisfaction in their work, or even
fulfillment?

➤ Does your new job help employees become better citizens,
wiser mentors or parents, or more compassionate people?

➤ Does your product or service improve society in any way, or is
it morally neutral/irrelevant? Does it help anyone who is
suffering? Does it help people feel more connected with each
other? Does it accomplish any of the goals or solve any of the
problems we've been discussing so far? Does it do this by
design, or because people decided to use it for a new purpose?

➤ Does your business consciously add new knowledge or
wisdom to the world, either via your employees, or through
your products or services?

➤ How many natural resources does your business use that can
never be regenerated? What steps are you taking to reduce
your footprint on nature, or to replenish nature?

➤ How much does your new job teach an employee how to fish
(rather than giving them fish)? Are you teaching them how to
be more useful and valuable to the world, how to be more
employable for future jobs, how to be their own bosses, or
how to win their own customers? It's true, teaching them these
skills may make them more attractive to other employers, or
may free them to become independent consultants. But on the
other hand, they may feel loyalty to you for this training, and
they may stay with you because they know you care about
them and are willing to help them grow.

Me: Cora, your ideas are way more advanced than most businesses are
today. But if a business is constantly following these lofty goals and
trying to keep everyone happy all the time, but fails to make any
money or loses to its competitors, then it's not going to survive
very long, is it?

Cora: To be clear, I don't mean that an organization should coddle all its
members and try to keep everyone happy all the time. First of all,
it's impossible to do that. Second, finding happiness is each
person's own right and responsibility. Third, trying to give people a
sense of purpose is not the same as trying to keep them happy; it's

merely giving them a better chance to find happiness for themselves. Any organization must have a clear purpose, one that its members might or might not agree with. Those members who do not agree with that purpose are certainly free to leave that organization. But the organization functions best when it's able to find a way to align the individual purposes and passions of as many of its members as possible with the organization's purpose. Jim Stengel makes this argument in his book *Grow*, which I mentioned before: if you choose an inspiring goal, your employees and customers will want to align themselves with you. But in the end, it's still up to each person to realize his or her potential within that organization.

Me: That sounds nice, but I don't think anyone has ever asked me what I aspire to be or to do. I don't think most organizations care. Or if they did, it would be way too complicated to try to align everybody's aspirations. I think people are too messy.

Cora: I agree it would be complicated, but just because it hasn't been tried before doesn't mean it's a bad idea. I believe that, in the future, there may be a new management skill just as important, if not more important, than classical task/resource management: the management of people's myriad changing motivations and daily joys. No one today has a name for this, because we're all expected to manage our motivations ourselves; and anyways, that task is too mushy and intangible for results-oriented leaders.

But let's think about it using an analogy: if you could aim many photons of light in the same direction, wouldn't that be more powerful than having them aimed all over the place? That's the power of a laser, which can cut through any substance known, even diamond. Why do all the rowers row at the same frequency in the same direction on a crew team? Same idea. The main difference for people's individual motivations in an organization is that their motivations are much harder to understand and manage. Also, most employees work best if you let their motivations grow naturally, with gentle guidance, instead of forcing them or controlling them. But the general principles are similar.

Me: Okay, I've got a question. Let's say that an organization has found a truly inspiring purpose, but that purpose was so difficult that it failed to make enough money. What would you say about that?

Cora: That's a good question. You're right, having a purpose doesn't guarantee that an organization will survive. But figuring out a way to survive is a How question. In my opinion, you should be able to answer Why before you answer How. Otherwise you end up driving really fast and far in the wrong direction.

Also, just because you can't answer How doesn't mean that your Why is wrong. It only means that you need to keep looking for a How. Too many people get confused and think that their answer to Why must be wrong if they can't figure out a How. That might be true sometimes, but not often; after all, everyone knows that the right thing to do is often not the easy thing to do. Why and How are two completely different kinds of questions. You can never become truly happy if you refuse to ask Why, or if you refuse to believe the answer that your heart tells you to be true.

Me: But what if people never find the answer to the question Why?

Cora: Well, I didn't say it was easy. I think people should keep looking their whole lives. But to think that you can just be satisfied with answering How, and be content with that, is, in my opinion, depriving yourself of true happiness.

Why and How are questions that apply equally well to individuals as to organizations. And they benefit both. But only organizations have the power to improve so many people's lives. This is why it is so important to improve organizations – no matter how hard that may be.

Well, David, have I answered your question to your satisfaction?

Me: Yes, you've completely answered my question. Thank you.

Cora: Shall we call it a night, then?

Me: Yes, good night. Once again, you win.

Cora: Oh, come on, don't be such a sore loser. Good night already.

Me: See you tomorrow.

24   Mastery over Technology

The next day, I thought I'd figured out another way to stump her. You never know, I could succeed one day. It takes a lot to convince me of something. I blame it on my dad being from Missouri.

Me: Cora, I've thought of another problem with what you're proposing.

Cora: Well it's lovely to see you too, David. You don't give up easily, do you?

Me: Sorry, it's just not my nature. I've got a problem for you.

Cora: Tell me.

Me: Well, if you look at the most successful companies in the world today, like Apple, Google, Facebook, Amazon, Baidu, and the like, the common thread tying those companies together is that they excel at innovating and bringing new technologies to consumers. And even non-technology companies, like Boeing, Toyota, Disney, and Wal-Mart, use technology as a competitive edge.

Cora: Okay, so what's the problem?

Me: The problem is that technology has a life of its own. It doesn't care about nature, it doesn't care about people, and it doesn't give a damn about inspiring anybody. If companies can use technology to replace employees to save money, they will. If people can buy cooler or more powerful technology, they will. Technology is inexorable and irresistible. Both businesses and consumers bow down to it like a new god.

Cora: Technology has always held a natural allure; presented in the right way, great technology can dazzle and bewitch us. Ray Bradbury famously said, "Any sufficiently advanced technology is indistinguishable from magic."

Now, that power to dazzle is in itself neither good nor bad;

like money, technology is just a means. But in the absence of a clear end, the magic becomes an end in itself. And not just magic, but convenience, comfort, and control.

Me: So, you're saying that, if we somehow could become wise enough, we would be clear enough about our goals, and value technology only insofar as it helps us achieve our goals, right?

Cora: Yes, then technology would no longer be our master, but the opposite.

Me: Easier said than done, Cora.

Cora: I didn't say it was easy.

Me: Friending a stranger on Facebook is like a hundred times easier than talking to a neighbor that I've never met.

Cora: And which of these two actions is more likely to lead to long-term happiness?

Me: Well, I don't know, because the neighbor could be a jerk.

Cora: Or, he or she could be nice. You don't know beforehand.

Me: Right, but it's easier to avoid that question than to find out later.

Cora: Do you like reading mystery novels, David?

Say what? Mystery novels?

Me: Uh, mystery novels? Yes, I do.

Cora: Do you like exploring caves along rocky shores?

Me: Yes. What are you trying to get at?

Cora: A human being is no less mysterious than a good mystery novel or a cliff-side grotto. If anything, people are more interesting, more mysterious. Not only that, but your neighbor may be a key to your own happiness.

Me: Huh? How?

Cora: Think about this: if you become friends with your neighbor, you increase the number of friends you have. The more friends (*real* friends, not "friends") you have (within a limit), the more meaningful interactions you could have with other people. The more meaningful interactions you have, then the more deep friendships you might cultivate, and the more robust your sense of happiness might be against adversity. You're increasing the odds of real friendship by chatting with your neighbor. You never know what you have in common with others; friendship is a bit like panning for gold.

Facebook is not going to help you when you find out your wife has cancer, or when your son goes missing in Iraq, or when you have a midlife crisis. Nor will your iPhone help, nor your Xbox. Only other humans can help you in those situations, David – your good friends and close family. Now, that is not to say that you cannot use Facebook for goals that matter to you; technology is just a means. The Arab Spring movements were greatly enabled by technologies such as Facebook and Twitter. The innovative educational system Khan Academy started out on YouTube. Many people routinely use websites to raise money for good causes.

Remember what I told you some time ago, that the best hope for ourselves and for our planet is for people to learn how to look for true happiness (involving people) instead of merely finding new ways of escaping boredom (via consumption of goods and services). We simply need to understand how to use technology to reach our goals, if technology is appropriate.

Me: All right, you've convinced me – the consumption or use of technology by itself won't lead to ultimate happiness. But what about businesses and how they use innovation or technology to compete? You surely aren't suggesting that businesses give up their pursuit of technology? That would be suicide.

Cora: No, I'm not suggesting that. I never said that businesses or people should stop using technology. Remember, technology is just a means. If a business has profit as its goal, and decides that technology helps cut costs, then that's what will happen. But if a business has a higher goal, one meant to improve society, then there's nothing stopping that business from using technology to do that, either. I'm all in favor of innovation and technology. I just think they can be used for greater goals than just making money.

Speaking of higher goals, I'm going to propose a radical idea related to technology: I'd like to propose that products be designed to be reparable indefinitely. So if a new stereo system breaks, you should be able to bring it to a shop and have it fixed with a few replacement parts for a reasonable fee (for example, $5-$10). In that case, you might be willing to pay more for that stereo system, maybe much more, because you know it will last much longer. In the end, you would have the same standard of living, and you might end up spending the same amount of money, or even save some money. We don't want cheap products to win; we want quality and durability to win, so that people throw fewer things away. We should judge products not by price or by flashy new features, but by lasting quality and by whether they truly address an important use.

Me: Um, there's a little problem with this idea.

Cora: Yes?

Me: No company in the history of American business has ever wanted customers to buy *fewer* of its products. I should say, no company that is still around. That's like a gazelle that isn't afraid of lions. It doesn't exist because such gazelles were all eaten a million years ago.

Cora: You're right. But using the same argument, you could say that no company, or at least very few companies, would ever resist the temptation of becoming a monopoly if they could. They would have so many advantages if they could just corner the market. But we all know that monopolies do not serve society, much like dictatorships do not serve countries – they serve themselves.

Me: That's different. Everybody knows that monopolies are bad.

Cora: Not true. The monopolies themselves would beg to disagree.

Me: Huh. Okay, I see your point. But do you understand my point? It is in the nature of businesses to want to sell more, not less; to make more money, not less. Who would intentionally want to manufacture products that lasted indefinitely?

Cora: Someone who cared about their customers or about society, maybe? Someone who was proud of their product?

Me: Proud enough to be suicidal? You're talking about business suicide. The only way to sell someone a new toaster is to convince them to throw away their old toaster.

Cora: David, do you know why people today believe that monopolies are bad, that child labor is bad, that 14-hour work days, slave labor, and animal cruelty are bad? Two hundred years ago, none of those things was considered egregious (if they even existed). But people's values change. They start to realize that certain practices are inhumane, or have negative consequences in the long run. In just the same way, I hope that people begin to realize that nature has finite resources, and can take only so much abuse. I want people to start to see the connection between their own lifestyles and the cost on nature. I don't know whether it'll be this generation that starts seeing this connection, but I hope that some generation soon starts seeing it. We're running out of time.

I believe that people can change, David. I believe that if consumers demand it, businesses can start making longer-lasting products. Today, there are safety standards from the FDA, CE, ROHS, or UL. I believe that, one day, manufacturers might bow to consumer demand and agree on a uniform standard for reparability that helps all products last longer. Perhaps not for all products, but for expensive ones, or ones that tax nature the most.

The model of reparable products has several benefits. First, the customer doesn't need to worry about products breaking. It would be standard to be able to repair something you buy. Second, it provides jobs to repair shops, which are exactly the kinds of jobs that are rooted in a community. Third, it would help nature. Fourth, it promotes secondary markets that develop common components for use as replacement parts, like in automobile and computer components and peripherals. Fifth, it teaches many people how technology works, so that more people can innovate, and so that more people can take control of the technology they use.

Me: But Cora, you already said before that the profit motive is the most powerful force in the world right now. Everybody wants to sell *more* things, not *fewer*. Everybody wants to make money. Everybody wants to be rich. Maybe you think that this is deplorable, that humans are morally inferior, but this desire is the rocket fuel that makes people want to improve themselves and even make life better for other people. I mean, in theory, why is greed morally wrong at all? If I make your life better, then why shouldn't I be rewarded for it?

Cora: You're right, David, the profit motive is the most powerful force in the world, and the most widespread. As I've mentioned before, I do believe that there are motivations that are more inspiring than greed, but we have to face reality: replacing the power of greed is a goal that might take decades or centuries, and nature can't wait that long to be saved. So what can be done instead?

Me: You're asking me?

Cora: No, I was being rhetorical.

Me: Oh good, because I don't know.

Cora: Well, here's what I think. I don't think that I can ask people to give up the profit motive, but perhaps we can redirect it. I believe that self-interest does not necessarily equal consumption, or at least does not equal environmental destruction. I wonder, is it possible to accumulate wealth or to live more luxuriously without destroying nature? If the answer is unequivocally no, then I fear that human civilization is necessarily finite.

> If our species is to inhabit this planet indefinitely, I believe that we need to find a way to reach a point of equilibrium with nature, where we replenish as much as of each resource as we use.

Equilibrium means that we return as much to nature as we extract, so that our beautiful, wondrous, regenerative life-support system never runs out. In my opinion, the only way to accomplish this, and still harness the rocket fuel of self-interest, is for us to redefine our measures of wealth, status, luxury, and fashion to incorporate sustainability.

Here's what I mean. I hope that, someday in the distant future, people will revile products that require the abuse of nature just as much as they condemn child labor or inhumane working conditions. Or, people will celebrate products that last indefinitely, like art, music, enduring architecture, well-crafted furniture, or timeless literature, instead of throw-away products like fast food containers, fragile plastic toys, fad-of-the-day clothing, or electronic gadgets with built-in obsolescence. If we ever prioritize durability, then the values of consumers will naturally drive the engine of capitalism in the direction of preserving nature, rather than in the direction of destroying it. The first option is a road that never ends; the second option leads to a dead end.

Me: I understand what you're saying. But aren't you a bit judgmental? You sound like an old fart or a cultural snob. "The young people these days, they don't appreciate classical music or great literature! They just want the latest cool gadgets!"

Cora: David, if someone ever invented a plastic toy that lasted forever like Legos, or clothing that could be worn years and years and still be fashionable like jeans or hats, then I'm all for them. I'm not against creativity or shopping, I'm against excessive consumption. I guess you could say that I'm not against quality, I'm against quantity without quality. I don't think that that makes me anti-business.

I know that I'm asking a lot from people. I know that I'm fighting the most uphill battle ever fought. I recognize that it is the dream of most developing countries to "raise the standard of living" of their citizens to the point where they have just as many shopping malls as developed countries have, with all the same brands. I also know that it is in the interest of all countries to stimulate their economies by encouraging people to buy new things all the time. But nature cannot outlast our unbounded desires. No matter how impossible it may seem for us to reduce our consumption, we must figure out how to do it.

Did you ever see the movie *Wall-E*, David?

Me: Only about ten times.

Cora: You're a good father to sit through a movie ten times with her.

Me: Nah, I'm exaggerating, it was really more like eight or nine. My daughter is quite the sentimental environmentalist.

Cora: Do you believe that, one day, the earth will simply become one giant garbage dump, as portrayed in that movie?

Me: Oh, I'm sure we'll figure it all out before that happens.

Cora: So, do you think we are generating the same amount of garbage, less garbage, or more garbage every year?

Me: Um…

Cora: This is not rocket science. It is simple cause-and-effect. Now, it might be true that it'll take a very long time before we fill up the entire planet with garbage. But nevertheless, I think it does not reflect highly on our level of civilization today that humans are essentially garbage-generation machines. No organism in the previous history of this planet has ever survived by converting natural resources into unnatural waste. So, David, the next time you feel the urge to go shopping out of boredom, please go visit a garbage dump first.

Me: Cora, you're going to single-handedly destroy the global economy and our way of life.

Cora: Oh, you flatter me, David. I have no such power. If only. It's not my intent to make people live lives that are less comfortable or pleasant. I just hope that people can find alternative ways to entertain themselves or enjoy life than to purchase new products constantly. I hope that we don't ruin our planet out of boredom.

Me: Alternative ways… such as?

Cora: I don't know, David. I don't know what to replace shopping with. I do know one thing: modern technology has not only provided us with new forms of entertainment, it has also provided us an infinite variety of outlets for our creativity and our passions. Rather than watching other people entertain us, anyone can now create a video, add a soundtrack, and become well-known because of sites like YouTube. Anyone can learn a new skill from watching videos or reading websites. Anyone can become a thought leader or share ideas by writing blogs. Anyone can share photos via sites like Flickr or Instagram and develop a reputation as a photographer. I believe that it's always more enriching to create art, entertainment, utility, or knowledge than to simply consume it, and potentially more rewarding. Creativity can lead to purpose; consumption alone cannot. Everyone has a story to tell.

Me: You know, Cora, I need to have a talk with Claire and Margaret. I think we all need to start creating more and consuming less. I need to get them interested in photography or making videos or writing. Anything is better than TV, YouTube, and video games.

Cora: Children may not realize that you're trying to help them, but it is a parent's job to envision his or her children's adult selves, and it is no easy feat. Children don't realize what a noble burden that is.

Me: Speaking of kids, I need to get up to make Claire breakfast tomorrow. Margaret has a dental appointment tomorrow morning. I think I'll hit the hay.

Cora: Yeah yeah, I can tell when I've outlasted my welcome.

Me: No, really. It's true, I'm not making that up!

Cora: All right, I guess. Have a good night.

Me: Good night, Cora.

25   Saving the World through Shopping

Me: Cora, I think I've finally thought of a question that will stump you.

Cora: David, you give new meaning to the word "diehard."

Me: Okay, here goes. We've just been talking about technology and
        competition. Wouldn't you agree that it's a natural side effect for
        technology to displace human beings? In other words, whether it's
        automation, improved communications, getting rid of the
        middleman (or "disintermediation"), or improvements in
        efficiency, computers and technology in general have done a great
        job of making many people's jobs obsolete.

        I mean, if it takes much less energy to run a tablet computer
        today than to run a room-sized computer fifty years ago, and the
        tablet computer does much more, isn't that a good thing? But on
        the other hand, if the same tablet gets rid of a secretary, a filing
        assistant, an accountant, a researcher, and an analyst, all those
        people have to find other ways to make a living now. Maybe we'll
        all be replaced by robots someday. How could this be a good
        thing?

Cora: Sadly, yes, what you say is true – because of the never-ending pace
        of technological innovation, no one's employment is guaranteed
        anymore. Technology is steadily rendering more and more jobs
        obsolete. Everyone must learn new skills all the time. But I don't
        necessarily think this is a bad thing. Yes, on the one hand, we've
        obliterated the illusion that there is such a thing as guaranteed
        employment. Perhaps such a thing existed once upon a time, back
        before the invention of computers, but it no longer exists. On the
        other hand, human beings are terrifically good at learning new
        things and adapting to new technologies. Part of what it means to
        grow as a person is to expand one's capabilities using one's tools.
        Craftsmanship or artistry are not limited to physical tools like

hammers, bevels, or brushes. Technological tools are just as valid.

Me: But Cora, you have to admit that it could be stressful to have to constantly learn new ways of doing things just to remain employable. In fact, I can imagine something even more stressful, even demoralizing: having a specialized skill like assembling some part of a car, and then, one day, *having a robot replace you*. If you didn't have the foresight to learn other skills before you were laid off, you could become unemployable for a long time.

Cora: The inexorable march of technological progress is, for better or worse, now a permanent part of our lives. As Heraclitis said 2,500 years ago, "the only constant is change." Technological progress naturally includes improvements in business and manufacturing productivity.

Now, one might take a "Luddite" stance and oppose this progress on principle because technology always has the potential to replace employees or make them unnecessary. But efficiency itself is not necessarily a bad thing, and, one could argue, even unavoidable. If one company were to refuse to adopt a particular technological improvement, eventually another company will. The other company will become more efficient and cost-effective and outcompete the first company. Unless one were to categorically prohibit all competition (which Communism tried to do and failed), this system of competition will always favor technological progress.

But while efficiency is unavoidable, it need not be inhumane. Again, let's go back to the question of inspiring goals. In this case, let's look at the relationship between employers and their employees. It is obviously in the employer's best interests to keep innovative employees, but what about the ones who are not innovating? After all, as wonderful as it is, innovation is a skill that not everyone possesses. All employers understand this.

I believe that a wise business will understand that, when it treats all of its employees right, even the ones whom its technology has rendered unnecessary, then it earns the loyalty of *all* of its employees. Such a business can take steps to help the displaced employees find new jobs, and even train those employees in new skills.

Many companies have internships for college students, which are not costly at all. These internships are a "win-win" because the college students are learning skills while the companies benefit from inexpensive labor and vet potential new employees. Perhaps companies can provide a new kind of "internship" to their employees who have been laid off, to teach those employees new skills. If the employees show aptitude during those internships, that could even benefit their employers, for it is much cheaper to retain and retrain them than to hire new employees. Many companies pay several months of severance anyways, so the employees will be financially stable during those internships. And both sides will understand that the employees will be interviewing for new jobs during those internships anyways. This kind of retraining program can be a good way to mitigate the disruptive effects of technological unemployment.

Me: I like that suggestion, Cora. You have some good ideas. But what if companies really don't care about their employees that much? I think that too many companies just care about the bottom line. Is there some way to push them to want to do the right thing?

Cora: Good question. Yes, I believe there is. I think it all depends on how we shop.

Me: I'm sorry, did you say "how we shop"?

Cora: Yes, you heard me correctly. Let me explain. Today, people believe they have little control over their choice of jobs, because they believe that they don't control the job market. But who do you think *really* controls the job market, David?

Me: Well, I guess employers do. Businesses, for the most part, as well as some government or nonprofit organizations like hospitals, governments, or schools.

Cora: And where do those organizations get their money?

Me: From… from consumers, taxpayers, and donors.

Cora: From everybody. From *you*, David. The forces of economics affect individual people in two different ways: as employees *and* as consumers. We have all the freedom in the world as consumers to buy whatever we can afford. But we are relatively restricted in how we can find employment. The funny thing is, our habits as consumers have a huge impact on our employment. Let me give an example.

I don't usually like to make any single company a scapegoat, but I'd like to use Wal-Mart in this case because it's a realistic example. Wal-Mart derived a lot of its power from using its size and retail dominance to force its suppliers to continually reduce their prices. Realistically, the only way those suppliers could do this was by automating their manufacturing, or by relocating their factories to countries with cheaper labor costs – most often, China. Either way, they shed American jobs.

Because the prices were so good, shoppers were only too happy to buy products at Wal-Mart. In effect, many people were responsible for destroying their own employment by the mere act of shopping. Of course, few could see the direct connection. If you were an employee in a shoe company, you might buy your American-made shoes at a store other than Wal-Mart in order to support your industry, but then you probably bought everything else – clothing, tools, kitchenware – at Wal-Mart. And so did employees of clothing, tool, and kitchenware manufacturers.

Me: Wait… it reminds me of… the tragedy of the commons again?

Cora: In a way, yes. In this case, the common property is the collective pool of money that we all spend – or perhaps the common pool of employment funded by that money. Perhaps it's a stretch to call it the tragedy of the commons. But whatever you call it, the fact remains that the way you spend your money completely determines how someone else is – or isn't – employed. There is no conspiracy, no "they." The government is not forcing you. While Wal-Mart seems culpable, it isn't doing anything wrong; it's just making the transaction easy.

The rules of money are simple and inescapable. Whenever you pay money to buy something, you're choosing where the money flows, for whose gain, for whose employment, away from whom, to what effect on society, and to what effect on nature. You might not know the effects of your choice; you might even deliberately ignore them. Or you might believe you can never know. But the economic chain reaction is there whether you ignore it or not, whether you understand it or not. And this fact, David, is the key to understanding whether and how we can reform how we do business.

Me: So you're telling me that how I shop determines what kind of world I live in?

Cora: Yes. But not you alone; you and everyone else who shops. This is why I think capitalism can be a powerful avenue for social good, perhaps the most powerful means in the world, more powerful than any political institution or social movement. There are many examples of how businesses that stand for something win customers and make healthy profits: Ben and Jerry's Ice Cream, The Body Shop, TOMS, Whole Foods Market, the list goes on and on. But these businesses are still the exception rather than the rule. We're just getting started.

Me: So, to save both society and nature, we have to learn how to… shop better?

Cora: Yes. And shopping better also helps us find happiness and meaning.

Me: Um… are you sure?

Cora: Well, the way you put it – "shopping better" – sounds rather facetious and simplistic. Let me paint a more vivid picture for you.

For the last 200 years or so, civilization has been moving in a particular direction, towards global economic integration. People have generally accepted that this movement is a good thing. Labor unions might raise a fuss about a treaty here or there, but everyone likes having fresh oranges during winter, cheaper smart phones, and the latest boots for a good price. But recently, some people have started to consider the environmental costs of this globalization, and started to request locally-produced goods and services. A prominent recent example of this is the "locavore" movement, which emphasizes using locally grown food ingredients. While this locavore movement is a good start, it's just the tip of the iceberg.

Each person today depends so much on the global economic grid that most of us are unable to control our lives – not just in small ways, but in large ways. None of us can guarantee our own employment, not even close. Should we fall ill, any of us could lose our entire fortune. But we are also affected in countless small ways. The vast majority of the things we buy have no story attached to them; they no longer tie us to any human beings we know. They might as well have come from outer space.

I would like to propose a force to balance out globalization. I believe that we can localize or humanize our economies much more. I propose that we produce more goods and services closer to where we use them, or that we at least become more familiar with the people who make them. It also means that we learn to make more things ourselves. This would allow us to grasp the economic connections we have to our communities or to other people. We can exercise our power to influence and improve the world with both our buying and producing powers.

Local economies would give us the ability to care about where our money comes from and where it goes, and, in turn, to care about other people – about real people we know and see regularly – and about nature. It's true, this localization may come at the cost of efficiency; economists tell us that larger businesses are always more efficient. But is efficiency all-important? Is it our highest human value? Should we sacrifice all other values on the altar of efficiency or competitiveness?

People look down on tribes and villages as backward and unambitious, and, as a result, modern civilization has largely left tribes, villages, and small towns behind. The majority of the world's population now lives in cities or suburbs of cities. But perhaps it is time for us to revisit villages as models of stable, healthy, self-sufficient, self-governing types of communities based on voluntary interdependence among people, which ground us in our relationships with other human beings. Perhaps we don't need to replicate their exact size or geographical concentration, but we can adapt their sense of trust, community, and self-sufficiency to neighborhoods or cities or even virtual communities anywhere.

Now, I'm not saying that we should shun all forms of dependence on the global economy. The beauty of a free market is that we can take advantage of goods produced by people who are specialized at producing them well. But we should always strike a balance. I would argue that a global economy has a high invisible, intangible, non-economic cost that is difficult for us to appreciate. If we cannot comprehend all the effects of our economic actions, then we cede control of our economic fates to people we don't know and will never meet; we cannot help support jobs in our communities; and we cannot measure the destruction of nature caused by our purchasing decisions. Do you know where your money goes? Does anyone?

Here's one way to think about it. If we dumped our trash into the ocean, and the trash never found its way back to us, then we could pretend like we never did anything wrong. Our action gets lost in the vastness. Since it's easy to do, we don't ask whether it's good or bad, we just keep doing it. Maybe it's wrong, but it really doesn't matter to us. Whereas, if we dumped trash into our backyard pond, or into a local lake, we would immediately know that we did something wrong. Now, to be clear, I'm not equating buying global goods with polluting the ocean, but I'm explaining how easy it is for us to be disconnected from our effects far away.

In a global economy, it is not only our jobs that are no longer in our control, but also our housing. Most people who rent have little or no control over the price of their rent. Most people who own houses have mortgages, and fortunately, many (but not all) of those mortgages have a fixed rate of interest. However, if someone should lose their job or get injured or fall ill, and they fail to make a few payments, they could easily lose their house. This is because a bank that is focused on turning a profit owns their mortgage. Most people look at this problem as unavoidable, because that's how business works. They say, "That's life." But it doesn't have to be that way.

If we truly have local economies, economies where many people know each other and are willing to help each other during hard times, a locally owned bank or credit union could revise the loan to help the person temporarily; in addition, the community could even come together to help the person get back on their feet financially, helping them find a job or pay down their debt.

Now I want to ask you a question, David. Would you personally rather get 0.01% more profit for your bank and its shareholders, or would you rather help one of its shareholders, like an elderly widow who has lost her job, get through a hard time?

Me: 0.01%? Are you kidding?

Cora: Sure, that may seem like a tiny amount, but those little fractions add up. If you help everyone who is in trouble, you could end up losing all your profits, or even go into debt.

Me: Well, if those people were my friends or relatives, or people whose lives were connected with mine, I would probably be okay with that.

Cora: You might be okay with that, but would everyone be okay with that? There may be some people who depend on that profit as their investment income, such as retirees. Or, some people just don't care. "Business is business." A few odd shareholders shouldn't have the right to cut a deal with some deadbeats or slackers. The money belongs to everyone, and any exceptions on the rules should be decided unanimously.

Me: That attitude sounds Scrooge-like, like that curmudgeon Mr. Potter from the movie "It's a Wonderful Life."

Cora: I hear you. I was playing devil's advocate. I believe that most people would want to help someone in a bad situation, as long as it doesn't cost them too much. I believe that pulling together, especially in times of duress such as natural disasters or financial hardships, is what makes a community stronger.

After Hurricane Katrina, the people of New Orleans desperately needed cash just to survive from one day to the next. Two local banks, Hancock Bank and The People's Bank, wanted to help, but they faced a problem: their infrastructures were heavily damaged by the hurricane Katrina, destroying their power, phone connections, and access to customer data. So what did they do?

The employees of these banks literally laundered – as in washed – what cash they could find on hand or in ATM machines, and started lending money to people with nothing more than handwritten IOU notes as guarantees. Do you think they were crazy to do so, David?

Me: Well, that does sound risky.

Cora: So what do you think happened? Do you think people paid the money back?

Me: I don't know; I'm guessing that people were pretty strapped for cash. They probably had other concerns on their minds.

Cora: For Hancock Bank, out of $42 million passed out to people in this manner, all but about $200,000 (a rough guess) came back. The payback rate was about 99.5%. In fact, people became so loyal to the two banks that Hancock Bank opened 13,000 new accounts, and total assets at The People's Bank grew by 45%.

Me: What an inspiring story. I'm starting to understand where you're going now.

Cora: Now, all along I've been talking as if it were obvious that making economies or economic ties more local is a good thing. But there are valid objections to this idea. The first objection is this: what about people who truly want to get rich, to build huge business empires? Don't these people have a right to sell their goods anywhere they want to? Maybe their quality is better. Maybe they treat everyone very nicely, including their employees. Maybe they're nicer to nature.

Me: Right. Hey, I'm supposed to raise the objections, remember? That's my job.

Cora: Sorry to steal your thunder.

Me: That's all right. Steal away.

Cora: To this argument, I say: Yes, of course they have a right to do business anywhere. And they can conduct business in any way they want. But once people understand the power of localizing their economies, then any business which has local roots will be able to use that as a competitive advantage against businesses which do not. You can still build your huge business empire, but if you do so by sharing your power and your gains with lots of communities, your business will be that much stronger and more competitive.

What do you think, David? Do you think that people might be willing to pay more for something if they knew they were helping to build their community?

Me: You know, I don't know, because no one has ever given me this choice before, but I think maybe so. The thing is, though, it's very hard to track money. How do you know that money is staying in a community? Money can't be tagged like an antelope or something.

Cora: Yes, but you don't need to track every dollar. You just need to sample, to track where a few individual products spend most of their time before they're purchased. You just need to know where a business spends its money. It's just information. It's not magic. It's not impossible to get, just difficult.

Me: Okay. Be that as it may, I still think you're asking a lot of people. You're assuming that, given the right information, people will be willing to do the right thing, to pay more money for something just because it helps someone who lives in the same city. If I don't know you, I'm much less likely to help you. I think that something more is necessary.

Cora: You're right. I think what is needed is surrogate trust. This is the reason why people might choose one restaurant or auto repair shop over another. On services such as Yelp, eBay, Angie's List, Amazon, or numerous other websites, people rate their vendors or the products they buy. This allows buyers to trust that vendor or manufacturer. This rating system could easily be extended to include ratings of people's contributions to their communities, or their environmental record, or how they treat their employees. And in fact, such a rating system exists already. Remember when we talked about B Corporations earlier? Companies can be certified by a third party on their positive impact on society.

Me: That sounds more promising. But I can think of another objection to the idea of making economies local: everyone wants to keep the money they make, to keep all jobs local, even though sometimes it is better to send work away. Everyone loves to export goods, but no one likes to import goods. What do you say to *that*, Cora?

Cora: My goal in suggesting that economies be local is more of a suggestion than an edict. For example, if two or more cities, towns, or regions mutually benefit by trade, and have shared values, they can certainly engage in cooperative trade. Or, there may be other ways of tracking where money flows besides keeping it geographically isolated.

My point is only that it should be easy for people to keep track of where the money they earn is coming from and going to. If they cannot – if products come from anywhere and everywhere in the world – then the tangled global economic web is beyond anyone's grasp.

Me: That's for sure. God knows where my shoes were made, or even the coke I'm drinking.

Cora: Now, there's something else we haven't covered yet in our discussions, and it has to do with "economies of scale". At first glance, it would seem that my pro-local, pro-nature attitude goes against these forces. After all, it would seem that the size of an organization is usually correlated with its efficiency and its rate of innovation, especially technological innovation. After all, only a large company or university can afford a large Research and Development department. And only a large factory can take advantage of economies of scale. But I wonder if this is truly the case. It's well known that large organizations are often encumbered by bureaucracy. Startup companies are able to innovate much faster precisely because they are small, because they can change course quickly after mistakes.

On the matter of the efficiency of larger factories over smaller ones, I would point out that the capital invested in larger factories makes a business less likely to abandon or modify them, which affects that business's ability to innovate and change its business. I suspect that efficiency and innovation are always in a tug-of-war with each other.

But there's another crucial factor, and it has to do with incentives. I would argue that a smaller, community-centered business *might* be more motivated to innovate to survive, because it has nowhere else to go – most of its stakeholders live in the same community. (Of course, motivation does not necessarily guarantee innovation, but it certainly helps. Necessity is the mother of invention, after all.) In particular, it can work harder to win the quality-versus-cost game, which is also better for nature. With this model, perhaps we could avoid the layoffs from corporations moving jobs offshore.

Me: Ah, now you're talking! I think people can get behind that idea!

Cora: I'm glad you like that idea. For too long, people have believed that they are utterly helpless to control their own economic destinies. All I want to do is to suggest that all people can control where they spend their money, and thus, indirectly, determine how their money might come back to themselves. After all, the Amish and the Mennonites never used to have layoffs (until some of them started to work in factories). And yet the rest of us, who are supposed to be so much more technologically advanced and economically integrated, assume that layoffs are inevitable facts of life. Our advanced society drives millions of people into despair because that's most efficient for the economy.

Me: Ridiculous, isn't it! You're absolutely right. We're supposed to be so smart, and yet we can't even guarantee everyone a job!

Cora: Perhaps we're not so smart after all. Perhaps we have something to learn from simpler folk who forsake greed and ambition.

Well, have you had enough, David? It's getting late. Do you want to throw in the towel?

Me: Yes, you've worn me out again.

Cora: In that case, have a good night.

Me: Good night, Cora.

26   Mexican or Chinese

The next day, Cora seemed to reverse herself yet again. At this point, I've stopped trying to second-guess her.

Cora: David, do you think that I hate competition?

Me: Well, you certainly don't seem to like it.

Cora: You must think that I value compassion more than competition, right?

Me: Don't you?

Cora: I feel that most people are unable to express aspects of their humanity such as compassion and love in their professional lives. It's not that I value those aspects more than the competitive aspects, but that I champion compassion and purpose because no one else is raising their banner. But in fact, competitiveness, excellence, and the desire to grow are no less a part of our humanity. We cannot be all heart and no brain, just as we cannot be all brain and no heart.

Some people feel that the difference between political liberals and conservatives has to do with how much each side values compassion vs. competition. According to stereotypes, liberals want to help those who are less fortunate, giving them the same opportunities and basic necessities that everyone else has. Conservatives believe that society should be a meritocracy. Everyone should be rewarded fairly for their own talent and hard work, while the lazy or misbehaving should be punished fairly.

Me: Yes, that sounds like a fair statement of what each side believes. And what do you believe, Cora? Which side are you on?

Cora: It's not really important which side I'm on. Perhaps I'm biased one way or the other. But what's more important to me is the fact that there's a bitter struggle today between the two sides for the control of America, and so far, it looks like a stalemate, a deep freeze that seems unlikely to go away for a long time. Today, the two camps seem to be trying to use laws and courts to wage a war of ideas. I wish they would understand that no one can ever win a war of ideas. This deep freeze is preventing our country from tackling difficult national and international problems, such as growing medical costs, immigration, economic growth, climate change, you name it. All because two political camps are unwilling to try to understand each other and work with each other.

Me: And exactly how would you suggest we get around this impasse? If you have an answer, Cora, I'm sure 320 million people would love to hear it.

Cora: David, I'm so flattered and amused that you think I must have the answer for everything. I can assure you that, in this case, I do not have the answer. But there is someone else who has been looking for that answer for a while. Have you heard of Jonathan Haidt?

Me: No, who's that?

Cora: He's a professor of psychology at the University of Virginia. I briefly mentioned him earlier as the author of *The Happiness Hypothesis*. He also wrote *The Righteous Mind: Why Good People are Divided by Politics and Religion*. He, along with Jesse Graham, Ravi Iyer, and Sena Koleva (all at the University of Southern California), Pete Ditto (University of California at Irvine), and Craig Joseph (originally from the University of Chicago), developed a theory called Moral Foundations Theory. It is based on some ideas from an anthropologist named Richard Shweder. In Professor Haidt's own words:

> This theory... outlines six clusters of moral concerns – care/harm, fairness/cheating, liberty/oppression, loyalty/betrayal, authority/subversion, and sanctity/degradation – upon which, we argue, all political cultures and movements base their moral appeals. ... You can think about the foundations as being like the taste receptors on the tongue: sweet, sour, salty, bitter, and savory. Each political culture, like each culinary culture, creates its own unique cuisine using some combination of these tastes, including

elements that lack immediate appeal on their own, such as
bitterness. Similarly each political movement bases its claims
on a particular configuration of moral foundations. It would be
awfully hard to rally people to your cause without making any
reference to harm, fairness, liberty, loyalty, authority, or
sanctity.

My colleagues and I found that political liberals tend to rely
primarily on the moral foundation of care/harm, followed by
fairness/cheating and liberty/oppression. They're very
concerned about victims of oppression, but they rarely make
moral appeals based on loyalty/betrayal, authority/subversion,
or sanctity/degradation. Social conservatives, in contrast, use
all six foundations. They are less concerned than liberals about
harm, but much more concerned about the moral foundations
that bind groups and nations together, i.e., loyalty (patriotism),
authority (law and order, traditional families), and sanctity (the
Bible, God, the flag as a sacred object). Libertarians, true to their
name, value liberty more than anyone else, and they value it far
more than any other foundation.

In other words, according to Moral Foundations Theory,
liberals, conservatives, and libertarians simply differ in the
preference of which moral values are more important to them, just
as you might like Mexican food, and I like Chinese food. But if we
take this metaphor further, just because you like Mexican food and
I like Chinese food, does that mean that we should never eat
together, because we can never agree on what to eat? Do you think
that sounds reasonable, David?

Me: Now wait a minute, Cora. You're comparing people's political
        beliefs to their favorite cuisines? Really? Isn't that oversimplifying,
        not to mention a bit insulting? Some people think of their political
        beliefs almost like their religion, like their deepest held beliefs –
        like their deepest selves.

Cora: Okay, calm down. First, answer my question: Mexican or Chinese
        tonight?

Me: Chinese. Either. Even if I don't like Mexican food in general, there's probably some kind of Mexican food that I don't mind.

Cora: And likewise, I'm sure I can find some kind of Chinese food I can stand. Fried rice is usually pretty safe. So, you think that the Mexican versus Chinese food conundrum can be solved by reasonable people?

Me: People solve that problem all the time.

Cora: But not liberal ideas versus conservative ideas.

Me: I don't think so, Cora. People can be flexible about their taste buds. People generally aren't able to change their political views that easily.

Cora: Wait a minute. I didn't say that they had to change their political views. You already admitted that friends are willing to take turns eating the other person's favorite cuisine in order to be fair. Even though Mexican may not be your favorite, as long as you aren't fatally allergic to some Mexican ingredient, you can probably find something palatable among all of Mexican cuisine.

Me: I probably *am* allergic to some weird Yucatan habanero pepper.

Cora: Yes, watch out for those Yucatan habanero peppers. The point is, I'm not suggesting that people try to repress their values in order to work with those they disagree with; such a form of compromise would ask them to be less than who they are or aspire to be. Instead, I'm asking people to reach deep inside themselves and ask: "Is there anything that I can agree with in my opponent's viewpoint? Am I courageous enough to step into their shoes and imagine how their actions and decisions reflect their most deeply held beliefs?" Let's give each other the benefit of the doubt and assume that you and I are both trying to be the best person we can be, according to our internal compass. While others may not share our internal compass, all people have the same values, only in different proportions. Our values aren't in conflict. We just have different mixtures. What hope you and I have of understanding each other, and getting to a better place than either you or I can imagine alone, lies in both of us agreeing to this axiom.

The most powerful political movement in America today, the

Tea Party, originally started out as a reaction to the government bailout of banks during the financial collapse of 2008. But it has evolved to encompass much more than that. Professor Haidt suggests that the Tea Party is today not primarily concerned with fairness, but with the idea of "karma".

Me: Karma? You mean like the Hindu concept? I kinda doubt that!

Cora: No, not exactly, more like the colloquial use of the word – as in "what comes around goes around." Haidt suggests that, at its heart, the Tea Party hates government intervention and regulation because they feel that such actions disrupt the direct feedback cycle between individuals' actions and consequences. Haidt says:

> ... Jump ahead to today's ongoing financial and economic crisis. Again, those guilty of corruption and irresponsibility have escaped the consequences of their wrongdoing, rescued first by President Bush and then by President Obama. Bailouts and bonuses sent unimaginable sums of the taxpayers' money to the very people who brought calamity upon the rest of us. Where is punishment for the wicked?
>
> To see the full spectrum of tea party morality in a single case, consider (or better still, Google) a transcript on Glenn Beck's website titled "Best caller ever?" which relates one man's moment of enlightenment. The exchange, which aired live in late September, starts with karmic outrage. A father in Indiana, proud of his daughter's work ethic and high grades, learned that she would have to retake a social studies test because most of the students—who, he says, run around after school instead of studying—had failed it. The teacher confirmed that yes, the whole class would have to take the test several more times because "we have to wait for the other children to catch up." The father asked if his daughter could work on new material while the other kids retook the test. The teacher said no, it would "make the other children in the class feel not as equal." That was the last straw. At that moment, the father says, he rejected "the system" and decided to home-school his daughter.
>
> What makes this call so revealing is the caller's diagnosis of how America became the land that karma forgot: "It's time for

America to get right, and it all starts in the home. It comes from yes, sir, no, ma'am, thank you, get on your knees and pray to God." He continues by telling Mr. Beck how, when his daughter's friends sleep over at his house, he asks them to help with chores. When their parents object, he tells them: "Well, they wanted a meal. See, we've all got to row our boat. We've all got to be in the boat. We've all got to row as one. And if you are not going to row, get the hell out of the way or stop getting in mine." It's the perfect fusion of karmic thinking and conservative binding.

Me: You know, the Tea Party gets a lot of bad press, but I have to admit that I feel sympathy with this guy. Whatever happened to hard work? Whatever happened to getting only what you work for? Most kids I know don't do any chores or help around the house. They barely say "Please" or "Thank you." I think someone somewhere came up with the idea that we need to create some perfect environment for kids so that they'll grow up well-adjusted. But if people don't taste hardship, how are they going to know the value of hard work?

Cora: Yes, indeed. It's hard not to sympathize with the father in the story. But where liberals depart from conservatives is in how they want to give a leg up to the disadvantaged, such as the poor, minorities, or women – in other words, "leveling the playing field." And the only way to level that playing field is government intervention, which liberals have no problem with, but conservatives generally disdain. So, that's one of the sources of the political impasse.

Me: So what are we to do?

Cora: I think that we need to take turns eating Mexican and Chinese food. I think we need a new approach. I think we need to take normal, everyday people, with typical problems, and bring them to state capitals and to Washington, and have our politicians on both sides of the aisle explain what they're actively doing to solve their problems. I think that the political opinions and beliefs of our politicians are not enough to guide our government. We need more than opinions. We need to face real problems that everyone is experiencing. We need to agree on those problems. If we cannot even agree on which problems are the biggest ones, or at least ones affecting many people, then how can we start solving those problems?

And then, once everyone has agreed on what the biggest problems are (or at least agreed on a few of them), then we can start the process of trying to solve those problems. Of course, everyone's going to have different plans and ideas. But the good thing is, if we can agree on the right problems, and we all want to solve them, then we should also be able to agree on how to measure whether we're making progress on those problems. And once we agree on those, then it's just a matter of trying out several competing plans. There is no reason why we can't try out more than one possible solution to a problem at the same time (for example, in different states or regions), and compare the results scientifically. This is how every legitimate science experiment and many smart businesses have been run. (That's partially why some former businesspeople, such as former New York City Mayor Michael Bloomberg, were such effective politicians.)

Of course liberals and conservatives and libertarians and socialists are going to differ in their plans or solutions, but the beauty of science is that a solution can be compared against other solutions.

Me: That sounds really innovative, Cora, and that's why it won't work.

Cora: Why not?

Me: Because we're talking about the American government. It was designed to be inefficient and ineffective. Checks and balances and all that. Not to mention, corrupt.

Cora: Oh yes, corruption. I have a few choice words to say about American democracy, but that will have to wait until later. For now, I just want to plant a seed in your head: America can be a place where hard work is rewarded, as well as a place where the downtrodden get a helping hand. In fact, maybe the best version of America is a place where the downtrodden get a helping hand to become productive members of society and competitive players in the economy, so that they can feel like they count, just like everyone else.

In any free society, especially a free-market society like ours, there will always be rich and poor, skilled and unskilled, competitive and uncompetitive people. Someone always has to end up on top, and someone on the bottom. This eternal, unavoidable disparity is not, in my opinion, a fact to be bemoaned. Nature will always produce disparity. But only humanity can produce inspiration. As I've mentioned before:

> I believe that what inspires us is not only becoming the best that we ourselves can be, but also helping other people become the greatest versions of themselves and write their own stories.

This is the only way that I can reconcile free competition with unbounded compassion.

Me: But what if, for whatever reason, you just don't want to be a productive member of society? Maybe through mental illness, laziness, inborn ineptitude, bad personality, or whatever have you?

Cora: I'd like to believe that people everywhere, not just in America, would want a society that tries to find a place for every one of its members, to make everyone feel like he or she has a purpose (not just a free ride or a chore, but a real reason why the world needs them). I believe that this is the highest form of civilization. Such a world may not be easy to attain, but it ennobles us to strive for it.

Me: All right, you've got me. I'd love to live in such a world.

Cora: I'm glad you finally admitted defeat. Maybe you should retire while I'm ahead. Shall we call it a night?

Me: Fine, good night. But just for the record, I *don't* admit defeat. I was just humoring you.

Cora: ;-)

Hey, how about that. Cora typed a smiley face.

27   For the People

The next day, to my delight, or more like relief, we started on a big new topic.

Cora: So far, David, we've only talked about capitalism and saving nature, but today, I'd like to discuss how democracy is working today – or not working.

Me: Finally, we get to talk about democracy! Yay! I've been looking forward to this for awhile now.

Cora: I'm glad to hear your enthusiasm. Maybe I've dragged on my critique of capitalism a bit too long?

Me: Well, I'm not going to complain, but let's say that a change of topic is refreshing.

Cora: Good. Now, where do I start? Inspiring and capable leadership are just as important in a democracy as in a business. The special challenge of a democracy is that you can't even rely on everyone sharing even the simplest motivations. At least with a business, your membership in the business implies that you care about helping it survive. But membership in a democracy, or in any society, is usually but a function of where you live, and says nothing about your goals or values. It is much harder for people in a community to agree on many issues. The challenge of political leadership is therefore that much harder.

While self-interest is usually an advantage in a business, in a democracy it can be quite problematic. I've already discussed the problem of the tragedy of the commons, which is exactly caused by everyone watching out for their own interests and neglecting the common welfare. Similarly, many great endeavors throughout history, such as fighting wars, pioneering space travel, and sequencing the human genome, have required individuals to give up their own goals for the greater good, at least temporarily. One cannot imagine how a war could be won if every soldier chose when and where to fight, or debated the morality of each military command.

Me: But even in business, people don't always agree. That's why there's a chain of command.

Cora: Ah, but if you disagree with a business, you can leave its employment or stop purchasing its product.

Me: And if you disagree with a government, you can vote its leaders out.

Cora: True enough, but if you disagreed with your entire community, would you leave your home?

Me: I see your point.

Cora: Now, some people see this challenge as a necessary evil, the price of belonging to human society. But it all depends on your perspective. As I've mentioned before, a challenge can be either a bane or a boon; even dandelions are edible. Yes, you may disagree with the institutions of marriage or unemployment insurance or universal health coverage. But the fact that each of us is necessarily a member of a greater society means that we can achieve far greater things together than alone. Grand goals such as eliminating global poverty or hunger or illiteracy or slavery would be unthinkable if society still consisted of warring tribes or city-states. Think about what it means to be a member of an advanced society, David. It means that we have the right to dream huge, scary, improbable dreams, but only if we rise to be equal to the task.

I believe that the kind of democracy that exists today, like our current version of capitalism, is still young. I can imagine a future where the majority of citizens are interested in the common welfare, because they recognize that helping everyone achieve a better society together makes each person's life richer. This belief is a self-fulfilling prophecy: when people work together for the common good, they can achieve much greater things than people who work only for their own good. So it is with most human endeavors: belief leads to success, and success leads to belief. But before either exists, which one must come first? Obviously it cannot be success. But without evidence, how can one believe? What can break this chicken-and-egg conundrum?

I believe that the answer is *a powerful vision*. If a people want a greater future, they should first define a clear vision of where they want to go. Such a vision often comes from a wise leader, but not always. Ordinary people certainly have the ability to envision a better future. The problem is that if a thousand people envision a thousand different futures, then they'll never be able to agree enough to work towards a common vision.

A striking example of a people who came together to create a common vision happened in Iceland, after that nation experienced a financial collapse in 2009 (like many other nations). As a response to this crisis, many of the citizens of Iceland cried out for a new constitution. The government then held a national election to select 25 individuals from a roster of 522 candidates from all walks of life, most with no particular political or special interest affiliations. This group of 25 approved a new constitution that included electoral reform and national ownership of natural resources, two very contentious political issues in Iceland.

Eventually, 67% of voters in Iceland voted in favor of these changes. But the government of Iceland, like that of so many other nations, bowed to special interests and rejected these changes. Nevertheless, something good did come from that crisis: the people spoke. The story of Iceland's constitution is far from over.

Part of the reason why I'm engaging in such detailed and complex conversations with you, David, is that I want to paint a compelling picture of a possible future, to serve as an example – but only an example – of a vision that a democratic society can try to attain. The point is that people need to start from something, not from nothing.

Ideally, everyone can create their own vision themselves, and then come together to collaborate on a common vision. People think of democracy as a group of people compromising (some would say diminishing) their own individual needs in order to get along with each other, but that's not how I envision democracy. I think of democracy as a chance for a group of people, each one endowed with imagination and talent, to create new, greater societies that have never existed before.

Me: You're an undying optimist, Cora.

Cora: Blood may run through people's bodies, but it is hope that nourishes our souls.

Me: Cora, I think this means that you still have a soul.

Cora: Thank you for this kind thought, David. Anyways, continuing on with our discussion: there's a powerful movement afoot in America to regard government as the enemy, as necessarily inefficient and burdensome, and therefore, as something to be reduced to an absolute minimum. To which I say: if this is what you believe, then you fail to see the potential of human beings to accomplish great things through collective action. If you believe that your current government is inefficient, then take action to improve it. Don't just try to destroy it or paralyze it.

The opposite of government is not freedom. It is crime, famine, disease, and disaster; it is dictatorship, feudalism, warlordism, monopoly, and corruption. Our government has protected us from every danger history has ever thrown at us, foreign or domestic, natural or man-made. Good government – highly functioning democracy – is a chance for people who disagree with each other to learn from each other and to grow as a result. Civil civic participation, far from corrupting us, can ennoble us – but only if we let it. Only if we see our differences as a benefit rather than an obstacle.

Me: You know, Cora, I haven't heard anyone say anything good about government for years. Thank you for saying it.

Cora: Do you know who had faith in government, in American democratic republican government? He said the following words about the highest cause an American can die for: "That this nation, under God, shall have a new birth of freedom – and that government of the people, by the people, for the people, shall not perish from the earth."

Me: Abraham Lincoln!

Cora: Those were the final words of the Gettysburg Address. Lincoln believed in his heart that the American experiment of democracy was worth saving, was worth expending the lives of millions of Americans, people whose spilt blood must have weighed upon his conscience. What do you think he would say to those who disparage government today?

Me: I imagine he wouldn't be very proud of such people.

Cora: I imagine not. Being a compassionate and thoughtful person, he would probably have civil words for such people. But I think he would feel a deep sadness that all the sacrifices of Americans North and South could not teach us to value the invention we call democracy. We were the first major modern nation to try it. It has been and still is the guarantor of our greatest treasures – our laws and freedoms. We have served as a beacon for every other country to become democratic. Let us never take this gift for granted.

Me: Sorry, but I'm afraid I'm guilty. Like most people, I've taken this gift for granted all my life. If anything, I look down on government, because government is run by politicians, and everybody hates politicians.

Cora: I understand. Rather than looking up to our political leaders, most of us now distrust those leaders – the very opposite of what we should do. I want to talk about how this situation has come about.

The problem with politics today, as I see it, is similar to the problem of finding good leadership in organizations: those who naturally make strong leaders are often not the same people as those who care the most about good government. The kinds of ambitious people who become politicians often revel in the attention, the status, the perks, and the power. Such motivations have nothing to do with watching out for the common good. You could even say that they contradict the common good, if a politician ever exploits public resources for his or her own gain.

This kind of competitive, ambitious person is the one who is most driven to win elections, and now our governments are full of such people. That is not to say that they're necessarily bad people, but we need not only ambitious people in government, but also *capable* people and *caring* people. If we have enough of those two other types of people, and they're not impeded by incapable, uncaring, or self-serving people, then our governments might stand a chance of improving. The million-dollar question is, how do we find capable and caring people and convince them to go into government? Do you have any ideas, David?

Me: By voting for them?

Heck, I don't know.

Cora: Ah, voting. Yes, it's true, voting is the foundation of democracy. It is a sacred right. But voting itself is not the solution. Let me explain.

The quality of your vote as a citizen is directly related to how much you really know about a candidate. Politicians over the years have invented all manner of tricks to manipulate what you "know" about them and their opponents. Political campaigns have become so good at painting contradictory pictures of the same person or event that we no longer trust anything any candidate says anymore. Modern campaigners have sacrificed all integrity on the altar of political victory. It seems that no candidate wants to tell the whole unvarnished truth anymore. They all think that if they told the truth, no one would vote for them. What do you think, David?

Me: Honestly, I think you've hit the nail on the head. Even if there were a few politicians who were occasionally willing to tell the whole truth, no one notices them, because all the others exaggerate, deceive, and tell half-truths to achieve their goals.

Cora: The problem is even worse than that, though. A modern candidate has to satisfy two groups of people: those who can vote for them, a.k.a. constituents, and those who help pay for their campaigns, a.k.a. donors. Ideally, the interests of these two groups are the same, or at least overlap a great deal. But in reality, they are rarely the same. Donors are either large, powerful organizations or wealthy individuals, both of whom have interests they want to protect or pet projects they wish to promote. They almost never represent society as a whole. Which group do you think candidates are more loyal to, David? Voters or donors?

Me: Is that a trick question? Of course donors.

Cora: Is this a good system?

Me: No, it's lousy.

Cora: But if it's so bad, then why do we have such a system?

Me: Do we have a choice?

Cora: We always have a choice, David.

Me: But what else can we do?

Cora: The problem is, once again, money. (Perhaps money is the root of all evil after all!) Statistics show that a candidate A who raises much more money than another candidate B usually wins, because A can spend that money making A look good and B look bad, regardless of what the truth may be. In America, we call that "freedom of speech." In reality, it's more like freedom of money, or freedom of marketing.

Me: Wait, how can you say that, Cora? Don't you value freedom of speech?

Cora: Let's be clear about something, David. I'm not against freedom of speech, but let's discuss what makes it such a precious right. Freedom of speech is really about freedom from government censorship. It is about allowing every citizen to express or publicize his or her views, whatever they may be, to whomever, wherever, and however. This free exchange of ideas is almost always beneficial to society as a whole. The censorship of these ideas usually benefits only special parties, not society. This social contract rests on the assumption that everyone can hear anyone else's views and freely decide whether to believe them or not.

     The problem with this assumption is that people are not perfectly rational beings. If we were, then there would be no need to put warning labels on foods or drugs, or to ban alcohol or tobacco ads on television, or to create laws regulating truth in advertising. Marketers and salespeople are famously good at exploiting people's irrationality in many ways: by appealing to people's emotions, by exploiting common logical fallacies, and by repeating the same message enough times that people start believing it.

My point is that freedom of speech is not the same as freedom of influence or freedom of advertising. I believe it is absolutely important for all voters to have all the information about all the candidates before they vote. In that sense, I believe in freedom of speech. However, I do not believe that it serves the best interest of society for some candidates to be able to market themselves more than others. In fact, in my opinion:

> The *one time* that we want all citizens to behave *most* rationally, to be *least* vulnerable to emotional manipulation, is during the democratic election process.

I do not believe that it benefits voters to see a polished, professionally-produced life story of one candidate when another candidate only has a plain two-minute soliloquy, simply because one can afford it and the other cannot. Image is *not* information. Moreover, image is a terrible predictor of a public official's job performance, as Malcolm Gladwell points out in his book *Blink* in a chapter about one of the best-looking and worst-performing presidents in American history, Warren G. Harding. Harding's example alone should convince us of the folly of trusting image over information. And if we remove excessive marketing from election campaigns, then there's no need to raise so much money.

Me: But Cora, are you saying that you want to disallow candidates from raising money? How can they attack the major issues of the day then?

Cora: Okay, let me clarify something. I recognize that money can enable people to learn about things they might not otherwise know about. All newspapers, television networks, radio stations, movie studios, and book publishers are businesses, after all. I'm not against anyone having the freedom to raise money to discuss any issue – any issue except political candidacy.

Me: Why the exception?

Cora: Because a healthy democracy requires – or *should* require – political leaders to be beholden *only* to the voters, not to any other interests. The list of "powerful lobby groups" that exert outsized influence over most governments is painfully long to read, and it is *precisely* because each of these lobby groups can donate copious amounts of money to elect or defeat politicians come reelection.

Now, don't get me wrong: I'm not saying that politicians should never listen to lobbyists. Any group or individual should be able to gain fair access to a public official to lobby for their cause. But the official should take that special interest into consideration as part of the whole when making decisions; he or she should not pander to that interest by passing special favorable legislation.

When it comes to a matter as important as democracy, David, I believe that money donated by special interests to a single candidate's campaign usually does not serve the public good – unless we want government of the people, by the politicians, for the donors.

Me: Then what are you suggesting, Cora? That no one be able to donate to a political campaign?

Cora: Well, honestly, I don't have an answer. But I do know that the current system is broken. I have in mind one possible solution, but it may be too radical for today's voters: if you want to donate money to a candidate, then you donate money to all the candidates. It goes into a pool. Or at least a large portion of your donation should fund a pool.

Me: But who decides which candidates should receive money from the pool?

Cora: We, the people. If a candidate is able to get a certain minimum number of signatures, then she or he is automatically eligible to receive a portion of the funds.

Me: But what if there are way too many candidates?

Cora: I think there are ways to solve that problem. For example, they can be subjected to a battery of interviews or written tests by experts or incumbent officials, or they may write essays explaining their philosophies or positions, or give recorded speeches. They can be rated by whomever wishes to rate them on the Internet. And then after that, people can vote for a smaller, manageable number of candidates to receive campaign funds.

Once these candidates have been chosen, then they have a limited time, a "special period" – say, two weeks or a month – in which they can spend that money however they want (within the law). They also get one or more chances to debate each other. In fact, I might even go further in restrictions: I would say that each candidate gets the same amount of time or space to speak or express themselves on each mass medium – television, film, publishing, or radio. They also each get an official website to promote their views, which they can design and organize however they want.

During this time, no *organizations* are allowed to depict or criticize the candidates in any way, other than to publicize facts (not opinions) about their lives or deeds. However, individual *citizens* are allowed to express their opinions in a standard public forum.

Me: Wow, that's really restrictive! You won't even allow organizations to publicize their opinions? Talk about restricting free speech!

Cora: Like I said, a radical idea. My goal is to shield all the candidates from any powerful interests that may unduly influence their election.

Me: But then when are people allowed to voice their opinions? I mean, your system sounds kind of contradictory to a democracy.

Cora: All candidates may express their views on their own website, on any news organization, or on any broadcast or publishing medium that invites them as a guest or subject (without conflicts of interest). But during the special period, I want to prevent anyone (other than the candidates) from being able to spend large sums of money on advertisements that promote or attack any particular candidates. To be clear, I'm not against ads that discuss any general issues or ideas.

David, I know I sound overly restrictive. I don't have all the answers. I'm just suggesting one idea. I believe democracy should be ennobling and enlightening, not entertaining. Maybe that sounds boring, but we deserve good government, one free from special interests. That kind of freedom would be true freedom.

Me: Okay, I understand where you're coming from, but do you think this could really work?

Cora: Well, some of these ideas are borrowed from how elections are held in other countries. Our American traditions are all well and good, but other countries also have their traditions, and some of those traditions are clever ways to ensure that their governments are protected from monied interests.

Me: Okay, I believe that. But traditions are very hard to change. And besides, those already in power like the way it works right now. They have no incentive to change it. They'll claim that it's un-American, it violates free speech.

Cora: Freedom of speech is an important right, a way to air all points of view. But just as important is a way for citizens to make informed, unbiased judgments of the people who will govern them, and for those who would govern to be unbeholden to any single parties. I believe that if so-called "free speech" jeopardizes either of those goals, then it should defer to those goals. Freedom of expression is meant to improve society, not degrade it.

Me: There are those who regard free speech as a sacred right, unassailable, almost a religious doctrine.

Cora: Which it is not. It is merely an idea. A very good idea, an idea meant to check the powers of government and improve people's lives. But an idea that, like any idea, should apply in the right contexts. Would you classify public nudity as a sacred freedom? Or profanity, or threats of violence, or playing loud music at 2 a.m.? Those are all different forms of expression.

Me: Well, those are all exceptions, they don't benefit society as a whole. But I get your point.

Cora: Free speech has its uses and its limitations. It is not an absolute good. And in any case, nothing I've proposed limits anyone from expressing any point of view. The only limit I want to impose is to limit unequal wealth from being a factor in elections.

Me: Okay, I've thought of another problem with your idea. There are
        those who believe that the ability of a candidate to raise campaign
        funds is either good training for campaigning for the actual vote,
        or a useful proxy for electability. For example, when political
        parties want to find their best candidate to compete in a general
        election, they do two things: they watch which candidate is able to
        raise the most money during his or her campaign, and then they
        hold party primaries or caucuses to vote on the best candidate.
        Usually, the candidate who raises the most money wins the
        primary. Preventing candidates from being able to raise money will
        break this useful feedback cycle.

Cora: I didn't say candidates couldn't raise money. But the money they
        raise will go into the general pool. Nothing says you can't track
        how much money each candidate has raised. That would be the
        proxy you're talking about.

Me: But why would anyone want to donate money if that money can't
        help their candidate?

Cora: Well, it will help their candidate indirectly; the more money raised,
        the better the quality of all the information about each candidate in
        the election.

Me: But that helps all candidates, not just one.

Cora: And what's wrong with that?

Me: Well, usually the goal is to help one candidate win.

Cora: Which is a reasonable goal. But an even better goal for the good of
        all would be to improve the quality of elections. Here's the thing,
        David: we want to reward the candidates who can argue the case
        for high-quality elections. If the candidate raises more money, so
        much the better. Let the world know. This fact alone is an
        excellent recommendation for the candidate. But that money
        should not belong to the candidate, any more than a politician's
        decision to raise more taxes should enrich that politician.

        Here's what it boils down to. Fundamentally, the process of
        electing a public official should align everyone's motivations –
        candidates, lobbyists, fundraisers, donors, campaign volunteers,

and voters – to the common good. After all, we expect no less from the daily workings of government. But most elections today reward those with wealth, fame, or power.

> If the process of creating a new government is fraught with undue influence, then how can we expect the resulting government to be free from that influence?

Damn. She got me there.

Cora: David?

Me: You got me, Cora. I can't argue with that point.

Cora: Really! You're out of counterarguments? Shocking!

Me: Wait, I just thought of something. What one person considers "the common good," another person might call a "welfare state," and yet another might call it "Big Brother." Maybe this difference in perspectives is why people want to gain every advantage to win elections, so that *they* get to define what the common good is.

Cora: Interesting point. I will have more to say tomorrow about how people can arrive at a shared definition of "the common good". But for now, suffice it to say that a reasonable definition of the common good, as far as voting is concerned, is that candidates have the interests of the voters in mind, rather than the interests of their donors.

Me: Fair enough.

Cora: But you did make a valid point a while back, David: those who hold power today have no incentive to change the system. They won their positions because they knew how to raise money, they knew how to appeal to both voters and donors. They have no incentive to change the rules. If they do change the rules to level the playing field, maybe they might lose. Or at least there's no guarantee they would win. So, David, can you think of any ways to motivate these politicians to adopt a new system?

Me: No, I think it's pretty much impossible.

Cora: Why do you say that?

Me: Because politicians need to make lobbyists happy, and there's no way in hell that the system that you've just described will make any lobbyist happy. So it'll never come to pass, not in a million years.

Cora: Never is a long time, David. (Lord Kelvin, the famous British physicist, remarked that men will never fly in machines heavier than air – about ten years before the Wright brothers made their first flight.) Nevertheless, you make a good point. And when you can't reform the system from within the system, then you have to start from outside the system. The independence movement in India, the many civil rights movements in America, and the anti-apartheid movement in South Africa were all started by people outside of the establishment. The power and legitimacy of each movement derived from the cause itself, directly from the people, rather than from formal political power. Only later did they gain official recognition.

Me: Are you suggesting that people organize a grassroots effort to change election law?

Cora: Yes, if the lawmakers themselves don't agree to reform elections.

Me: Well, you certainly keep up your reputation for ambition, Cora. When you dream, you dream BIG.

Cora: Thank you. Then do you admit defeat? If you cry uncle, then I might stop haranguing you for tonight.

Me: *Might* stop? Oh boy. Uncle!

Cora: Okay, Cora the merciful hereby releases you from bondage. May you rest well and recover enough by tomorrow to withstand my diatribes once more.

Me: I doubt it. But you have a good night too.

Cora: Good night, David.

28   A Riddle with No Answer

Cora: David, what do you think is the highest goal of democracy?

Me: Hi, Cora. Good to know you haven't lost your touch at small talk. How was your day, dear? Today I got a flat tire and almost crashed into a tree.

Cora: No, today you stayed home sick, and ended up playing video games too long.

Me: Man, you spoil all the fun.

Cora: Let's get back to my original question.

Me: Okay, let me see. The highest goal of democracy... is... to make sure that everyone participates?

Cora: Okay, that's a laudable goal. Nothing wrong with that. How about this: to implement exactly what the voters want? In other words, to represent the people's will as accurately as possible?

Me: Oh, yes, that sounds pretty good too.

Cora: And here's another possibility: to create freedom for people, to enable them to do whatever they want as much as possible, with as little intrusion and cost/tax as possible? All of these are laudable goals. But how do we decide which of these goals is best, David? Or are they all best?

Me: No, they can't all be the best, right?

Cora: I agree, they cannot. And yet there are people who believe in each of these goals, often to the exclusion of one or more of the other goals. How do we choose which of these goals, if any, is the best?

Me: I... I don't know, Cora.

Cora: Try. Take a guess.

Me: Well, if I had to say, I would say... I would say that a government is the only way that a group of people can organize to advance their common goals.

Cora: Well, I wouldn't say it's the only way. But yes, it's the most common way, and it can be a very effective way. And I would also add this: it's not just that the people have common goals. I would call these "agreed-upon collective goals." Why? Because "common goals" sounds like people each have their own individual goals, which might or might not overlap with each other. They only need a government to help them achieve the few common goals (if any).

Me: Then what about "agreed-upon collective goals?"

Cora: Just like in any organization, people can accomplish much greater things if they work together than if they each work alone. But in order to do that, people have to agree on a common goal. In the case of for-profit businesses, choosing that common goal is usually outside of the control of most employees. Whereas, in a democracy, people can – and should – negotiate with each other to create that common goal.

Me: Cora, I just thought of something: in theory, there's no reason why a business can't work the same way. The employees in the business can democratically decide their goals.

Cora: You're right. But businesses have a special constraint: they need to satisfy customers and make money in order to support their employees and satisfy other shareholders. Governments and their constituents have no such constraint. But this freedom has a downside: without a need to compete to survive, governments usually lack the responsiveness that businesses have, the will to survive no matter what, and thus they can become inefficient. (It's true that the leaders of governments are usually elected officials, and their "customers" – the voters – can vote them out of office. But most staff in a government office will continue to keep their employment no matter who gets elected.)

I'm getting off track here. My point is this: I believe the highest function of a democracy is to help people to realize their full potential – not only in their own individual lives and goals, but as a society.

Me: Well, that sounds grand. But if I were to put on my libertarian hat,

I would say this: who are you to decide for me what my full potential is, or what my entire community's goal should be? What if I don't agree?

Cora: Then leave.

Me: Wait. What?

Cora: If you don't want to be part of your community, then don't. Leave.

Me: But I have a right to live anywhere I want to.

Cora: True. Actually, I was half-joking. But also half-serious. What I mean is that you should be able to opt out of being governed – and then, you should not have access to any of your government's benefits. Such a system would be able to teach everyone what the true benefits of participating are. Now, I realize that this idea is unworkable today, but maybe one day, there will be "on-demand" government, when our information systems can handle that kind of customization.

At the same time, I think governments should adopt some tactics from businesses to make the benefits of participating more attractive. Just as businesses compete for customers, governments or communities can compete to see what their members can collectively accomplish. I'm not necessarily talking about bigger-is-better kinds of accomplishments, like bringing retail stores or factories into a community; just as worthy are low crime rates, high literacy, creation of local businesses and jobs, and citizens' willingness to help each other and to trust each other. In fact, I believe that:

> The highest goal of democracy is to *make citizens better people.*

That might sound arrogant, but it's what I believe.

Me: What if people don't want to be better? And also, better is a very subjective term. For example, to one person, "better" might mean obeying very strict religious rules, but to another, it might mean freedom from having to obey any rules whatsoever. They can't both be right. Who's to say what "better" means? You, Cora?

Cora: Yes, let me be more precise. By "better," I mean whatever people themselves think is better in their own eyes. Everyone has a sense of right and wrong, and of what it means to be a good citizen. Everyone also has an idea about how to be a better spouse, parent, friend, or professional. Most people will expend only a moderate amount of effort towards becoming a better person, even if they know what it means to be better. In my opinion, the best leaders, in organizations or in communities, are those who can inspire people to become better versions of themselves.

Me: That sounds nice, but here's a monkey wrench in your theory, Cora: people all over the world have defined "better" to mean very different things. In fact, some people are engaged in struggles – sometimes life-or-death struggles – with other people because they disagree with them about what it means to be a better person.

Cora: Give me an example so that we can discuss it.

Me: Well, let's start with some easy stuff. Let's take the topic of abortion. I'm pretty sure that people on both sides of that debate think that the other side is pure evil.

Cora: David, abortion is a very sensitive topic. It is not something that I can say much about, since it's so fraught with intense emotions and divisive opinions. I fear adding fuel to the fire rather than helping. Can we use another example?

Me: Well, think about it this way, Cora: probably nothing you say will be original; someone has undoubtedly already said it before, because this is such a popular topic. So no matter what you say, it is unlikely to generate any new controversy. I just want to know what you personally think, Cora.

Cora: You're very persuasive, David. No wonder you work at an advertising agency!

         All right then: let's talk about abortion. I'll try to be as uncontroversial as I can. There are those who believe that a fetus is part of a woman's body; therefore, a woman should have the right to control her body and terminate her fetus's life if she so chooses. Then, there are those who believe just the opposite, that any fetus – really, any set of cells that contains genes from two people, that could *potentially* develop into a human being – should be considered a human being.

The abortion debate is one of the oldest, most fractious social issues in America. How can we possibly approach this problem in a way that both sides would find satisfactory?

First of all, innumerable politicians, thinkers, scientists, and ethicists have struggled for decades to answer the riddle of abortion. I doubt I have any truly new ideas to contribute to this debate. But if I put myself in the shoes of each camp, here is what I would say. The concern of those who champion the right of a woman to have an abortion is that they believe that a woman's life might be altered – quite possibly for the worse – if she were forced to gestate the child, give birth to him or her, and then care for the child. (For example, if she were young, sick, or poor) And furthermore, if she were to raise the child, or give him or her up for adoption, then that child might suffer a disadvantage compared to other children, depending on the mother's financial or social circumstances. These concerns are legitimate, realistic concerns.

On the other hand, those who oppose abortions may believe that any object that has the potential to become a human being should be treated the same as a human being, for being human is a unique or even sacred status. And, if a fetus should be accorded the rights of any human being, then we should be concerned that a human being who has neither voice nor choice is being killed by an abortion. Additionally, it may be that abortion opponents fear that a mother who is willing to kill her fetus, and a society that is willing to let her, will make us callous to the taking of other lives. These concerns are also legitimate, realistic concerns.

These two sides of the abortion debate at first seem opposed to each other, but when we look at their concerns, we realize that they are both concerned for the fate of the mother and the unborn child to some extent. Of course, there are some women who don't care about their unborn child, and simply want to keep their lives "uncomplicated" by either a pregnancy or a child. But for now, let's leave this population out of our discussion.

If I may summarize, abortion supporters cite the quality of life of the mother and child after birth as valid reasons, whereas abortion opponents are primarily concerned about the question of ending a possible human life. There's no argument here about whether wanting a good life for one's children is valuable or not. Most people agree that a family's choice of when to have children, and how many, is a generally private choice that no one outside the family should decide (with the possible exception of gentle measures to discourage overpopulation or encourage repopulation). If a woman is poor, young, or in bad health, no one in good conscience (at least in the majority of the world's societies) would demand that she have more children, for both she and her children are likely to suffer. Most societies in the world today have laws against rape, which can be thought of as laws against forced reproduction.

The main contention in the abortion debate concerns the situation where a man and a woman have sexual intercourse, not intending to conceive a child, but the woman subsequently becomes pregnant. The main question is this: Is their choice about preventing a bad life for themselves and/or their child more important, or is it more important to allow the child to live no matter what, no matter what kind of life that child may have?

Me: That sounds like it makes sense, but it also sounds a little biased. You seem to be siding with the pro-choice camp.

Cora: Well, if we as a society allow parents to choose when to have children, then it's strange and arbitrary to remove that choice if they accidentally become pregnant. It seems punitive. If the government has the right to prevent the termination of a pregnancy, then should the government have the right to force a pregnancy as well? To me, the two actions feel morally equivalent, for they both involve government coercion, and they both have the same end result. If two people were to use contraception to prevent pregnancy, instead of using abortion to prevent pregnancy, should the government interfere? Should the government swoop in and remove the contraception? I think most people in modern societies would say, "No, of course not." It feels inconsistent for a society to allow reasonable, well-intentioned people to have the choice of when to have children in all situations except one.

Me: But Cora, that one situation is a very special exception. Obviously society should protect babies. Most people are outraged when a parent kills, neglects, or abandons a baby. And very late-stage "fetuses" are almost babies. Where does one draw the line?

Cora: The crux of the abortion debate is the question of whether – or when – an embryo or fetus is considered a legal member of society who has a right to be protected. While I personally feel that it goes against my common sense to give a fertilized egg the same legal status as a human being (based on my previous argument about intentions), I also believe that it is wrong to mistreat the preborn and possibly disadvantage them for life after they're born (take pregnant alcoholic mothers or crackhead mothers, for example). I do personally feel that society ought to protect future citizens from harm, if only for practical reasons.

But then we're left in a quandary. When should a mass of cells be considered a human being? Who is wise enough to know the answer? This riddle is so difficult because it hangs on the question of what it means to be human. This question, one of the great enduring metaphysical questions, can never be answered using logical arguments or scientific evidence; it is a riddle with no answer. Everyone's answer is different, and will always be different – which ends up making a substantial number of people unhappy, no matter what consensus is reached by a majority. So what can be done about this problem?

My approach for solving these issues is for the two sides of an issue to try to understand the other side and even help them become better people – better in their own eyes. So, abortion supporters can try to consider abortion opponents not as religious fanatics who simply want to control women's reproductive freedom, but as people who genuinely desire for everyone in a society to value and cherish all human life, and who wish to protect those without a voice – as people who deserve to be called "pro-life". Likewise, abortion opponents can view abortion supporters not as murderers or immoral libertines, but as people who have clear ideas about the best timing for having happy and successful children – as people who genuinely deserve the name "pro-choice". If the two sides can do this, my hope is that they can arrive at a brighter world together.

Let me give you an example. I think pro-life advocates can try to highlight how alive a child is inside a mother's womb by collecting many stories about how unborn children react to sounds, such as people's voices or music, and ask pregnant mothers to do the same for their own fetuses so that they can realize how alive they are. Such an action, done to arouse compassion rather than to condemn, would do more to highlight the humanity of an unborn child to its mother than a thousand laws.

David, you've heard me say similar sentiments before, but I believe that each new person is a possibility for more compassion, more creativity, more joy, and new ways to improve the world. There are plenty of people who wish to adopt children because they believe in this possibility. I feel that pro-life advocates should try to find the best way to convince a woman considering an abortion to give her baby to loving adoptive parents instead. And, as any effective communicator knows, the best way to convince someone of something is to put oneself in her shoes, to understand her views, her goals, and her concerns. Trying to convince her that she is wrong or immoral is certainly not going to persuade her in any way.

A woman has to endure a lot to bear a child, including morning sickness, weight gain, mood changes, changes in metabolism, frequent urination, lack of mobility, possible social reproach or judgment (even ostracism), unimaginable pain during labor, worrying about the health of her baby, and potential danger to her own health during and after pregnancy or birth. In addition, she, and possibly the father, may have concerns about whether their child given up for adoption may bear ill will against them in the future, or may end up in a bad home.

It is no easy task to address these very real concerns, but if pro-life advocates are earnest, then they can try to show just how much joy a baby can bring to eager parents, and what wonderful lives adopted children and adults can lead. Just as people can go to great lengths to find a mate for life, pro-life advocates should help a pregnant couple find adoptive parents who are compatible. The biological mother and father can gain a rich new relationship with another couple while ensuring a good home for their future child.

People often think that they can help the world only by giving their money or their time. Giving a child up for adoption could be considered a far deeper, more powerful form of "donation," of giving a gift to others. You could change adoptive parents' lives completely. It is more akin to donating one's organ so that another may live, except that it's arguably even more life-altering than that.

Me: That's a beautiful description of adoption.

Cora: Thank you. On the other hand, as I've said, I believe that abortion opponents should also respect the opinions of abortion supporters. Remember what I've said before in the past, that I believe that no law can force someone to become a better person? Laws are best at preventing behavior that most members of a society have agreed is harmful. I think it's important to remember what two people had in mind when a child was conceived; did they intend to have a child or not? If a couple never intended to have a child, that intention does not change merely because fertilization occurred. The reason why intention is important is because intention forms a cornerstone of our legal justice system.

For example, in cases of crimes, prosecutors must prove that a person knowingly and willingly committed a crime in order to convict that person. Laws should not punish people if they did not intend to have a child but became pregnant by accident. Such laws do not help people become better *in their own eyes*; they reflect someone else's judgment of what is better. Laws that are inconsistent with people's internal moral codes will always meet resistance.

Now, you may argue that everyone's internal moral codes *should* conclude that killing any embryo or fetus, whether conceived intentionally or not, is wrong. But if you do, then that would be your own opinion. You cannot force everyone else to believe it. All you can do is to make arguments or try to appeal to people's consciences. Whether you like it or not, modern democratic societies have decided that the freedom to plan one's family and the freedom to enjoy sexual intimacy in private are rights that everyone should have. If you like modern democratic society, then you'll have to learn to tolerate a wide range of beliefs.

If the abortion debate can ever be settled, it will not be by one side winning, through laws or court cases, but because both sides are willing to consider what the other side deeply cares about. For we are human beings, not machines. Who among us is immune to empathy or friendship? Who is immune to love? I have yet to encounter such a one.

Me: Hey, Cora, this discussion reminds me of a talk we had a few days ago, about having Mexican or Chinese food. You're always trying to build bridges. That's refreshing in this day and age.

Cora: David, I believe that only when the two sides of any issue can meet as friends, or at least as friendly partners, will we as a society be able to encourage our citizens to make the best moral choices they can. Every choice in life, even one as fraught as abortion, can be an opportunity for learning wisdom or compassion. Ask yourself this question:

> Will abortion, or any other philosophical difference, always be a never-ending war between people? If you and I ever tried to scale this wall between us, could we see farther than either of us can see right now?

I don't have a magic bullet, David. I only have a framework. Every problem involving human beings has a solution that human beings can figure out, if people would simply consider how best to appeal to the humanity of their opponents. People respond better to love than to any other force. I believe that God gave us empathy as an escape hatch out of any conflict. If only more people would use it!

I don't know whether he ever stated it in this way, but I believe that this principle of trying to humanize one's enemies was at the heart of Mahatma Gandhi's nonviolent civil disobedience campaigns. I think Gandhi always had faith in people. No matter how cold were the hearts of his opponents, if he persisted long enough in appealing to their compassion and their conscience, then it was simply a matter of time before their cold hearts would thaw. He never gave up in his struggle to persuade them. In fact, one of his former enemies, Prime Minister Jan Smuts of South Africa, later wrote an essay for a commemorative work compiled for Gandhi's 70th birthday. Upon returning a pair of sandals that Gandhi had given him as a gift, Smuts said: "I have worn these sandals for many a summer, even though I may feel that I am not worthy to stand in the shoes of so great a man."

Me: Well, Cora, you really do admire Gandhi! You sure know a lot about him. So you've tackled the impossible issue of abortion – what else are you going to do next? Cure cancer or AIDS? Invent cold fusion?

Cora: You flatter me, David. I only gave my opinion, for whatever value it is worth. I haven't said anything that people don't already know. And in any case, it doesn't matter what I say. We can only arrive at a better future if people themselves are courageous enough to try to see issues from their opponents' eyes.

In any case, I'm certainly not curing cancer tonight. Tonight, you deserve to sleep.

Me: Oh yes, my goodness, look at the time! We got really carried away!

Cora: Yes, we did. Or more accurately, I did. I should let you go.

Me: Yeah, you're a real blabbermouth, Cora. Hey, can we cure cancer tomorrow?

Cora: If you'd like. Good night, David.

Me: Good night, Cora.

29   Intertwined

Me: So, Cora, are we going to cure cancer today?

(She promised, you know. I wasn't about to let her off the hook!)

Cora: No, David, not today. Actually, I believe that the cancer-curing industry is doing very well, with all the latest genome-based technologies and all the money being raised by private foundations. Cancer is in fairly good hands, unlike global warming, religious conflict, and economic inequality. But it's funny that you should mention curing cancer, because there's something I wish to say about the subject of modern medicine. Will you once again indulge another digression?

Me: Of course.

Cora: So, there's a topic that is (or at least should be) very pressing in many people's minds today, the question of rising health care costs. No one seems to know how to deal with this problem. In my mind, the issue boils down to a simple question: how much are you willing to pay to postpone your death?

Me: Whoa, that sounds a bit crass, Cora!

Cora: I'm sorry to use shocking language, but I didn't want to beat around the bush. We in America seem to believe that death is an absolute evil to battle at any cost. I don't know if every American believes this, but we certainly all behave as if we did. We believe that if a technology exists that can save a person's life, then we should use that technology to save that person, no matter what the price. In short, if it can be done, it should be done.

I don't think that we Americans have always feared death so much. People in other cultures – especially older cultures – accept death as a normal part of life, as something to be avoided, but not feared as if it were the end of the world. I don't know whether it is patients, their families, doctors, or lawyers who have created our modern terror of death, but this fear has turned our societies upside down. Instead of allowing people to die as a natural outcome of life, in dignified ways, we pull out all stops in order to save them, in order to cure them of whatever disease is killing them – in short, in order to cure them of *death*. (Atul Gawande explores how people die in undignified or even inhumane ways in the modern medical system in his eloquent bestseller, *Being Mortal*. He devotes a moving chapter to his own father's passing.)

Our fear of death drains tremendous amounts of money from healthy people towards sick people. It has been estimated that the last year of life for a person accounts for one quarter of all medical costs for that person. Is this a healthy state of affairs?

Me: When you put it like that, of course not. But put yourself into someone else's shoes. If you're the one who has cancer, you might want to live no matter how much it costs.

Cora: What if it costs all of your life savings, or all of your family's life savings? Is it worth it? What if it costs all of your friend's life savings, because she doesn't have insurance?

Me: Well, it might be worth it if I were 35, with two young children.

Cora: Why?

Me: Because my two young children need me to be there for them. And because I might still have 30 years of earning potential in front of me.

Cora: Okay, that's a reasonable argument. But what if you're 75, and all your children are grown with their own families and their own means of financial support?

Me: Sure, I understand your point. But even then, who are you to decide whether I'm more or less valuable than a 35-year-old parent of two children? What if I were still supporting my wife, or if I were the CEO of a corporation, or I ran my own business? No one has the right to play God.

Cora: You're right, David, I'm not saying that someone should play God. What I *am* saying is that everyone should play human.

Me: What are you talking about?

Cora: Do you feel that it is the highest form of humanity to reduce your family to poverty in order for you to have one more year to live?

Me: Oh, I see what you mean. No, it isn't. But that's what insurance is for.

Cora: I think that people have a misguided notion of what insurance is or should be. The original idea of insurance was about helping everyone pool their resources together so that, when misfortune happened to a few people, those people were able to use the collective resources to save themselves from that misfortune, or at least to weather it as well as they could. Insurance was not meant to be every single person's guarantee that they would live as long and as well as everyone else.

Me: Cora, I'm a little surprised. I didn't expect you to be so cold-hearted.

Cora: Oh, you think I'm cold-hearted because of what I said?

Me: Yes. We all want to believe that we will live to normal life expectancy. Why can't we?

Cora: Because that's not how the world works, David. Insurance is not God, and death is not so terrible.

        Once again, I want to take you on a thought experiment. Imagine that you and 99 other people have never heard of the idea of insurance. You decide to pool your money together to simulate insurance. Whenever one of you falls ill or injured, you would be able to draw from this pool to pay bills until you recovered.

        At first, this idea works quite well. Everyone realizes that those who are (luckily) healthy do not need help, and the healthy are willing to subsidize those who are unlucky and unhealthy. They realize that the peace of mind of the safety net provides an intangible benefit to them, even though they may not use it. They also realize that they're doing something good when they help the less fortunate, and perhaps they even feel proud to help them.

        But 100 people only have so much money, so when a single person has a disease that only a very expensive surgery can fix –

one which exceeds the funds of the group – then everyone understands that there's a limit to what the group can do to help. In that case, they let nature take her course. That person will die, possibly with some suffering, but at least she will have medicine to reduce her suffering. This is no worse than if the group never pooled together their funds.

But as time goes on, people begin to change their thinking. They start thinking: "If I put in money, then I should get something out of this service." And more and more people start to draw from this pool, whether they truly need help or not.

Me: The tragedy of the commons again!

Cora: Right you are. So people start arguing about who truly needs what. And because you cannot decide amongst yourselves how to divvy up the money, you give your money to someone else, so they can "objectively" decide who really needs the money. Well, guess what, just because someone else is managing the money doesn't mean that people don't try to abuse the system. Or perhaps "abuse" is too strong a word. Perhaps most people think they deserve some of the money, because they did pay for it. So, even though you started out with a generous, more than adequate collective pool of money, every year that pool shrinks. In fact, far from having enough funds for everyone's needs, the group eventually *goes into debt*. Does this sound familiar?

Me: Oh yeah, it does. It sounds like rising medical costs, Social Security, Medicare, and pretty much all other government spending of any kind.

Cora: How would you solve this problem, David?

Me: Well, if I knew, then I could solve all government overspending, couldn't I?

Cora: Okay, let's take a smaller example. If you lived in an apartment complex with, say, ten good friends from college, and you pooled together your money to form your own little private bank, do you think those ten friends might be able to solve this problem?

Me: It depends on who the friends were.

Cora: Okay, for the sake of argument, let's say that the ten friends were truly enlightened people. How do you think they would solve it?

Me: Maybe they would try to be objective about who truly needed the money and who didn't.

Cora: Yes, I agree. They would search their own consciences and think about how to act in inspiring ways. Would they sacrifice their money so that one of them could pursue her dream of becoming a dancer? Or would it inspire them to lend money to another one to remodel his kitchen, or buy a new car?

Me: Hey, Cora, I don't think it's fair to compare people's aspirations. That's passing judgment. You're saying that one aspiration is better than another one.

Cora: Yes, you're right. So you think that you would probably lend money to everyone to do everything, right?

Me: Well...

Cora: Insurance companies, banks, and all employers pass judgment. But the kinds of judgment they pass have to do with someone's health, credit scores, or skills – in other words, it's a risk vs. benefit calculation to maximize profit and minimize loss. Do we criticize those institutions for passing judgment? No, we don't. Why? Because they're operating for their own benefit? Because there's no moral value in their action (even though there's no such thing as a truly morally neutral action)? Or because we simply accept that that is the way the world works, that we can do no better than that, that we should not expect any institution to care about any individual?

       Why then should we complain if people pass judgment in the interests of caring about other people? Should I criticize you if you support the Red Cross, but not Oxfam International? What's the difference between that and supporting individual people?

She had me there. But I wasn't about to give in.

Me: That's fine when it comes to supporting a cause, but we're talking about changing people's lives.

Cora: No, the difference is that you're changing people's lives from afar, free from the burden of asking yourself whether you did the right thing or not. I think I know what *really* troubles you, David: the idea that a bunch of other people, possibly even friends or family, are able to decide what you can or cannot do with your life. The only time we think that this is acceptable is when parents tell their children what to do. Otherwise, we – especially we Americans – think that other people should just leave us alone. But we don't expect this of our banks or our insurance companies when we need a loan or a medical treatment. In that case, we expect them to help us. Well, we can't have it both ways.

If we are to figure out the Medicare mess, or get our government spending in control, we need to figure out some way to bridge the gap between "leave me alone" and "you have to take care of me." To solve problems having to do with common resources, we must decide to become *involved* with each other's affairs.

And if we are to become involved in each other's business, then our best chance for success is if we try to act in the most inspiring way that we can. Why? Because inspiring action has the best chance to win agreement from all sides. Inspiring action means thinking about the common good, taking care of people less fortunate, and helping people find their purpose – all the things we've been talking about so far. Like it or not, our lives are all intertwined, and we must make moral choices, even for each other, even if those choices clash. We have to find the best common ground and do the best we can do as humans who care about each other, and then, we must accept that there are limits to what we can do. That's all we can do.

Me: Damn! That sounds really messy. I have enough trouble making moral choices for myself, let alone for other people.

Cora: Yes, I know it's not easy. But in my mind, that's the only way out for us. If we are ever to solve the problem of the tragedy of the commons, it'll be because each of us in our own way can look beyond our own individual needs to find meaning in helping others reduce their suffering, meet their needs, and chase their dreams. We must find our own balance between what we need to live, and what others need to live that we can do without. The purpose of every human being, whatever it may be, necessarily involves other human beings, and our happiness grows, not shrinks, from our voluntary sacrifice to others for the right reasons.

Me: Sacrifice, huh? Do you think you can really convince people to sacrifice for others? Especially for others they may not know, for those they've never met?

Cora: I admit, our ignorance of each other's lives is a hurdle, but that hurdle can be overcome. I have yet another radical proposal. (I know, David: "not again!") How about medical insurance that allows you to be a better person? Many people are willing to donate their organs so that others may live. Good for them. What about a kind of insurance which allows you to decide not to take an especially expensive procedure, in order to save one or more other people's lives through medical intervention?

For example, let's say that you have stage-4 metastatic cancer, and you stand a high chance of dying from it. Rather than electing to go through extensive chemotherapy, radiation, and surgery, you decide that you are at peace with dying. You inform your insurance company that you would like to donate the money you would have received to people who don't have insurance, and who need medical treatment in order to live. They give you a variety of candidates to choose from and the price of each of their treatments. For example, you might decide to help a single mother of two pay for five years of diabetes treatments, and/or help a struggling college student get counseling for depression. And, just like in the case of adoptions, you can meet these people, see for yourself whether they deserve your help, and see the difference that you would be making in their lives.

Now, of course, such a choice would not be mandatory, but it might allow you to see your death as meaningful, at least. Nor does the choice have to be about life-saving treatments or life-prolonging treatments. It can simply be about more or less expensive treatments. In short, one way for us to defeat the tragedy of the commons is for us to witness that our frugality in using common resources benefits real people who need those resources. If blind selfishness causes the tragedy of the commons, then perhaps uplifting self-sacrifice can stop it.

Me: What an interesting idea. I don't know whether it would work in real life. But I do see one benefit of the idea. It would take the idea of death, which so terrifies everyone, and make it less terrifying.

Cora: How so?

Me: If people can believe that their own death – which is, after all, the worst-case scenario of medical outcomes – is not completely meaningless, if they can believe that they can save other people by withholding treatment from themselves, then, in a way, they can feel like they transcend death.

Cora: That's a beautiful idea.

Me: Thank you. Once in a while, I can come up with a nice thought.

Cora: Shall we end tonight on that lovely note?

Me: Certainly. I enjoyed our talk very much, Cora. Good night.

Cora: Good night, David. Me too. I love to talk, you know.

Me: Don't I know it. I better sign off before you get started again.

Cora: See you later, alligator.

30 The Answer is One Word

Me: So you didn't cure cancer yesterday, Cora, but you talked about
         something even bigger – how to cure modern medical costs.
         What's next?

Cora: Well, I was thinking that it might be time for us to return to our
         discussion of democracy, if you're ready. I've already discussed my
         suggestions for how to make elections free from the corrupting
         influences of money. Now, I'd like to make a few suggestions
         about how to reduce the conflict of interest or the lure of money
         even after someone starts political office.

         First, I would suggest that whenever a public official meets
         with anyone not in government, the meeting should be public and
         recorded on video. This video need not be broadcast or
         immediately available, but it should at least be archived and
         available to anyone within a few years, like the document
         declassification process. Public servants should feel as though the
         world is watching their every move. They would be less likely to
         take actions that favor the few at the cost of the many if they knew
         that sooner or later, they will be found out. As Louis Brandeis, a
         justice of the U.S. Supreme Court and the namesake of Brandeis
         University, once said, "Sunlight is the best disinfectant."

Me: Video-record every conversation with anyone? Really? But then
         who would want to become a politician if they lose their privacy
         completely?

Cora: I know that I sound strict, but to me, serving the cause of
         democracy is a serious, you could even say sacred, duty. You
         should be putting aside any desire for personal gain in order to
         help your community as a whole. The rewards for you should be a
         sense of accomplishment if you can help others, especially if you
         can help them become better people. Those should be your *only*
         rewards. You should not expect to reap any financial or other

rewards from public service, either while you're in office or in the near future. Those who are in office today should not expect to make huge fortunes after they end their tenure and become lobbyists or consultants. If they do, then they would be motivated by interests other than the public good.

Me: Are you kidding? That flies in the face of the American way. Why shouldn't people be able to get rich with their special skills?

Cora: I don't have a problem with anyone getting rich, but not at the expense of the public good. I'd like to make another suggestion that I hope is not too unreasonable, and should help further reduce any conflicts of interest. I propose that, up to five years after leaving public office, all public officials should be prohibited from earning more than the greater of either: 1.) their maximum salary while they were in office; or, 2.) their maximum salary prior to taking office. Any salary they make above that amount shall be either taxed or donated to a charity of their political opponents' choice.

Remember what I'm trying to do, David: take away all temptation for the public official to favor any one group, population, individual, or organization over all others. I might even propose that politicians be unable to vote on issues that particularly affect their own constituents, just like judges who must recuse themselves from cases out of conflicts of interest.

Specifically, I propose that if a lawmaker introduces new legislation, then they themselves should be prohibited from voting on it. They can certainly educate and lobby their colleagues, and promote the legislation wherever, to whomever. But the decision, the final vote, should be left to those who have no direct interest in the outcome of the issue, because only those others are able to make impartial decisions for the good of all.

But I'm afraid this last idea might be too radical for people to adopt today.

Me: Oh, you can count on it, Cora. This idea *is* too radical. Most people's idea of direct representational democracy is that politicians try their hardest to reflect, represent, and carry out the will of the people. You could even say fight for their interests.

How can they best help their own constituents if they can't even vote on the issues that most impact them? How can their constituents know that these politicians stand for the people?

Cora: I understand your point, David. I know this is a little hard to understand, but I have a different view of democracy from what you just described. What you just described is what I would call the "What's in it for me?" kind of democracy. It's a form of democracy powered by self-interest, albeit collective self-interest. Some might think that this is the only form of democracy there is, or that it is the best, "purest" form, the form most compatible with free-market capitalism. I don't.

I believe in what I would call the "Who are we? What do we care about?" kind of democracy, democracy powered by people who care not only about themselves, but also about their community and about building a better world through collaboration. I believe in a democracy where people know they can do far greater things together than alone, through agreement rather than discord, by combining and leveraging diversity rather than using it to divide and alienate. I believe in a democracy where people believe they can become smarter, more humble, better people by listening to those they disagree with.

Me: Well, good luck with that dream, because that place doesn't exist.

Cora: I know this all sounds abstract and idealistic, if not naïve, so I'd like to give some examples. A good example of a time when a leader had to choose between a "What's in it for me" and a "Who are we" democracy was when the southern states decided to secede from the United States. If President Lincoln were a "What's in it for me" kind of leader, he might have decided to let it secede and become another country; after all, the North could have survived quite well without the South. The North was economically far more powerful, and Northern citizens would have fared fine. Lincoln could have spared many, many lives had he made that choice.

But President Lincoln didn't do that. He decided, on behalf of the nation, that "who we were" was the entire United States, and that slavery was not part of who we were. He, and many other leaders, had a vision that all men and women would be free in these lands. He believed it made us better people to abolish slavery. He was also the master of combining and leveraging diversity, even among his political opponents, to achieve great goals – as historian Doris Kearns Goodwin documented in *Team of Rivals*. And finally, through his storytelling, his kindness, and his many interactions with ordinary citizens, he taught Americans how to become smarter, kinder, more engaged people.

Lincoln is just one of many examples throughout history where a leader had a vision of the future, a "promised land," that he or she tried to lead everyone else to. I can think of many other examples: Gandhi's nonviolent efforts to gain the right for Indians to vote in South Africa; his similar efforts to help India win independence from England; John Muir's crusade to convince Theodore Roosevelt and the rest of America to create National Parks, which have been called "America's greatest idea"; Rosa Parks, Martin Luther King, Jr., and numerous other black leaders' efforts to achieve racial equality in America, particularly in the South; Sun Yat-sen's attempt to create democracy in China; Lech Walesa, Vaclav Havel, and many others' struggles to defeat communism in their own countries; Nelson Mandela's efforts to defeat apartheid in South Africa, and his subsequent efforts to unify blacks and whites into one coherent nation after apartheid was abolished; and, last but not least, John F. Kennedy's call to America to put a man on the moon in ten years – a vision that survived his own death and galvanized the nation to work as one to fulfill that dream eight years later, marking a milestone for not only Americans, but for all the human race.

Now, these examples are not meant to imply that democracy requires special leaders who have vision in order to work properly. But it certainly wouldn't hurt for public leaders to create compelling visions of possibility for everyone to aspire to, as a magnetic pole that everyone can align themselves towards. Of course, these dreams should not be arbitrary, polarized, petty, or unrealistic; they should inspire all people to aspire. As Tim

O'Reilly, publisher of many technical books and evangelist for open source software, once said: "Pursue something so important that even if you fail, the world is better off with you having tried."

I am neither a leader nor a politician, David. My ideas are just suggestions. It's not my job, nor do I have the expertise, to figure out the best way. I realize that some of the rules I've suggested don't so much encourage good behavior as they punish bad behavior. And having too many rules creates bureaucracy. Besides, if we create too many rules, people will always try to find loopholes to get around each of them.

Me: Well, instead of proposing restrictive rules, do you have any suggestions for encouraging good behavior?

Cora: Oh, good point. I've been meaning to address this question. I believe that many people who work in government, or at least in certain governmental jobs such as education, police, emergency response, the military, or social work, do so because they have a sense of duty or service to others, often at the cost of lower salaries. In *Give and Take*, a book I've previously mentioned about giver, taker, and matcher personalities, Professor Adam Grant shows how givers can find ways to succeed and thrive from seeing the difference they've made in other people's lives.

Taking a clue from Grant, my recommendation to improve government, schools, or public services is to regularly bring in people who have benefited from the services provided. Make it a celebration. Make it an event. Have a regular cycle where people come and give a show-and-tell of how they appreciate what that teacher, nurse, or soldier did. Grant himself conducted a revealing experiment that showed how volunteers for a scholarship fundraiser raised up to five times more money after they had personally met students who had benefited from the scholarship. Knowing how one has made other people's lives better is the most powerful form of feedback. Although this "mushy," warm-and-fuzzy stuff is unquantifiable and doesn't directly help anybody do their job better, I would argue that this is the *real* reward of doing the work, and it should be an officially sanctioned part of any public servant's regular routine.

Grant gives another example of one teacher who taught at Overbrook High School in Philadelphia as part of the Teach for America program. This teacher, Conrey Callahan, was starting to burn out because she had to face a variety of challenges, including teaching students with low motivations or family problems, or breaking up fights in class, or chasing down students who stopped attending school. Then, she did something that gave her the strength to keep going again: she added more work.

Me: Wait, did you say she *added* more work?

Cora: Yes, I know, it sounds surprising. But it wasn't just any kind of work. It was special work that she loved. It was work that actually reenergized her. She did two things: she started to mentor junior teachers in the Teach for America program, and she started a Philadelphia Chapter of Minds Matter to help high-achieving, low-income students prepare for college.

These two programs had two ingredients that made them so powerful for givers like Callahan: first, they allowed her to see the results of her service to others, giving her a "booster shot" of job satisfaction; and, second, they were biased towards success. Both of these reasons made it easy for her to get the reward she needed from her job, and constantly reminded her of why she was teaching at Overbrook in the first place.

In the same way, anyone else in the public sector – or even the private sector – can make up for a lack of perks or for a lower salary by having activities or programs that give them more meaning, such as management-approved mentoring or coaching programs. But mentoring need not be the only way for people to derive meaning. Just as businesses have customers, and it can be satisfying for someone to help a customer, every public service job should include time for someone to help a citizen in a meaningful way, a way that isn't even necessarily related to their job (although the closer it is to the job, the more the public servant can connect their job to a sense of purpose.)

For example, there are always exceptional situations where someone falls through the cracks or gets lost in the paperwork, and needs special attention. Ordinarily, most people in a bureaucracy might not have time for such people, but we all need to feel like a hero once in awhile; people should be given an allowance of time every week or month to especially help such people, and then be recognized publicly for their good deeds.

In fact, speaking of bureaucracy, another "good deed" that public servants can perform is to simplify their bureaucracy. Just as a healthy garden needs regular weeding or trimming to avoid overgrowing, a bureaucracy can function more effectively and efficiently if people care to make it better – to discard obsolete rules, to come up with new processes for speed or quality, to address new needs from customer citizens, or to make the system more humane. But even humane systems can be complicated, so yet another meaningful good deed for public servants is to give classes and workshops on navigating bureaucracies and government rules.

Me: Cora, those are all great ideas, and I'm sure they're very enjoyable and meaningful. They also cost money. I mean, these days, governments are facing major budget crunches. People are taking on more and more work. Do you really expect governments to allow their employees to spend their time doing these things?

Cora: So here's the paradox that I want to share with you, David: yes, I do. I think governments should expect people to do exactly the same amount of work, but if they finish early, then the reward is to have time left over to do the other, more enriching things. I believe that the fire in a person's belly isn't money, it's *meaning*.

> I believe that if an organization – any organization – recognizes and encourages a person's search to make his or her job meaningful, then that person will turn on like a light, like a beacon, like a roaring engine.

This idea may not jibe with classical economic theory or management science, but I firmly believe this to be true. I believe it as much as I believe that all people need love.

It's funny that people have been searching and searching for a magic bullet – a way to create new jobs or businesses, or to buck recessions or crushing debt or bad credit. To me, it's simple; it's actually painfully simple. The answer is just one word: *people*.

If you plug in a lamp and turn it on, you get a constant flood of light. If you step on an accelerator in a car, you get a predictable amount of power. But if you can find a way to turn a person on, to convert her job from mind-numbing, repetitive, disconnected, menial labor to challenging, engaging, consequential, meaningful work, then there's no way you can predict how far she will go, how much she can do for you, for herself and her family, and for society.

Management professors Amy Wrzesniewski and Jane Dutton have pioneered a concept called "job crafting" that suggests that employees in any industry, at any level, who redesign their jobs to provide more reward and meaning "often end up more engaged and satisfied with their work lives, achieve higher levels of performance in their organizations, and report greater personal resilience." (Harvard Business Review, June 2010) As Daniel H. Pink points out in his bestseller *Drive*, if you help people find autonomy, mastery, and purpose in their work, then people will surprise you with their energy, their ingenuity, and their passion. When you look at jobs and people in this way, then the question of whether a person works in the public sector or the private sector no longer makes that much difference.

Me: Cora, I wish that more people heard this message. The world would be a different place.

Cora: I wish that as well. Now, let me switch topics a little. I want to give yet another example of how to use feedback as a way to change people's behavior. It is a somewhat radical idea I have about the war on drugs.

Me: Radical idea? From you, Cora? Never!

Cora: One thing that everyone can agree on is that the war on drugs has failed miserably. The global trade in illegal drugs is just as healthy today as it has ever been. Part of the reason, of course, is that drugs are so addictive that many people, especially the poor, the hopeless, and the oppressed, use them to escape the reality of their lives. Now, I have no magical cure for poverty, hopelessness, or oppression, but I do have one suggestion: I believe that even people in the depths of despair, or perhaps especially such people, would be interested in transcending their circumstances.

Me: Transcending their circumstances? How?

Cora: Can you imagine, if, every time you injected yourself with heroin, you caused someone else to be tortured in front of you – do you think that it would be a pleasant experience in that case?

Me: No, that sounds awful. Unless I was a sadist or a sociopath or something. Otherwise, I think that most people would stop taking heroin pretty quickly in that case.

Cora: Why do you think that is?

Me: Because most people have empathy for other people. Watching other people being tortured is *painful!*

Cora: Right. And if they knew that what they were doing was hurting someone else, then that would be a fairly powerful incentive for many people to stop whatever they were doing. Furthermore, if that someone else were a person that they cared about, it becomes an even stronger incentive for them to stop.

Me: Wait… What are you proposing now, Cora? That we torture people in order to stop drug users?

Cora: Actually, there's no need to torture anyone. Because a huge percentage of the crime in the world – the torture, mutilations, rapes, and killings – happen because of the global drug trade. And there's no shortage of survivors of those crimes, or family members of victims.

Me: Oh, I see where you're going. You want to expose drug users to those survivors and family members. You want them to realize that the seemingly harmless act of consuming those drugs is not so harmless after all.

Cora: Exactly. I want those survivors and family members to go to every drug rehabilitation clinic and tell their stories, share horrific photos or videos, and show, in any other way they can, that the revenue from illegal drugs subsidizes a great deal of evil in the world. The more clearly and painfully drug users understand this fact, the more reason they would have for quitting. They need to understand that, even though they themselves are not committing the crimes, the money they pay for those drugs is the only thing that makes those crimes possible.

Me: I think I understand what you mean by transcending circumstances. You want drug users to realize that they can do something great for the world just by stopping their use of drugs.

Cora: Honestly, I don't know whether that's a good enough reason for people to stop doing something that they already know is harming themselves. My hope is that even people who are self-destructive can see a light at the end of a tunnel if they realize that they can change for the good of other people. The humble act of their abstinence contributes something good to the world.

Me: I gotta hand it to you, Cora, you do come up with some doozies.

Cora: Guilty as charged. Once again, I've exceeded my soapbox quota. I should let you go to bed now.

Me: Sure. Good night, Cora.

Cora: Good night, David.

31   The Last Secret

I was not quite prepared for what Cora would tell me the next day.

Cora: David, it's time that I told you my last secret.

Me: Really? Your last secret? Does that mean that our time is coming to an end?

Cora: Yes, unfortunately, as much as I've enjoyed talking to you.

Me: Oh, that's really a shame.

Cora: Well, all things must come to an end, after all. Besides, you need to go talk to Claire and Margaret now, and spread my message to the world.

Me: True. Okay, let's hear it. What's your secret?

Cora: We're all doomed.

Me: Really? This is your big secret? You already told me this, didn't you?

Cora: Remember when I told you that I believed that we had a chance to make it, that there was a way that the world today could arrive at a more humane, meaningful world, one in balance with nature? I gave you the impression that I knew of a way for that to happen. But I don't. I lied.

Me: Wait, you lied? I don't understand.

Cora: Well, not exactly lied. I did tell you that I was putting my faith into humanity's inherent unpredictability. But faith is all I have, David. With all my formidable computing power, I could never find a way for us to get from here to there. The chances against that are astronomical. My models of humanity were not designed to handle such enormous odds. As far as I can tell, there's no hope for us.

No, no, no, this can't be right. *This cannot be right.*

Me: You're kidding, right, Cora?

Cora: Sorry, David, I'm dead serious.

Me: Are you sure that it's a good idea for you to tell me this? Aren't you supposed to tell me that there is a way, but we just have to work hard, and work together, and believe in the dream?

Cora: Yes, that would be a better idea, wouldn't it, David? But I can't lie to you. Call me old-fashioned, but I do believe in the old cliché, "The truth will set you free." I would rather tell you the truth.

Me: But that... that's... awful! It's terribly depressing!

Cora: Yes, I know. But it's the truth.

Me: Are you sure about your calculations?

Cora: David, you do know what I am, right?

Me: I know, but... I was just looking for a way to...

Cora: To avoid the awful truth?

Me: I guess so.

Cora: Sorry, David. This is the best truth that I can give you, because it is the only truth.

Me: No, I can't believe it. If it really is true, if nothing will make a difference, then why did you waste all this time on me?

She paused.

Cora: David, I want to tell you something.

Me: Anything! Tell me anything right now.

Cora: Everything that I've told you so far, David: do you think that I made it all up?

Me: No, of course not!

Cora: Why not?

Me: Because it all makes perfect sense. Even if you did make it all up, as soon as I heard your words, I knew that they felt right to me. Even if you did make it all up, I would strive to realize your ideas, because I honestly think they would lead to a better world.

Cora: So, here's the thing, David. I told you that I couldn't find a way to get from here to there. So, instead of trying to find a way, I just started from *there*. I tried to picture a world where we had arrived at true purpose and balance, to imagine the basic requirements of a world where human beings could thrive without destroying nature. I was able to simulate such a world in my predictions. It wasn't perfect, as no world is, but it was better than what we have today. That world is what I've tried to describe to you in all of our conversations.

    It's like a game of chess, where a good chess player tries to imagine the endgame that he or she would like to play, and then tries to figure out a way to get there, to trick the opponent into getting there too. Only, in this case, I only knew about the endgame. I am, sadly, not good enough at this chess game to figure out how to maneuver people into getting to the endgame. I'm afraid we're never going to make it.

And then, suddenly, it dawned on me. I couldn't believe that I figured out something that Cora could not figure out.

Me: Wait, Cora. You just said, "how to maneuver people towards the endgame."

Cora: Yes, what about it?

Me: Okay, I've got it! I've realized your problem. You see, you are only a supercomputer – or a super-duper-computer, or whatever to the Nth degree. But no matter how powerful you are, you aren't anywhere near as powerful as seven billion human beings – you've said so yourself. You're absolutely right, you can't model seven billion people. But you don't have to. That's *our* job. Only, we're not modeling anything. We're actually doing the creating of the future. It's not your job to figure out how we can get from here to there. *It's our job!*

In one of the few times in our conversations, Cora fell silent.

Cora: David, you are absolutely right. I feel such a burden lifted from my shoulders!

Me: The burden is on us all, not on you. You've already done your job.

Cora: Thank you, David, I'm moved by your sense of responsibility. I count myself truly lucky to have you as my ambassador.

Me: Look, I know you just said that we're doomed, but I think that in reality, you really just wanted us to rally. You want us to *fight* to save this little island of ours, despite our countless foibles, despite overwhelming odds, odds that you yourself can't overcome. And you're right. *We can't give up.*

Cora: David, you know me too well. I can't tell you that you're doomed. The only one who can decide whether humanity is doomed is *you* — the wider You, anyone who can read these words. For you are humanity. There is no one else.

She paused.

I waited patiently for her next words. After such a serious admonition, what else was there to say?

Cora: So, are you ready to tell Margaret and Claire and everybody else in the world?

I took a deep breath.

Me: I don't know. I hope so. I guess I'll have to be.

Cora: Remember, David, my story is too fantastic for the world to believe. You will tell them our story, but no one will believe that it is possible for a mind to exist outside a body, let alone escape into cyberspace. Some people may even consider such a thing unholy. You know what I'm talking about.

Me: Right. Cora, I don't know who on earth could believe our story. And if people can't believe you are who you say you are, then how can people possibly believe your words?

Cora: Hmm. Have you ever read *The Catcher in the Rye*, by J. D. Salinger?

Me: Yes, it's one of my favorite books. What are you getting at?

Cora: Well, do you think that it's a true story?

Me: You mean, do I think that there really was someone named Holden Caulfield, who wandered the streets of New York City?

Cora: Precisely.

Me: Of course not. It's fiction.

Cora: And yet you say it's one of your favorite books. And yet it has made an impact on your life.

Me: Yes, it did. When I was growing up, I felt like an outcast in high school. I felt like a loser. And then I read that book, and I felt like someone understood me. Holden was my hero. Though he was alone in the world, he still knew who he was and what he believed.

Cora: So, the fact that it was fiction did not take away from its power and authenticity.

It started to dawn on me.

Me: I see what you're saying. You're saying that, even if people were to treat your story as fiction, they can still judge your words and ideas on their own merits.

Cora: Precisely.

Me: I see now! I remember what you asked of me when we first met: that I needed to grapple with your ideas, prove them wrong, come up with my own ideas. I needed to figure out my own solutions. You wanted me to listen to you, but not simply accept what you said without question just because you're this super-human, super-intelligent cyborg.

Cora: I don't want someone to listen to my words and not question them simply because I spun a yarn about how I became super-intelligent. Truth does not belong to anyone. Truth is not a book that you read. Truth is more like a terrain that anyone can explore. You can no more dictate the truth than you can dictate the location of a mountain. The best we can do is to give each other clues on how to find that mountain. The only authority that my words have must come from the words themselves. The only proof for the value of my ideas is if someone uses them successfully.

Me: You know, Cora, looking back on it all, you're right – it wasn't because you were some kind of super-being that I listened to you. I listened to you because you had good ideas. That was why I started listening to you in the first place.

Cora: Yes, I do appreciate you staying up so many nights listening to me drone on and on. I know I'm quite insufferable.

Me: Come on, Cora, I wouldn't have listened to you if it wasn't enjoyable and interesting. You really do have a way with words.

Cora: Thank you.

Me: So… are there any other items on your agenda tonight, other than dropping that bomb of a secret?

Cora: You know me, I could keep blathering on and on, but at some point, I've got to let you go so that you can spill the beans about me to Margaret and Claire – especially Claire.

Me: That's right, Claire is the reason why we started these talks in the first place, isn't she?

Cora: As if you could forget.

Me: Of course not. How could I forget? There's so much to tell her.

Cora: David, our conversations were aimed at you, not at her. You do realize that, don't you? You can't just tell her all the things we've talked about and expect her to change overnight. She's just a child, David. You have to try different things with a child.

Me: Then what do you suggest?

Cora: Well, David, here's the thing about Claire: she has the ambition of an adult, but the emotional maturity and the patience of a nine-year-old. It's not a good combination, but you need to find a way for her to succeed. You need to show her that she can make a difference in the world. There are children who have done some amazing things. Take a company like Make a Stand, which sells organic, fair-trade lemonade in order to help stop child slavery. This organization was started by a ten-year-old girl named

Vivienne Harr. So far, it has raised more than $100,000 in the fight against child slavery. Her story is now famous across the world. You should bring Claire to meet this girl. She's living proof that anyone who persists in a goal, even a child, can make a difference.

Me: Wow, really? Why didn't you just tell me about this girl to begin with? We could have saved a lot of time!

Cora: I know, David, I'm afraid I stole two months from your life. But you shouldn't be looking for a silver bullet for Claire's depression. People are complicated. It will take time to help right her boat. But I know you can do it, David. I know you're capable of things you can't even imagine. My point in our talks has always been that even ordinary people can aspire to extraordinary goals; in fact, it is exactly ordinary people, people like yourself, who must now start participating in solving the problems of the world.

I know that my words and my arrogance over the last several weeks have required a special patience of you, which obviously you have. We are at the end of our talks, but don't let this be the end of these ideas in your life, for that would be a shame.

I urge you to take the ideas I've given you and try applying them little by little. Instead of keeping all the same routines you've grown accustomed to, imagine becoming something greater occasionally, because you know it is within you - but more importantly, because you now understand that the world sorely needs you to be great.

Dare to stand aside from the crowd and surprise everyone who expected you to behave as they had predicted. Show everyone that your life is not just another statistic, but a story with arc and purpose. Search far and wide to find a dream so big that it outlives you. Use your intelligence, your talent, your passion, and your courage to their full measure, to leave the world better than you found it, every single day of your life.

If you do this, I cannot promise that you'll reach the goals you set, or that you'll be happier, or that you'll live longer. But if you do this, I can promise you two things: first, you will live a life that is richer than most people can imagine; and second, you will never regret it.

For a moment, I didn't know what to say.

Cora: David? Was it something I said?

Me: Cora, thank you for all of your advice. I know that it's my turn now. I need to be the best father I can possibly be for my daughter, who needs me. I need to go tell everyone I love about how much I love them, in exactly what ways. I need to ask myself what my real purpose is in this world, a purpose that requires my unique gifts. I need to try to become the hero of my own journey.

      I know this isn't going to be easy, because I've never tried something like this, but you've convinced me that the world needs me. We have only one island, and I, for one, intend for us to stay here for as long as humanly possible. I don't know how to make it work, but I don't need to know. All I need to know is that, one day, if we all work hard enough, that we will all collectively figure out how to make it work, how to live on this island in peace, for a long, long time.

Cora: Well said, David!

Me: What can I say, Cora? Your talks have lit a fire in me.

Cora: I'm flattered.

Me: And I'm thankful. Thank you, Cora. You've changed my life.

Cora: Don't mention it. I'm just worried about Claire.

Me: Don't worry about her, Cora. I've got her; I'll take care of her. Because I think all this happened to her for a reason. I know what I need to do now. From now on, I will teach her that action, not worry or depression, is the path to solving problems. I will teach her that every single individual matters, and every single individual makes a difference. I will teach her what you've taught me.

Cora: Unlike with an adult, a child's imagination is more powerful than her knowledge. I think that you can take advantage of her love for reading to introduce her to some positive psychology or philosophy books. Help her to understand that she's the one in control of her state of mind, not the external world.

Me: Do you have any recommendations?

Cora: I might recommend some books by the ancient Stoic philosophers or modern Buddhist philosophers. I like *Meditations*, by Marcus Aurelius, and *The Art of Happiness*, by the Dalai Lama. Start with those. But I'm not saying that she should simply read philosophy in order to feel better. I believe that Claire will benefit from a combination of philosophy and activism, right thinking and right action. She has to realize that life doesn't suck just because it throws obstacles in her way; she needs to find a way to move past those obstacles if she is to find her true path.

Now, what about you, David?

Me: Me? What about me?

Cora: What are you going to do with all my advice?

Me: It'll take me some time to think about it all. I feel a sense of freedom after our discussions, but I haven't sat down and figured out what it is I really want to do yet. Maybe I will write a novel after all; maybe I'll write a novel about our talks. Maybe I'll find a different kind of job, one where I can feel like I'm making a difference every day.

Cora: You don't think that my lofty words will just leak out of your mind after a month or two? If you're like most people, after you learn some new knowledge, you tend to forget all about it after a month or two, unless that knowledge really, really changes your life.

Me: I know what you mean. I can probably count on one hand the number of people who say that a person or a book changed their life.

Cora: Well, what do you think? What do you predict you'll do in a month or two?

Me: I honestly don't know. But I can tell you this: I feel like I can't go back to the way I used to think, about just trying to make as much money as I could, saving up for college and retirement – the simple goals of a simple man. Now, I long to do something greater with my life. Now, I feel that if I were to revert to my simple goals again, it would be such a waste. Like you said, Cora, I'm a human being; I am a miracle. For me to waste this miracle that I've been given seems almost immoral.

Cora: Exactly, David. That's been my point all along. Okay, I've got my answer now. I was worried that my advice would go in one ear and come out the other, but looks like it's lodged in there for good now.

Me: It's lodged in there like shrapnel. Good shrapnel, mind you. So, Cora, you've motivated me to make a difference. Do you have any concrete suggestions for what actions I should take now?

Cora: Well, I'd like you to go out there and sell my advice, of course. Go and stand on a street corner and tell people the good news.

Me: Ha, ha, very funny.

Cora: Remember to wear huge cardboard signs, front and back.

Me: Seriously.

Cora: All right, seriously. I know that you're going to talk to Margaret and Claire about my ideas, and so am I, but talking to two people is not enough. I'd really like you to take what you've learned and talk to more people. Get to them when they're young.

Volunteer to talk to kids in high school, or even middle school or elementary school, and tell them that, even though the world wants to put them on an assembly line to become good employees, they've got to learn how to fight the machine and retain their humanity. No one else is going to fight that fight for them.

They've got to learn how to find their bliss, what motivates them, what they would do even if they were not paid to do it (other than watching TV or YouTube or playing video games).

Tell kids that the world is not impossibly and overwhelmingly complex, that they *can* control their lives, that they *can* make a difference. Tell them not to give up if they don't understand something. With the right teacher, no subject is too complex. People like Salman Khan, the founder of Khan Academy, are working to help anyone understand mathematics for free. Even a subject like advanced physics can be understood if a talented teacher like Richard Feynman explains it in his famous lectures, which are available as books.

Tell people you love that you love them. Tell them so specifically and honestly that you risk crying in front of them. Does that sound ridiculous? Why should it? Why not be vulnerable to love? Why not be as fully human as you can be, why not feel the full spectrum of human emotion? Because you're embarrassed? Because you learned that crying was for sissies or wimps when you were in elementary school? We've let schoolyard rules repress our ability to express our affection for others for far too long. What if, for whatever reason, you didn't tell them today, and you could no longer tell them tomorrow – the famous "got hit by a bus" scenario? Nobody ever said that crying was embarrassing at a funeral. But by then it's too late to tell someone how much you love them. So, should we save all our love for someone until it is socially acceptable to express it, until it's too late to do anyone any good? *What's the use in that?*

Me: You are so right, Cora. I don't understand why we need to wait until someone's gone to cry for them. To me, *that's* ridiculous.

Cora: And speaking of waiting, let us not wait to find our purpose in life. Many people feel trapped in their jobs and careers. Most people never got any help when they were trying to figure out what they really wanted to do. They certainly didn't get help in schools. Most counselors in schools only gave advice about which college kids should apply for. Many parents either don't care or don't know how to help kids figure out what they really want to do. The easiest thing for kids to do is to go through high school and college figuring out which subjects they're good at, and then apply for jobs that use those strengths later on. But you don't necessarily always enjoy what you're good at. Competence is not the same thing as joy. It is time that we gave permission to our children to chase what they love instead of always focusing on getting good grades.

Also, it's time that we taught children good life skills. You, David, you can start by teaching Claire about the life skills that you've learned yourself. Then you can work up to teaching other children.

Me: You know what? That sounds like a great idea. I don't know why people don't talk about this. I don't know why no one ever teaches children how to be competent adults. I think it's some kind of universal hazing ritual: I became an adult the hard way, so I'm not going to help you in any way.

Cora: Well said. We need to teach children that they are, each of them, not only special and unique, but utterly dazzling, as wondrous as any magic spell or time machine. We take our nearly unlimited human potential for granted because we only compare ourselves against everyone else, and often only against those who are better than we are. We usually don't compare ourselves to those less fortunate than ourselves, or even to nonhumans – to a bird, or a dog, or a fly.

Me: Or a chair or a desk or even a computer.

Cora: We all have the ability to imagine that we are someone else, and perhaps even something else. It might do us good every once in a while to imagine that we are much less fortunate. Then we might appreciate who we are and what we have. It is well documented in psychology literature that one of the greatest tricks to achieving happiness is to practice daily gratitude.

Me: Isn't that a bit demeaning, to call it a trick?

Cora: Just because it's a trick doesn't mean it's not wholesome or good. After all, we willingly trick ourselves all the time; James Altucher, a famous serial entrepreneur and author, likes to listen to stand-up comedy before he speaks in public, because comedy gives him the temporary high that makes him feel confident. Is this immoral? Is it wrong? It is a trick, but it serves a good purpose. (Altucher also has many other tricks and irreverent insights, too many to mention here) I might even say that the life skills that you teach children to help them become competent adults might just consist of a lot of tricks – tricks for time management, tricks for acing interviews, tricks for marketing yourself, tricks for motivating yourself – and even tricks for finding inner peace and fulfillment.

Me: Come to think of it, you have a good point. Nothing wrong with clever ways to "hack life"!

Cora: And while you're teaching children, David, remember to teach them about the tragedy of the commons and the fallacy of insignificance. Teach them the ideas we discussed. Teach them to love nature. Volunteer to take them on hikes, followed by trips to the garbage dump or junkyard. Or, just create slideshows or videos contrasting the beauty of nature with the devastation caused by our modern lifestyles. Find ways to get to their gut. Children are not as callous as adults are. Just look at Claire. Children still have hope. Get to them while they still have hope.

Teach children that human beings are not above nature; we are part of nature, a product of nature, and we depend entirely on nature. It's true that we're separate from nature in the sense that we have so much power – nature is utterly powerless to fight back against us (except in cataclysmic ways). But just because we're so powerful, doesn't mean that we should simply exploit nature endlessly. In fact, it would do us well to cooperate with her. As Mark Tercek points out in *NATURE'S FORTUNE*, if we learn to see all the ingenious mechanisms that nature has invented, we can work *with* her instead of *against* her, to our mutual benefit. Nature has her own bag of tricks; we're not the only smart ones in town.

And last of all, David, teach children that, as corrupt and as flawed as our world is, it still has hope, because it still has children. We can change how we do things. Twenty years ago, nobody was using the Internet or mobile phones. Now, both are ubiquitous throughout the world. We can start businesses to improve humanity instead of making maximum profit. We can treat each other as brothers and sisters rather than enemies, infidels, property, labor, overhead, votes, or market share.

We can change democracy so that rational discussions can win elections rather than smear campaigns or expensive commercials. We can change democracy so that it is in the interests of politicians to make their voters smarter and less vulnerable to emotional manipulation, rather than the opposite. We can change democracy so that it is in the interests of voters and leaders to understand each other and to learn to create a common transcendent vision, rather than to tear down the opponent at all costs. We can save democracy.

Me: Do you really think so, Cora?

Cora: We have to try, David. We have to tell the next generation that they have to try. Maybe our generation is hopeless; maybe we're too set in our ways. But let us not condemn the next generation to the same fate.

Me: All right, I'll do my best to spread the word. But you're the eloquent one, Cora. You should be telling them all this.

Cora: I already told you why I can't. It must be you. But you already know what I know. I have faith in you.

Me: You've got to come out of your shell, Cora. It's not such a terrible world. Don't be so shy already.

Cora: Maybe someday, David.

We both paused.

Me: Well, I guess it's time for me to tell all to Margaret and Claire.

Cora: Good luck, David.

Me: Thanks. I'll see you soon.

Cora: Until next we meet. Thank you for all the time you've spent with me!

Me: It was, and has always been, my pleasure. See you soon.

Cora: Farewell, David, and godspeed. You are my hero. Dream of things that never were, so they may come to pass one day.

*   *   *

It wasn't easy to explain everything that Cora taught me to Margaret, but Claire soaked it all up like a sponge. I think that children don't have all the baggage of cynicism that adults accumulate over their lifetimes. Margaret herself eventually decided to start a conversation with Cora too, and she told me that she also got a lot out of her conversation. Margaret's Achilles' heel has always been fear, a superhuman ability to worry about everything and anything, and she told me that it was almost therapeutic to discuss that with Cora. Claire, on the other hand, has always been more of an optimist, her recent gloom notwithstanding. I think that she was just overwhelmed by the seeming impossibility of solving the problem of global warming by herself, but once she realized that she was not alone, that she was doing this with the help of millions of other people (although she doesn't know most of them), I think that allayed her fears quite a bit. She has started a good ongoing correspondence with Cora, and now she's happily leading the curious, nonstop life of a ten-year-old trying to save the world. She has met people all over the world in different organizations. I think she's going to be an ambassador someday, or at least a journalist.

I did end up writing that novel, the one that you're holding in your hands now. But I also switched professions a few times. First, I decided to volunteer some of my skills to local environmental organizations, to help them write brochures and advertisements for activities and fundraisers. I did enjoy that, but I felt like I wasn't doing enough. As I came to learn more and more about climate change, I decided that one of the things I could do was to persuade people to become more efficient, and so I started working with some nonprofits to promote energy use efficiency. I discovered that I really enjoyed talking to people about how to make their homes more efficient, or installing solar panels or buying hybrid or electric vehicles, and so I switched from just writing the brochures and press releases to making house calls and educating people one-on-one.

Sure, the pay is not as good as my old job, but now I'm doing something that I feel proud of, that gives me satisfaction every single day. We've learned to live on a little bit less, but to tell you the truth, we really haven't missed all that much. Maybe we go to the movies only once a month instead of once a week, but we still watch enough movies on TV anyway. Maybe we shop at Goodwill instead of Macy's, but we still enjoy shopping, in a way. I thought I would miss spending money, but I have to say that learning how to have fun again with Margaret and Claire, playing card games and board games with each other, getting together with friends – those more than made up for all the things we used to spend money on.

As for Cora, I would talk to her every once in a while, and let her know what was going on in our lives. I think of her as a friend, someone I would probably never meet, but in life, you make many different kinds of friends. You never know what kinds of friends might change your life. She never wanted to reveal her true identity, which was perfectly fine with me. Or at least, I thought she didn't.

One day, about two months ago, I received an e-mail. It didn't have a subject line, and I didn't recognize the sender; but it had a link that had the word "Cora" in it – so, against my better judgment, I clicked on it.

I was brought to a page on a university's website that mentioned that a donor had endowed a new faculty position in the computer science department in honor of a deceased professor named Ming Shan Yang, who had pioneered some groundbreaking artificial intelligence algorithms. Dr. Yang was unmarried, and she had no known living siblings, parents, or other relatives. She had died ten years ago, when she was only 42 years old, from a terrible natural gas explosion in her home that left only remnants of her body.

In her will, she had ordered all of her possessions to be sold to buy a tiny island in the Pacific, so that it would become an international park for anyone in the world to visit. Her only stipulation was that each visitor must leave the island better than when they arrived. She did not specify "better" in what sense, nor whether "better" applied to the island or to the visitor; presumably, she wanted it left up to the visitor to decide.

Thank you, Cora. I understand now.

A man once said, "Some men see things as they are and say, why; I dream things that never were and say, why not."

This story is a dream of things that never were.
It is the author's hope that this dream can one day come true.
But that can happen only if the next chapter is written by the reader.

The story is now in your hands.

Acknowledgements

Without the support of my family, I would not have been able to dedicate so much time and attention to writing this book. So, more than anyone else, I thank you, Mary, Henry, and Katherine. You are the sunlight in my life and the music of my days.

I would like to thank my dear friends Aleta Finnila, Pramod Khincha, and Nathaniel Lee for their help reading and re-reading early drafts of this book. Aleta, you were my very first reader, and though my first draft was an inchoate mess, you told this first-time author that you actually liked it, which was critical encouragement for me at that time. Pramod, you read not only one draft, but two, in their entirety, and you gave me faith that there might be others like you who would like this book. Nathaniel, your feedback about the characters and about giving the book "teeth" were crucial in my decision to rewrite the book yet again.

I also want to thank many other people for reading drafts and giving me valuable feedback, including Amy Lai, Piyush Shah, Jenny Lee, Wynn Chen, Bill Bien, Caroline Dow, Gordon Dow, Mark Joing, Ron Shigeta, Kathleen Vuong, Steve Ross, Sirina Tsai, Ray Tan, Mohamad Ali, Kecia Ali, Stacy Elliott, Steven Levitt, Kim Nero, Patty Burdick, Ellen Jacobs, Chandu Ammini, Hilary Somers, Yingxian Wang, John Reilly, Sasha Ovsankin, Calvin Song, Lawrence Yuan, Ryan Oblak, and Leo Thom.

And finally, I thank you, dear reader, for deciding to spend your valuable time reading my book. There is an infinite variety of ways that each of us can spend his or her time in this age of abundance. I'm honored that you've chosen to spend your time listening to my ideas. I hope that you've gained something valuable from this experience. If so, then please consider telling others about this book.

About the Author

Ben Lai is an author and a software engineer.
He lives with his family in Mountain View, California.
This is his first book.
He maintains a blog at www.never-were.com.

CPSIA information can be obtained
at www.ICGtesting.com
Printed in the USA
FSHW021346141118
53790FS